I0804167

"Christian de Chergé tells his community that they have taken a vow of permanent catechesis, and this valuable book allows us to share in that. He addresses familiar monastic themes: stability, silence, *lectio*, and much more, with a compelling urgency. This is rich material, made all the more poignant since we know the end of the story."

—Esther de Waal, author of *The White Stone: The Art of Letting Go*

"Christian de Chergé took seriously his duty as abbot to provide his brother monks with substantial input on a wide variety of topics. His notes from hundreds of informal teachings in chapter are a window into his mind and heart. The selection of talks presented and translated here gives us privileged access to the reflections that nourished Christian and his brothers in the years leading up to their final self-offering."

—Fr. Elias Dietz, Abbey of Gethsemani

"*God for All Days* offers us the first book-length taste, in English, of the writings of Christian de Chergé. His chapter talks nudge monastic and ecclesial teaching in fresh ways and open a window into the thinking behind the community's decision to stay alongside their Muslim neighbors during the Algerian civil war. Matthew Cheung Salisbury and Jennifer Rushworth deserve our thanks for translations that faithfully convey the flavor of Christian's 'speaking notes' and for their helpful commentary. This book is a welcome step in making more of the writings of the Tibhirine community available in English. More please!"

—The Rev. Dr. Jane Foulcher, Charles Sturt University

MONASTIC WISDOM SERIES: NUMBER SEVENTY-THREE

God for All Days

The Final Monastic Chapters of Christian de Chergé

Christian de Chergé

Translated by Jennifer Rushworth

Edited and Introduced by
Matthew Cheung Salisbury

Cistercian Publications
cistercianpublications.org

LITURGICAL PRESS
Collegeville, Minnesota
litpress.org

A Cistercian Publications title published by Liturgical Press

Cistercian Publications
Editorial Offices
161 Grosvenor Street
Athens, Ohio 45701
cistercianpublications.org

Cover Image: Photo of the cemetery gates leading to the grave markers for the martyrs of the Tibhirine Monastery in Algeria. Used with permission.

Cover design by David Drummond.

This selection of talks is translated from *Dieu pour tout jour: chapitres de Père Christian de Chergé à la communauté de Tibhirine (1986–1996)*, edited at the Abbaye Notre-Dame d'Aiguebelle with the permission of the Association des écrits des moines de l'Atlas and Les Éditions du Cerf.

Library of Congress Cataloging-in-Publication Data

Names: Chergé, Christian de, 1937-1996 author | Salisbury, Matthew Cheung editor | Rushworth, Jennifer, 1987- translator
Title: God for all days : the final monastic chapters of Christian de Chergé / Christian de Chergé ; edited and introduced by Matthew Cheung Salisbury ; translated by Jennifer Rushworth.
Description: Athens, Ohio : Cistercian Publications | Series: Monastic wisdom series ; number seventy-three | Includes translation or is translation | Includes bibliographical references. | Summary: "Christian de Chergé was the prior of the Trappist community of Our Lady of Atlas in Tibhirine, Algeria, until his assassination with six of his fellow monks in 1996. Drawn from the last two years of his life, these chapter talks to his brothers offer deeper insight into the monastic search for God in community during tumultuous times"—Provided by publisher.
Identifiers: LCCN 2024051100 (print) | LCCN 2024051101 (ebook) | ISBN 9780879073633 trade paperback | ISBN 9780879073664 epub | ISBN 9780879073695 pdf
Subjects: LCSH: Trappists—Algeria—Tibehirine—History—20th century—Sources | Tibehirine (Algeria)—Church history—20th century—Sources
Classification: LCC BX4147.A4 C5413 2025 (print) | LCC BX4147.A4 (ebook) | DDC 271/.125—dc23/eng
LC record available at https://lccn.loc.gov/2024051100
LC ebook record available at https://lccn.loc.gov/2024051101

Contents

Abbreviations

CCC *Catechism of the Catholic Church*

CST Constitutions of the Cistercian Order of the Strict Observance

DPTJ Christian de Chergé. *Dieu pour tout jour: chapitres de père Christian de Chergé à la communauté de Tibhirine (1985–1996)*

LG *Lumen Gentium*

RB *RB 1980: The Rule of St. Benedict in Latin and English with Notes*

SC *Sacrosanctum Concilium*

Introduction

The Trappist monastery of Our Lady of Atlas in Tibhirine, near Médéa, Algeria, was founded in March 1938.[1] Throughout the history of the community, the brethren lived fruitfully alongside their Muslim neighbors, working with them to cultivate the land and serving the needs of the wider community by providing medical care and clothing. During the Algerian Civil War (1992–2002), the community declined to offer preferential treatment to one side or the other or to share its resources exclusively with one faction. In the face of increasing danger from conflict that did not involve them, the brethren resolved, on several occasions, not to escape to a safer location in Algeria or France. In March 1996, seven of the monks were kidnapped and then executed, bringing the monastery and its work to global attention. They were beatified on December 8, 2018, together with the other Martyrs of Algeria.

Central to the brothers' common life, and indeed to their decision to remain in the face of danger, was the spiritual counsel of the then prior of the community, Christian de

1. The Trappists, formally known as the Order of Cistercians of the Strict Observance, are Cistercian religious who follow an austere rule of life that, at its foundation in the seventeenth century, was a reaction against a perceived relaxation of the discipline of the Cistercian Order. They gained formal independence as a distinct order in 1892. The name comes from La Grande Trappe, the first such community to be reformed.

Chergé (1937–1996). Christian's thrice-weekly lectures in chapter to the community, from 1986 until his kidnapping and death, reveal much in general about the experiences and thought processes of a Roman Catholic religious community in North Africa at the end of the twentieth century and offer a remarkable account of the challenges and opportunities that the monks faced in particular. They also reveal something of the reasoning behind the community's encounter with Islam and, from Christian de Chergé's perspective, how both Christian and Muslim faiths might benefit from such encounters. In this volume, Christian's chapter talks from late November 1993 until his disappearance in March 1996 are presented for the first time in English translation. We have translated them here from the French transcriptions, which have been published as *Dieu pour tout jour: chapitres de Père Christian de Chergé à la communauté de Tibhirine (1986–1996)*, edited at the Abbaye Notre-Dame d'Aiguebelle with the permission of the Association des écrits des moines de l'Atlas.

The Monastery, its Prior, and the Chapter Talks

The monastery of Our Lady of Atlas at Tibhirine was founded from Aiguebelle Abbey, a Cistercian foundation with medieval origins in southeast France, the result of Cistercian presence in French Algeria for almost a century. Fr. Christian de Chergé entered the monastery in 1969 after having been ordained in 1964 in the diocese of Paris. He studied for two years in Rome at the Pontifical Institute of Arab and Islamic Studies (PISAI), where he studied the history of Christian-Islamic encounter in depth, having already had an opportunity in Algeria to experience such relationships for himself. As a child, Christian had had an insight from his mother that Muslims and Christians direct their prayers to the same God: "I remain profoundly grateful to my mother, who taught us, my brothers and me, respect for the uprightness and attitudes of this Muslim prayer: 'They are praying to God,' my mother would say. And so I always knew the God of Islam and the God of Jesus Christ are not two."[2]

As a seminarian Christian did national service for eighteen months in Algeria as part of a military unit that attempted to win over the local population during the Franco-Algerian war through the provision of public health, education, and protection.[3] While working in this capacity, he met a local policeman named Mohammed who, in the course of many conversations, became his friend. Of this friendship, Christian wrote,

> I was given the gift of meeting a mature man who liberated my faith by teaching it to express itself as a climate of simplicity, openness, and surrender to God, taking in quite naturally the relationships, the events, and the minutiae of daily life. Our dialogue was the expression of a peaceful and trusting friendship which had God for its horizon.[4]

Ultimately Mohammed defended Christian in a tight situation with another faction, and, though Christian was spared harm, Mohammed was found murdered the next day. "In the blood of this friend," Christian wrote, "I came to know that my call to follow Christ would have to be lived out, sooner or later, in the very country in which I received the token of the greatest love of all."[5] It is this revelation of an imitation of Christ that committed Christian to a life of service to Algeria, for, he said, Mohammed "had given his life like Christ."[6]

2. Christian de Chergé, "Prier en Église à l'écoute de l'Islam," cited in Christian Salenson, *Christian de Chergé: A Theology of Hope*, trans. Nada Conic, Cistercian Studies 247 (Collegeville, MN: Cistercian Publications, 2012), 179.

3. Salenson, *Christian de Chergé*, 23.

4. Cited in Salenson, *Christian de Chergé*, 24.

5. Cited in Salenson, *Christian de Chergé*, 24.

6. Salenson, *Christian de Chergé*, 25.

At the monastery of Our Lady of Atlas, the community met for chapter meetings three mornings a week as well as coming together each evening for conversation and to receive information from the Cistercian Order and the wider church, and to practice the chant and prepare liturgical materials for subsequent days. Throughout his period of office as prior, from 1984, Christian gave a talk at each morning chapter; these "mini-series," to use Christian's term, were occasionally punctuated by his absence from the monastery, by retreats and talks by others, and by the demands of the busiest seasons of the liturgical year. From April 1985 on, these talks were based on a general theme or a train of thought that Christian would continue for weeks or months, writing notes for the talks on a third of a sheet of A4 paper. He delivered them during the Office of Terce (around 9 a.m.), with the brethren sitting around a large square table. In the place of the short sentence from Scripture towards the end of the service, Christian would speak for eight to ten minutes.[7]

Six hundred and five chapter talks survive (those before February 1986 do not). The mini-series treat the following subjects: the Psalms, Christian communities in the Near East, conversion, the fourth chapter of the Rule of Saint Benedict, humility, Saint Bernard of Clairvaux, the Song of Songs, the Constitutions of the Cistercian Order, catechesis and the liturgy, "in the church, here and now" (treating the situation all Christian communities in Algeria faced at the time), and (last, from November 1995 until the kidnapping) "the charism of a martyr." We have chosen to focus on the last three mini-series not only because they offer a compelling witness to the years of greatest danger and tumult, but also because their

7. Introduction to the French edition of the text: *Dieu pour tout jour: chapitres de père Christian de Chergé à la communauté de Tibhirine (1985–1996)*, 2nd ed., Les Cahiers de Tibhirine 1bis (Montjoyer: Éditions de Bellefontaine for the Abbaye Notre-Dame d'Aiguebelle, 2006), xiii–xiv. References to this edition are marked DPTJ with the date of the chapter given.

subjects—liturgy, catechesis, and interreligious encounter—are of great interest to the contemporary church.

Catechesis and the Liturgy. This series begins the year after the promulgation of the *Catechism of the Catholic Church* and thirty years after the Church's promulgation of the Constitution on the Sacred Liturgy, *Sacrosanctum Concilium.* In addition to reflections on the reception of the work of the Second Vatican Council, and on the particular context of the monastery and its encounter with Islam, Christian offers a personal commentary on the introduction and first chapter of Section One of Part Two of the Catechism (CCC 1066 through 1130), "The Paschal Mystery in the Age of the Church," treating the liturgy as a work of the Holy Trinity and the paschal mystery in the sacraments of the Church.

In the Church, here and now. Christian considers the changing vocation of religious communities in Algeria, and that their life in 1995 was becoming much more dangerous. Henri Teissier, archbishop of Algiers, had asked these communities to consider whether they might leave for safer homes, while seeking to maintain a "core" around the bishop to allow the mission of the Church to continue in Algeria. Christian returns, again and again, to his own community's choice to remain.

The Charism of the Martyr. How could a vocation to the religious life be consonant with grave danger? For Christian, there is no contradiction. This moving series reminds us that the desert fathers too made an offering of martyrdom, that the incarnation together with the cross and resurrection stands at the heart of Christian witness and ministry. Christian shows that the paschal mystery and the Cistercian charism were not incompatible with the community's circumstances.

The Shared Search for God

One of the central features of the monastery's life was "praying among other people at prayer," *priants parmi d'autres priants.* In February 1995 Christian wrote, "The new threat that weighs over us does not change anything about this reality. The best way for us to stay safe is to keep this in mind. This is the SIGN that God dared to make by gathering us here."[8] Christian's teaching to his monastic brothers is sensitive to their pragmatic circumstances but always faithful to the desire to be with the Other. After Mohammed's death Christian wrote, "He exists. He evokes for me all others." Jane Foulcher, who believes that Christian was familiar with Emmanuel Levinas, adopts the vocabulary of the Other here and elsewhere:

> For de Chergé, the recognition of his own identity, being created by and for God, immediately necessitates consideration of the other. This is of central importance. He continues: "We do grave damage [de Chergé uses a strong word here, '*mutilations*'] because we forget that it is God who builds every human house, often without the knowledge of the tenant." For de Chergé, Saint Paul's words are not confined to the Christian community: all human beings are temples of the Spirit.[9]

As monastic superior, Christian occupied the position of leader of the community at Tibhirine and as such had the responsibility of pastor as well as teacher. As the Rule of Saint Benedict indicates, the superior's teaching "should, like the leaven of divine justice, permeate the minds of his disciples."[10] Central to all Christian's remarks on Christian-Muslim encounter was the principle that "all seekers for God are brothers, [for] that quest creates fraternal character . . . and

8. DPTJ 2/23//95. Christian regularly indicates emphasis by all caps, capitals, or quotation marks. We have retained those in this text.

9. Jane Foulcher, "Nuit de feu: Christian de Chergé and Prayer with the Other," *Spiritus: A Journal of Christian Spirituality* 18 (2018): 221. The insertion is Foulcher's.

10. RB 2.5.

equally that all people are so created by the call of the Creator who made them for the same ideal."[11] This assertion, and Christian's aspirations more generally, can be said to go somewhat further than the principles of the Catholic declaration *Nostra Aetate* (1965) on "the relation of the Church to non-Christian religions." *Nostra Aetate* "urges all to forget the past [quarrels and hostilities] and to work sincerely for mutual understanding and to preserve as well as to promote together for the benefit of all mankind social justice and moral welfare, as well as peace and freedom."[12]

Similar questions of the limits of inclusion are also present in the Islamic tradition. In one chapter talk in 1986, Christian reflected on a verse of Surah 49: "The believers are but brothers, so make settlement between your brothers. And fear Allah that you may receive mercy." He notes that "For the majority of commentators and the great majority of the faithful, 'the believers' means 'Muslims.'" Other verses come to confirm the running theme: "only those versed in Islam are truly brothers in God." However, "if we were to ask our friends the mystics, they would say to us that all seekers for God are brothers . . . ."[13] Nevertheless, Christian argues that "many will tell us at least that 'believers' denotes all people of the Book, and those who have a brotherhood through Abraham."[14] He observes that Christians occupy a place close to "the believers," citing the passage "You will find the nearest of them

11. DPTJ 2/7/86. Throughout Christian's chapter talks he adopts an unusual use of the ellipsis, usually to imply the end of an idea and not to indicate omissions from a text. In this book, therefore, ellipses indicating omissions from printed texts are enclosed in square brackets.

12. Declaration of the Relation of the Church to Non-Christian Religions *Nostra Aetate* 3 (October 28, 1965), https://www.vatican.va/archive/hist_councils/ii_vatican_council/documents/vat-ii_decl_19651028_nostra-aetate_en.html.

13. DPTJ 2/7/86.

14. DPTJ 2/7/86.

in affection to the believers those who say, 'We are Christians.' That is because among them are priests and monks and because they are not arrogant" (Surah 5.82).

The importance of love in the two great Christian commandments, on which the Law and the Prophets depend, may also be seen in the Qur'an. "It is sure," writes Christian, "that the root of LOVE is less frequent in the Qur'an than in the Gospel, but, as Rachid says, it is under each word for those who know how to see it, because the characteristic of a root is to be buried."[15] Self-giving, loving sacrifice is also a theme not ignored by Christian, who more than ten years before his own death was reflecting on the sacrifice of the twentieth-century Franciscan martyr Saint Maximilian Kolbe and on 1 John 3:16: "We too must give our life for our brothers."[16]

In this shared search for God, Christian pointed out to the brethren that certain practices are shared by Christians and Muslims, among which he singles out almsgiving, prayer, and fasting. The close connection of fasting to Ramadan, both in the imagination and in the Qur'an, is acknowledged by Christian. He observes that only a single verse in the first Meccan surahs refers to it (Surah 19.26) with the word *sawn* (صَوْم), "abstention" or "a fast": Mary says after bearing her child, "Indeed, I have vowed to the Most Merciful abstention, so I will not speak today to man." "And this," says Christian, "is called the fast of Mary, mother of Jesus. A very special fast, since by all appearances it is a fast from speaking . . . Just as corporal fasting is a good way of 'taking back the body,' so fasting from speaking allows for 'taking back the heart.' Here and now, fasting is in the service of an interior re-fashioning [*une RE-FECTION intérieure*]."[17]

15. DPTJ 7/31/87.
16. DPTJ 8/14/85.
17. DPTJ 6/19/93.

Christian's message about Muslim and Christian prayer strengthens the understanding that it is a shared enterprise. He draws a connection between the appeal to pray "seven times a day" (Psalm 119) observed by Christians (and religious in particular) and seven times for *salat* (the ritual prayer of Muslims) during the day.[18] On Eid al-Adha 1994 and as part of a series of talks on subjects from the *Catechism of the Catholic Church*, Christian pointed out that "our ears are full of an earthly liturgy that is associated with the great celebrations of the Feast of the Sacrifice in Mecca," similar to the earthly liturgy, which is "a foretaste of the celestial liturgy that is celebrated in the holy city of Jerusalem."[19] The liturgy

> sets us in motion in space and time, *hic et nunc*, towards that which is beyond space and time. Our *Kaaba* is not a specific corner of the world, not even Calvary or the Holy Sepulchre . . . it is Christ in glory who also indicates to us our *qibla* to the extent that, like him, with him, we turn ourselves towards the Father. It is in this way, as we can sense, that all prayer can join and merge with his to sing the hymn of glory: the *ilah'a illa Allâh* or *Sanctus*![20]

The Search for God in Reading, Prayer, and Common Life

Christian gives particular prominence to three practices that are shared by Christians and Muslims and of which his community has considerable experience, both in their own context and alongside Muslims. In reading, both Muslims and Christians do more than acquire meaning from text; they

18. DPTJ 7/27/91.
19. DPTJ 5/21/94.
20. DPTJ 5/21/94.

are also shaped in other more fundamental ways by the practice. Prayer alongside the Other is seen to have mutually supportive ends. Life in community prepares one for mutual tolerance (and even flourishing), even in situations where it is difficult to love the Other.

Like many commentators, Christian remarks that the first word of the Qur'an is *iqra* ("recite!"; Christian adds, "and not 'read' "). As he puts it, "The first word of the Qur'an is, in fact, the key word of catechesis."[21] Perhaps by no coincidence, the first word of the Rule of Benedict, foundational text for all coenobitic monasticism, is *Ausculta* ("listen!").[22] In both Christian and Islamic practice, the centrality of reading and listening cannot be separated from the art and science of memory. Christian studied the Qur'an alongside the Bible and used it in his didactic talks as a source of inspiration.

Daily prayer is another significant practice shared by Muslims and Christians, one that was particularly important for the monks of Tibhirine who embraced the Benedictine charism. Shared prayer had a particular importance for Christian, and he wished to encourage it in others. Praying alongside his Muslim friend Mohammed had, of course, been foundational to his early experiences in Algeria. In his chapter talks, he describes several instances where that time of prayer had been held in common and suggests that in addition to familiarity with both traditions, such experiences could benefit from the use of silence and from understanding unconventional elements of shared time as prayerful.

In August 1987 Christian describes a shared time of prayer with international participants, during which crucifixes had been taken down to create "a space where everyone could pray." Both Muslims and Christians recited the first surah of the Qur'an and the prayer taught by Jesus to his followers.

21. DPTJ 11/27/93.
22. DPTJ 11/12/91.

Of the Lord's Prayer Christian commented that not all would have followed it since it was not recited in every language of those present; the Muslim commentator observed, "but it was in the heart." The gathering also reflected that the forthcoming feast of the Assumption of Mary ("*alayha as-salâm*," said the Muslim, noting the gender) was a great feast for all.[23]

In 1989 in another chapter talk Christian, reflecting on recent mutual prayer, offered some guiding principles: "what helps me to PRAY freely with the Other . . . ensuring a solid coherence between FAITH and PRAYER: lex orandi, lex credendi!"[24] In repeated chapter talks he returns to the question:

> 1. I don't think it would be fair to speak of successive or juxtaposed prayers . . . if that were the case, we would obviously have to take care of the balance of time and words, so that each could express oneself as much as the other. Otherwise it would look a bit like the assembly of Carmel and the duel between the priests of Baal and the prophet Elijah. I was very sensitive to the fact that at the end of the ritual prayers, some of the Alawite brothers turned to us to say, "Peace be with you," this wish that is intended for one's neighbor. They thus treated us as concelebrants of their prayers and not as spectators, although we did not perform their rites.
>
> 2. The SILENCE that we experienced together could have the same consistency as our prayer and of our particular monastic vocation (almost forty-five minutes, on both sides in search of IHSAN [excellence in worship], of presence to God) . . . a silence that leaves the spirit free to cry out the prayer of the Other, of the multitude, in ineffable sighs. Our prayer, which often seems so empty, must consciously tend to be this silence where the cries of people are engulfed, mysteriously, so similar to those

23. DPTJ 8/14/87.
24. DPTJ 11/28/89.

> that our Psalms have preserved and that constitute our own office in the church. One of us also spoke of an almost palpable PRESENCE.
>
> 3. For me it was our entire meeting that constituted our office of Vespers on that day [and not just the structured elements of prayer], taking place somewhat in the way that an extraordinary celebration replaces the corresponding time of day. We did well to integrate elements of the hour of Vespers . . . but I would like to emphasize that if the worst comes to the worst, it wouldn't be necessary. An example? proof? We sang in the *Magnificat* words of thanksgiving similar to those that they had also sung. This served as a kind of responsory!
>
> 4. It is important to get carried away, as quickly as possible, in praying for the other, if you want to be more than a Christian present next to a Muslim. I have a vocation to unite myself to Christ, who helps all prayer to rise and who offers the Father, mysteriously, this prayer of Islam like that of all righteousness.[25]

In general, Christian's position is that words can be very powerful ("peace be with you," for example), but silence, or presence, can be equally significant, allowing the Spirit to speak "in groans too deep for words" (Rom 8:26). As he noted on a subsequent occasion, prayer is not the only possible spiritual link with Muslims: "With certain neighbors, the connection of contemplation is able to take place without an explicit sharing of prayer (even if this is the most frequent means)."[26] For both communities, the function of prayer as a public work or a public service (noting the λαός + ἔργον etymology of *liturgy*) is shared both by the Christian enterprise of prayer and by *salat*.

25. DPTJ 11/28/89.
26. DPTJ 8/22/91.

Monastic Obedience (*islam*) and Stability

Several of the series of talks focused on particular aspects of the Rule of Saint Benedict, including the ladder of humility, which forms a significant part of that document, and, elsewhere, on the Constitutions of the Trappist Order. "Our life is, by vocation, an ordinary life, a simple life. Very simple acts end up consuming a large part of our time, as they punctuate the lives of many men and women around the world."[27] Christian observes that Benedict's Rule and associated Benedictine documents have similarities to the instructions to neophytes of the Rahmaniyya (Algerian Sufi) Brotherhood:

> - My child, you will serve your BROTHERS with dedication. To serve them is like a title of nobility for you.
>
> - The one who reveals the guilty actions of his brother loosens the veil that covers his own sins.
>
> - Assist them in illness, come to their aid in adversity.
>
> - Beware of hypocrisy, lies, and pride in your relations with your brothers.
>
> - When you talk about your brothers, apply yourself to praise their merits and show that you are proud of their brotherhood.
>
> - Think with them with the same mind: act with them with the same heart.[28]

This is not the only occasion on which the "instruments of the spiritual art" in Muslim spirituality are mentioned.[29] As Christian explains, the special conditions of Benedictine monasticism offer the monks of Tibhirine a particular way

27. DPTJ 5/18/87.
28. DPTJ 11/16/88.
29. DPTJ 2/1/89.

of exploring submission to God (*islam*) and the stability of life especially found in the monastic charism, both of which offer lessons to ordinary Christians faced with similar (if less dangerous) challenges.

In February 1996 (just over a month before the kidnapping of the community), Christian wrote,

> At the very moment when it appears a choice of asceticism and deprivation, the monastic way seeks to be a way of peace and authentic freedom leading to what Jesus himself experienced by calling it "perfect joy." What matters is that EVERYTHING be received "with an even temper" as a GIFT from the Father and experienced for the glory of God [. . .] . I have already noted that nowhere is any mention made of "MARTYRDOM" (in the sense in which we understand this word when we speak of the martyrs of Japan today). Only once in the Constitutions is there mention of "SUFFERINGS." In the very beautiful Constitution 3, which talks about the spirit of the Order, "The Cistercian way of life is COENOBITIC. [. . .] By bearing one another's burdens they fulfil Christ's Law, participating in his SUFFERINGS in the hope of entering the Kingdom of heaven." (CST 3.1)[30]

In other words, everything (even the potential dangers the monks faced) was to be taken as a gift from God that might be borne together, and from which much good could be done. In his final chapter talk, eleven days before their capture, Christian wrote,

> [Of the Prologue to the Rule] This is the only place where the word "SCHOOL" is used. Soon after, the word *CARITAS* appears . . . and it seems truly to mark the Pro-

30. DPTJ 2/6/96.

> logue's culminating moment and thus the ultimate aim of the whole Rule, and of the Benedictine school that it describes: CHARITY, the DELIGHT OF LOVE, the OVERFLOWING of the heart . . . all this in the PATIENCE of stability and perseverance, our way of "shar[ing] in the sufferings of Christ," our "MARTYRDOM," which should thus be a "martyrdom of love," and just as well a "martyrdom of HOPE," since this passage is all about movement, about walking and running towards the kingdom of which the community is the image, but not yet the full reality.[31]

Loving self-sacrifice, therefore, is not only accomplished by the faithful towards God (as Jesus sacrificed himself for the world), or from one member of the community to another, but by the community (and each member of it) for their friends, and for the wider community they served. Christian presented a new way of linking their experiences to the monastic vows of stability, obedience, and *conversio morum*. *Conversio morum* does not simply take place at a particular point, he explains; the process of conversion is always ongoing.

Submission and Stability

Christian's chapter talks suggest that he viewed canonical obedience to the monastic superior (described in RB 2 as taking the place of Christ in the monastery) as a means of submitting to the will of God, an imperative that of course his Muslim friends shared. When thinking about prayer, Christian reflected often on the agony and passion of Christ, whom he once called the "only 'Muslim' " (as in "Submitter").[32]

31. DPTJ 3/16/96 (punctuated and formatted as in the original). The community was invaded on March 27, 1996.

32. DPTJ 10/26/89.

In the Garden of Gethsemane, Christ prayed, "My Father, if it is possible, let this cup pass from me; yet not what I want but what you want" (Matt 26:39).

> To ask God that his Will be accomplished IN US is to enter into the prayer of the Son in whom the Spirit whispers, I WANT, the same Spirit that says in the Father and in the Son, Yes, I WANT. It is for precisely this reason that the Son is the only "Muslim," and that in the sense that the will of the Father is accomplished in us, we all have a vocation to be subjected in the same Spirit, "Muslims" just like the Son.[33]

In discussion with a Muslim friend, Christian observed that his interlocutor said that in order to understand *islam* (i.e., submission), it was necessary "to tear up the dictionary: [for] submission, abandonment to God, which is the vocation of every man, cannot be locked in a dictionary."[34] If Jesus is a model for *islam*, it is because "*islam* preexists the creation of man."

On the eve of Pentecost 1992, Christian noted that in this context, Jesus is "not here. He is ahead of us": "we listened to him, contemplated him, imagined him, but he is no longer here . . . He has seized us, he holds us, he maintains us." The prayer of Jesus, he said, "unveiled in that of Mary, is summed up, as we have said, in these two words: ECCE . . . FIAT."[35]

> And the believer—I am thinking of the Muslim—who thus turns to God with all his enthusiasm, and who does not want more than what God wants, with a submissive and free heart at the same time, this believer is led by the Spirit of the Son in place of the Son, even if he ignores it. There is no other "Father's house." The Spirit

33. DPTJ 10/26/89.
34. DPTJ 10/25/90.
35. DPTJ 6/6/92.

> allows one to think, feel, want like Christ. Thus, "fraternity with others and filiation with the Father become inseparable."[36]

These thoughts enriched the community's reflection on the monastic vow of obedience (not only to the superior but, more important, to the will of God for one's life).

Christian's talks also reflected on the vow of stability, which in customary circumstances dedicates Benedictines to life in a single community. In the case of the monks of Atlas, Christian's talks suggest that this vow of stability was not just to the abbey but to the wider Muslim community that it served. In his talk on CST 13 (Coenobitic Life), Christian described the "law of common life" in one's own monastery as "unity of the spirit in the charity of God, a bond of peace in a mutual and constant love of all the brothers, and holding all goods in common."[37] The vow of stability made by each of the brethren at Tibhirine was no doubt on their minds as they considered abandoning the abbey in the 1990s, and especially after Christmas Eve 1993, when they were invaded by raiders looking for medical supplies. Christian's talks from January 1994 onward often return to the question of consciously deciding to remain. In February 1995 he wrote,

> We have privileged as far as possible the permanence of our community, as such, at the heart of this church core that feels itself called to continue to show forth the GIFT of his own life given by Jesus, once and for all, on behalf of all people, and so also on behalf of Algerians today. And it is our job—a little troubled and not at all certain—to feel that many of those who remain, like us, despite everything, rely on us, even if they do not come to tell us as much.[38]

36. DPTJ 6/6/92.
37. DPTJ 5/25/91.
38. DPTJ 2/9/95.

The personal stories of each monk, and the circumstances by which each came to spend his life in a Trappist monastery in Algeria, are all part of the story. Each had discovered a reason for which he was called to remain in that extraordinary and dangerous place: as Christian put it, "one person would always be there for poor sick people; another found it more important and easier to pray for Muslims; another remained tied to this country where he had always lived . . ."[39] Their shared vocation, he wrote, was greater than the community (that is, the monastery) to which it was bound. Even if a single one of the brethren remained, "he would be there to express our FAITH in what has been experienced and what is perhaps no longer possible . . . our HOPE also that this shared life may be resumed . . ."[40]

> This hope is legitimate because we know from experience that humanity is magnified by welcoming each other in this way, mutually, in the most demanding spiritual emulation, that of prayer and common life. We love the Algerians enough to continue to hope for this for them, with all those among them who have believed in this like us and who have helped us to grow in this hope.[41]

In March 1994, in the wake of the Christmas Eve incident, the abbot general of the Trappist Order, Dom Bernardo Olivera, OCSO, wrote to Christian saying, "The order needs monks more than it needs martyrs. So you need to do everything you can to avoid a dramatic end that would be of no use to anybody."[42] The diocesan bishop, too, had written expressing concern. Both of these reactions, Christian thought, reminded

39. DPTJ 2/21/95.
40. DPTJ 2/28/95.
41. DPTJ 2/28/95.
42. Recalled by Christian in the chapter talk on 11/7/95.

him that it was "profoundly true, and traditional in the Church [that] we do not have the right to hasten our own deaths, including through 'martyrdom.' "[43] They would not stay at all costs, but

> it is vital for us to be able to remain faithful to our conscience, to our monastic ideal, to our surroundings, and to our Church. And it is in this respect that there is something shocking about Fr. Bernardo's observation. It calls attention away from the essential question, which is that of knowing whether the Order needs us in this country, at the present time . . . You could say that Scripture is also helping us from day to day. Only today, Saint Paul to the Romans: *Be patient in suffering, persevere in prayer*.[44]

In his first chapter talk of 1996 (January 4), Christian wrote,

> I am strongly in agreement with what Gilles [Nicolas] told us in his Christmas homily about seeking in the mystery of the Incarnation for the true rootedness of our reasons for "remaining" despite the threat and turbulence. In a letter to his loved ones, he confirms, "Christmas is EMMANUEL, God silently present, but the presence of Love, which alone is revolutionary, which alone transforms the hearts of one another."[45]

The homily Christian cites continues by reflecting that the Eucharist, "celebrated on the TIBHIRINE mountain, inhabited by down-to-earth, hardy people who are attached to Islam and to 'their' monks, seems to me to have a very important meaning and one that is not only symbolic." In fact, as

43. DPTJ 11/7/95.
44. DPTJ 11/7/95.
45. DPTJ 1/4/96.

Christian put it, it was appropriate in these circumstances, and in keeping with the monastic tradition, to

> join the imitation of CHRIST here through this offering of a continual Incarnation in "the humble consecration of a hidden life" of prayer and work (the expression of *Perfectae Caritatis* no. 9), rather than assimilating it directly to the solitary reality of the CROSS and of a martyrdom isolated from the material context of a life lived together over many years.[46]

The life of Atlas was that of an incarnational, eucharistic community in that it was both anaphoric and anagogical: the life of the monks of Atlas joyfully committed to their Muslim friends recalled the life of Christ given for the world and pointed forward to their sacrifice, which beautifully closes the circle.

Christian argued that it was unthinkable that Christians, and especially religious, might imagine that the mission of the Church in Algeria was over as a consequence of dangerous conflict. In fact, "for us there is no break with that old decision to stay in Algeria; to demonstrate our Church's Algerian nationality. We wanted to draw ever closer, to be ever more united, connected . . . we cannot take advantage of our status as foreigners in order to leave this country in its misfortune."[47] It would have been a serious mistake to leave the country in the hour of need, he argued, when the services they provided to the locals and the house of prayer that sustained their own needs were sorely needed. He continued, "We need to live the hidden side of our lifelong mission, along with the millions of Algerians who do not have a choice, nor control over any choices."

46. DPTJ 1/4/96.
47. DPTJ 3/25/95.

After spelling out these reasons for the community's staying, in the chapter talk for March 26, 1995, just under a year before their kidnapping, he also articulates the manner of their remaining:

> 1. The necessity of a true spiritual life. It is not enough to pray in this situation but rather to pray, instead, about this situation, finding meaning day after day, preserving ourselves from the temptation of adopting a defiant attitude (towards the FIS[48]/towards ourselves). Like the second temptation of Jesus:[49] neither tempt God nor provoke people. If we stay, it is because this seems to us to be the will of God. Experience calm availability, which is the opposite of defiance. We are not called to a trial of strength but rather to a trial of faithfulness.
>
> 2. The necessity of preserving our love for the Algerians, our trust in them, at a time when they are uncertain about themselves. Maintain our kindness, which is the very kindness of God. Watch them "over God's shoulder." Contemplate people. Do not allow our forces to be exhausted by the storminess of a debate that escapes us, over which we have no control. Let our gaze go beyond, deeper.
>
> 3. In our communities, to be humane in our relationships; to have positive encounters based on shared humanity; to create among us first of all the condition of remaining here. It is a matter of living through what we are living through together: our inadequacy in relation to Algeria, our waiting for Peace. Living through our present ministry, which is probably, essentially, that of SURVIVING.[50]

48. *Front Islamique du Salut* (the Islamic Salvation Front).
49. Matt 4: *Do not put the Lord your God to the test.*
50. DPTJ 3/26/95.

Christian's chapter talks were intended to be pragmatic and timely teaching and counsel for the brethren, who were engaged in common life together but also in dialogue with the Islamic society around them. Christian encouraged the community to think of the Muslim co-inhabitants of Tibhirine as brothers, with whom they shared various common tools with which to carry out their common search for God, including common prayer, but also silence and abiding peacefully together. That the brethren were followers of the Rule of Saint Benedict meant that they were well equipped for Christian's discourse on obedience/submission, and for the argument that even in straitened times the vow of canonical stability made by the monks of Tibhirine was not only to the abbey, but also to the people around it.

Enfolding all of these points was the enduring model of self-giving, Jesus Christ, whose loving sacrifice was recalled not only in the worship but also in the actions of each member of the community—even to the last of those actions that, in seven cases, took them to their death. As Christian wrote, prophetically, "my call to follow Christ would have to be lived out, sooner or later, in the very country in which I received the token of the greatest love of all." The loving sacrifice of Mohammed the policeman set the scene for a life of self-offering and a death that, in its love, reflected the greatest love of all.

Christian's teaching was based upon his own experiences, not only as a long-term friend and resident of Algeria and its Muslim population, but also upon nearly thirty years of life in community. In his talks to the community, which sought both to inspire them in their everyday experiences of Muslim encounter and in the particular challenge of deciding whether to leave or to remain in Algeria during conflict, Christian argues that "fraternal character" between Christians and Muslims is created by their shared search for God. In particular, he identifies three general practices shared by both faiths (reading, prayer, and common life), which could be part of that shared search in community.

A Note on Translation

Every text presents its own challenges and idiosyncrasies for the translator. The specific challenges of translating Christian de Chergé's chapter talks include the oral nature of these particular texts, their own dense citational habits, and the author's use of gendered language.

First, the published French texts are transcriptions of handwritten notes on sheets of paper, intended as aids to oral delivery. As such, the chapters are not the written record of complete speech, but rather retain a notational, elliptical quality as prompts for speech. This orality is especially audible in cases where sentences are fragmentary, leaving the main verb implicit, where transitions between points and sentences are abrupt and/or unexplained, and where comments are even reduced to bullet points and the highlighting of single words. We have resisted smoothing out the evidence of this orality, except where the sense is impeded. We have also retained formatting and punctuation where it is non-standard (including the use of ellipses and colons in particular), as characteristic of Christian's documentary style for those who will only read the chapters in English. Such editorial questions remain the subject of lively debate in the context of the publication of written notes originally intended for oral delivery. The term *mouvance*, proposed by Paul Zumthor as a synonym for "textual instability" including (and perhaps especially) in the context of textual transmission, might helpfully remind us that various textual states—Christian's notes, his oral delivery of the chapters, the published edition in French, our translations—are all in some sense different but equally legitimate versions of a work that remains dynamic.[51]

51. See Paul Zumthor, *Toward a Medieval Poetics*, trans. Philip E. Bennett (Minneapolis: University of Minnesota Press, 1992), and Jennifer Rushworth, "Barthes and *Mouvance*," *Exemplaria* 33 (2021): 312–26.

Second, Christian draws on a large constellation of texts in his chapters, ranging from the Jewish, Christian, and Islamic Scriptures to the Desert Fathers to modern ecclesiastical documents to books of all kinds that we assume were present in the community. Christian also makes reference to homilies and lectures that he and his audience would have heard together but that have not been preserved. We have clarified his more elliptical references where it has been possible to do so. Biblical scholarship and translation is one of the *fontes* of modern translation theory, and it has been an interesting experience negotiating the citation and translation of Scripture here.[52] It is not always possible to determine which version of Scripture Christian has in mind, or even whether he cites or paraphrases familiar material, whether in liturgical paraphrase or directly, from *La Bible de Jérusalem* or the *Traduction œcuménique de la Bible* or some other source. We have adopted the New Revised Standard Version. But in some places this version obscures Christian's point, and we have added a footnote where we diverge. In some cases, for other material, we draw on the official published text in English (for instance, in the *Statute on Unity and Pluralism*, which exists in multiple languages for the international, multilingual Cistercian Order). Where this is not possible, we translate directly from Christian's own words or citation.

Finally, it is worth noting that English is less gendered than French (the chapter on December 12, 1995, speaks of "serviteurs et servantes," for instance, where English can have just "servants"). We avoid gendered language for people where this is possible. However, in some cases the masculine is retained because Christian is addressing the community of monks specifically. It is sometimes difficult to say whether he

52. John Barton has recently provided a magisterial and accessible introduction to biblical translation: *The Word: On the Translation of the Bible* (London: Allen Lane, 2022).

is enunciating a general truth (non-gendered) or something specific to the community (where the masculine should be retained). At other times the question of gender is about the Church (feminine, in both English and French, as the Bride of Christ), or about the Holy Spirit. We have opted for "it" or "the Spirit," again taking advantage of the greater neutrality of English compared to French grammar (though the Holy Spirit is "he" in the official translation of the *Catechism of the Catholic Church*, referred to in the chapter on May 24, 1994).[53]

We provide commentaries on almost all of the chapter talks. The commentaries appear after the heading and date in italic type, followed by the text of the talk in roman type.

Up until now we have been discussing the question of how to translate. But the question of why to translate Christian's texts is of equal importance. We see this as an opportunity to preserve and share with a wider readership the heroic, holy lives of the seven martyrs of Atlas, their remarkable and shining example of faith, hope, and charity. The French edition with its lack of notes and gloss on the individual chapters is directed primarily at those who already have ears to hear. But with this commented edition in English translation we hope to find new ears for Christian's words.

Acknowledgments

This project began during the Covid-19 pandemic of 2020. We thank those who offered us kindness, care, and hospitality during that time.

We are grateful for the encouragement of the Association des écrits des moines de l'Atlas via Hilaire de Chergé to

53. But also see Nicholas Adams on God's pronouns: "Language is strange. It gets especially strange as it approaches God. There is no language, only languages. There is no divine pronoun, only pronouns" (Nicholas Adams, "God's Pronouns," *Scottish Journal of Theology* [2024]: 1–16, here 16).

undertake this project, and we thank the original publishers, Éditions de Bellefontaine, and Éditions du Cerf, via Laurence Rondinet, for permission to translate and reproduce Christian's chapter talks, and to Professor Marsha L. Dutton, Executive Editor of Cistercian Publications, for her support and care in bringing this work to completion.

Oxford
Feast of Saint James, 2024

GOD FOR ALL DAYS: THE FINAL MONASTIC CHAPTERS OF CHRISTIAN DE CHERGÉ

PART 1

Catechesis and the Liturgy.
November 23, 1993–August 23, 1994

Tuesday, November 23, 1993
A school of catechesis

This chapter is the first of a series on the practice of catechesis, otherwise known as religious instruction. The series engages at length with the promulgation on October 11, 1992, of the Catechism of the Catholic Church *(CCC), marking the thirtieth anniversary of the inauguration of the Second Vatican Council. On this feast of Saint Columbanus, a sixth-century Irish abbot who founded monasteries in France and Italy (including Bobbio, home of one of the most famous medieval monastic libraries), Christian borrows words from the second reading of the Office of Readings for the day, which are drawn from a sermon by Saint Columbanus "on faith."*[1] *For Columbanus's monks as much as for those at Tibhirine, they are apt words, for, as Christian points out, the search for God*

1. *Instruction* or *Sermon I on Faith*, sections 3–5, in the Office of Readings for Thursday of Week 7 of the Year: *Sancti Columbani Opera*, ed. and trans. G. S. M. Walker (Dublin: Dublin Institute for Advanced Studies, 1957), 62–67.

in monastic life is linked to an ongoing and lifelong catechetical commitment.

Tonight's reading, taken from one of Saint Columbanus's *Instructions*, is a good introduction to our effort at catechesis: it is the words of a monk to his brothers. Thus it is of particular interest to us:

- God is everywhere, fully everywhere, vast . . . . He lives in us just as the soul lives in the body.
- But who will be able to follow the Most High into his inexpressible and incomprehensible being? . . . who will dare to discuss the eternal origin of the universe? . . . let no one have the presumption to plumb God's impenetrable depths, the what, the how, the why of his being. This can neither be expressed, nor scrutinized, nor penetrated.
- Simply BELIEVE,[2] but with conviction, that God is what he has been and what he will be . . . if you seek the ineffable through reasoning, it will get further away from you; if you seek it through faith, wisdom will abide where she resides: at your door (Prov 1:21). And where she abides, she can be SEEN, even if only in part.
- "Since God is invisible, we must BELIEVE in him, and yet, God can be SEEN in a way by the pure in heart" (Matt 5:8).

FAITH and SIGHT are mutually exclusive and at the same time call one another. This explains why the place of the life of faith is also that of sight: *when did we see you? When you*

2. Christian regularly indicates emphasis by all caps, small caps, or quotation marks. We have retained those in this text.

fed, dressed, visited [me], etc.[3] There is a knowledge of God that is acquired by faithfulness to the grace of our call and to its concrete demands on existence. This is why the life choices that we make are not innocent when it comes to seeking God. And we feel strongly that the monastic way of life can be in its entirety a place of CATECHESIS, about God and about humankind.[4] We cannot associate monastic profession with baptism, which is the secret of initiation into the FAITH, without dedicating it at the same time to the formation of FAITH that accompanies baptism. We have taken a vow of permanent catechesis. The monastery is a school of catechesis.[5]

Saturday, November 27, 1993
Κατέχειν [*katechein*, "to hold fast"]

What is *catechesis? In this conference Christian helpfully notes that in its original sense* catechesis *transcends both the finitude and the fixity of the written version; the "bestselling book" to which he refers is the CCC, published in French in the previous year. He hints at the advantages of the long-held practice of oral, collective transmission (over the "private perusal" implied by the book format). The public ministry of Jesus on earth begins with teaching in the synagogue (Luke 4: reading from Isaiah and declaring the prophecy fulfilled) and ends with teaching the unwitting disciples on the road to Emmaus. Jesus was a catechist! The etymology Christian*

3. See the previous Sunday's Gospel, Matt 25:31-46 (*I was hungry and you gave me food*).

4. Here as elsewhere this translates *l'homme*.

5. Christian here uses the colloquial French abbreviation *école de caté* in quotation marks.

refers to is κατα ("down from") + εχο ("to have, possess"), thus "to hold fast."

Κατέχειν: the etymological Greek root entails a form of oral teaching, a spoken word that resonates and that has the aim of instructing, of educating. The word itself is rare in the New Testament (five or six occurrences). For instance, in the prologue of Luke, it is necessary for the honorable Theophilus to verify "how well founded the teaching is that [he has] received," his "catechesis" (see Luke 1:4). In Galatians 6:6, Paul asks the one who has received the teaching of the Word, the CATECHIZED, to "give his teacher," his CATECHIST, "a share in all his possessions." In Arabic, the term is translated as his *mu'allim*. Another significant text is 1 Corinthians 14:19: *in the assembly I would rather say five words with my mind, to* INSTRUCT *others as well, than ten thousand words in a tongue*. Catechesis is thus a public discourse destined for practical, efficacious teaching, involving a meeting between two abilities to understand, two forms of understanding. This is why the same word also refers to the fact of listening, not only to that of speaking. Going back to etymology enables us not to allow ourselves to be confined to the narrower understanding conveyed by the CATECHISM when it presents itself as a book, as a form of words fixed in writing and lending itself to private perusal.

For a long time, the catechism was first of all the *school of faith*, where an oral tradition that demanded to be received orally, to be recited, was communicated: *Iqra*: RECITE! The first word of the Qur'an is, in fact, the key word of catechesis.[6] The catechetical sermons of Saint Augustine, and even many of his homilies, preserve for us the trace of a dialogue with the people, of a questioning requiring the active participation of those assembled. And we know that even the gospels themselves—like all the narratives of the Old Testament—were first

6. *Iqra* is said to be the first word revealed to the Prophet Muhammad.

transmitted orally. They were established to meet the needs of oral teaching and oral catechesis, and in accordance with a specific public for whom they had to be adapted. The Word subsequently embedded in a scroll has remained living only because it has not ceased ricocheting from one meaning to another, from one moment in time to another, from one public to another. At heart, it is important that the catechism of the Catholic Church be entrusted to the oral transmission of bishops rather than destined first of all to be what it has been, a bestselling book . . . with the risk of remaining a closed form of language that is distorted and badly interpreted. JESUS, in Luke, reveals himself essentially as a CATECHIST: his "public" life is encompassed by two lessons of catechism, that of the synagogue in Nazareth and that of the road to Emmaus . . . without forgetting the additional lesson sought at the temple when he was twelve years old.

Thursday, December 2, 1993
catechesis and liturgy: the same PUBLIC function

Christian continues reflecting on the catechetical work of Jesus, noting that at the beginning and the end of his public ministry his teaching took place in an essentially liturgical context: first in the synagogue, then in the sharing of bread and wine. Both liturgy and catechesis are naturally carried out orally and in public. Indeed a resonance between them may be found in the structure of the Catechism, which structures its first part on the declarations of the Apostles' Creed, followed by an exposition of the liturgy.

Jesus as catechist! And beside him, we are and remain "catechumens" (those on whom the "oral" words of Jesus' public life are bestowed). See today's Gospel (Matthew 11:11-15 [*recte* Matt 7:21, 24-27]): "To be assembled around him, to listen, to put into practice."[7] This formation, this catechesis, has always had a more specific place: the LITURGY. The first time Jesus taught, at the synagogue in Nazareth, this teaching took place in a wholly cultic setting, one Sabbath day, and Jesus, taking the scroll,[8] undertook, carried out a liturgical act. Likewise, on the road to Emmaus he created a meal-time liturgy in the ritual gesture of the sharing of bread. Etymologically, LITURGY comes from the Greek λέως or λαός: public, and ἔργον: work. The liturgy is thus essentially a "public service." It is striking that the liturgy (etymologically, again) shares with catechesis a common vocation of being PUBLIC, externalized: on the one hand, voice; on the other hand, gesture (and voice too) . . . the sign that the word accompanies is the definition of the "sacramental economy."

ECONOMY: this word, rich in meaning, makes the connection: it encompasses "the laws of the house."[9] The House-Church is regulated according to a dual discipline, both catechetical and liturgical. Fundamental catechesis is rooted in and leads back to the liturgy. For centuries, theology was itself first of all constituted as a commentary on the gospels, on the Bible, inserted into a liturgical context. Acts gives the first witness of this pedagogical function experienced there where the people have gathered to pray, the liturgy of catechumens. In the East, catechetical discourse continues to be constructed on the basis of the living experience of a Church made to CELEBRATE the Covenant with God in the paschal Word.

7. Seemingly an expansion by Christian. He has mixed up the reference: the Gospel at Mass on Dec. 2, 1993, was in fact Matthew 7:21, 24-27: "Everyone then who hears these words of mine and acts on them," which must be the passage he intended.

8. See Luke 4:16-21. Fr.: *le livre*.

9. Christian is perhaps suggesting that οἰκονομία comes from οἶκος, "house," + νόμος, "law," though νέμω, "to distribute/dispense."

(Cf. *God is Living*, an Orthodox catechism.[10]) The CREDO was first of all a cultic proclamation. The West turns it slightly away from this function by taking it as the first part of its expression of faith (the first part of the catechism), deferring the liturgy to a second part.[11] *Lex orandi, lex credendi.*[12] This saying bore for a long time all the developments of the faith. The bishops of France used to be in agreement with this tradition when they presented the faith (more or less fifteen years ago) by commenting upon the fourth Eucharistic Prayer.

N.B. During the retreat: dwell, each one of you, with these two questions:

- What mode of liturgical sharing?
- What expression of mutual, fraternal assistance?

Tuesday, December 14, 1993
Lex orandi, lex credendi

Like catechesis, daily prayer is potentially less helpful when it is restricted to private reading of words in a book. Such reading must be in the invisible company of all the saints or, indeed, the words should be recited in community if their true significance is to be understood. If Vatican II was an opportunity for the Church to reflect on and teach about its position in the modern world, it is significant that its first teaching document is the Constitution on the Sacred Liturgy:

10. *Dieu est Vivant* [God is Living] (Paris: Cerf, 1979).

11. Section 2 of the First Part of the *Catechism of the Catholic Church* is based on headings taken from the Apostles' Creed; this is followed by Part Two, "The Celebration of the Christian Mystery."

12. "The law of faith is the law of belief."

Sacrosanctum Concilium. *But what better place to begin a catechetical enterprise than in the liturgy?*

[after Fr. Sanson's retreat from December 3 to 10]

It is perhaps one of the specific functions of monks in the Church to bear witness to this link between prayer and faith, between public prayer and public catechesis of the faith. Some might say that monks are devoted to the public prayer of the Church (in the East as in the West), but not directly to catechesis. Without here too bringing up the "one" image of the BODY[13] that has different members bound to each other . . . and thus entering into the mystical vision of the communion of saints (cf. Fr. Sanson's last day). It is interesting, incidentally, to note that when the Office once more becomes private prayer, it runs the risk of no longer teaching anybody, not even the person who recites it (in the breviary). In this way the Psalms, which were first of all the cry and praise in which a whole people recognized itself, can no longer evoke anything when they intervene in private life, unless one makes an effort to join the vast crowd of those at prayer, and the even vaster crowd of those who have not been taught to pray and who do not know that there is a God who is swift to turn the human heart to prayer.

It is necessary to quote here the magnificent text from Zephaniah given to us by the eucharistic liturgy for this feria (the third Tuesday of Advent):[14] *At that time I will change the speech of the peoples to a pure speech, that* ALL *of them may call on the name of the Lord and* SERVE *him with one accord. From beyond the rivers of Ethiopia my* SUPPLIANTS, *my scattered ones, shall bring my offering* (Zeph 3:9-10). The Christ himself, "the ideal of the monk,"[15] presents himself first as the

13. Or the image of the "one body," as 1 Cor 12: *un seul corps*.

14. First reading at Mass: Zeph 3:1-2, 9-13.

15. A reference to *Christ, the Ideal of the Monk: Spiritual Conferences on the Monastic and Religious Life*, by Columba Marmion, OSB (London: Sands, 1926).

Worshiper of the Father, it has been said.[16] The first catechesis is wanting to be and being "about the Father's business" (cf. the retreat).[17] Opening Vatican II, John XXIII challenged the Church to respond to the question of our time: "Church, what do you have to say for yourself?"[18] What is surprising is that the first text adopted by the Council, in its response to this question (and the only text approved as soon as the second session, on December 4, 1963, only just thirty years ago), was the Constitution on the Sacred Liturgy: *Sacrosanctum Concilium*, which, subsequently, in the conciliar acts, only appears in third place (which seems to me in the end unfortunate). Instinctively, the Church felt the need to go back to the liturgy in order to express ITSELF for itself and in order to welcome, in new words, the ancient treasury of its faith.

Thursday, December 16, 1993
Opus Dei, liturgy, *salât*

The work of the assembly, whether liturgical or catechetical, is a response to what God has already accomplished for his people. Among those in dialogue with Islam, the shared interest in collective daily prayer can be useful common ground, recognized in the activities of the other tradition. Salât ("prayer" or "supplication" in Arabic) refers to the obligation of daily prayer in Islam, one of its "five pillars."

16. See, for instance, "Jesus is not only the revelation of the redeeming God; he is also the supreme worshipper of the Father, the supreme realization of all religion" (Edward Schillebeeckx, *Christ the Sacrament of the Encounter with God* [Lanham, MD: Rowman and Littlefield, 1987], 18).

17. Luke 2:49.

18. Paraphrase of the speech of John XXIII on October 11, 1962, at the inauguration of the Council, https://www.vatican.va/content/john-xxiii/la/speeches/1962/documents/hf_j-xxiii_spe_19621011_opening-council.html.

Let us return to the etymology of LITURGY: λαός, ἔργον. Like catechesis, liturgy is a public function (matter). And a WORK, too, and therefore a "public service." We can compare this etymology, which comes from the Greek, to the Latin expression that designates our choir office in the Rule of Saint Benedict and the tradition of the Church: *OPUS DEI*. Work: "the WORK of God."[19] In both cases, then, liturgy is work. In both cases, equally, liturgy means an assembly, a people, an oral expression that is public and community-based. The work of God, *OPUS DEI*, means both that it comes from God (he does the WORK) and that it leads back to God (this WORK is for him, and we are the ones who do it). In the same way, the liturgy is the work of the people and the work for the people (and this then means that God does it).

We return to Jacob's ladder (or that of Nathanael)[20] with the liturgy of the angels *who ascend and descend*.[21] We also return to the Son of Man: *The one who came down is also the one who goes up* (John 3:13).[22] There is here a work of "back-and-forth" between God and man, man and God, which is the specific "service" of the HOLY SPIRIT. We can observe that the same thing happens in the *salât*, the ritual prayer of the Muslim, which is designed to be oral (said aloud or reasonably so) and public. This prayer has a "call from God" (*hayya 'ala salât*). The response comes from humans: it consists in ablutions and preparations, the formulation of an intention (which is said to constitute half of the *salât*). And then there is the ritual psalmody—and the Qur'an is to

19. Christian here uses two different French words for work: *œuvre* and *travail*.

20. See John 1:51: *Very truly, I tell you, you will see heaven opened and the angels of God ascending and descending upon the Son of Man.*

21. Gen 28:12.

22. John 3:13-14: *No one has ascended into heaven except the one who descended from heaven, the Son of Man. And just as Moses lifted up the serpent in the wilderness, so must the Son of Man be lifted up, that whoever believes in him may have eternal life.*

be received and interpreted in this context, just as the Word of God is the heart of our *Opus Dei*, in our liturgies.

Receiving the Word in this context, in this work of prayer, is very different from dissecting it in the work of exegesis. And there will probably be a gap between the often-disenchanted analysis (which, however, is necessary) of the text and the faithful reception that opens itself to what the Spirit gives the churches to confess. This is indeed why we are lucky, as monks, in the dialogue with Islam, to be able to share in the experience of Muslims at prayer and also to let ourselves be recognized by them. In the three states that Fr. Sanson outlined—active, contemplative, and intellectual —it is clear that the liturgy (*Opus Dei*, *salât*) is situated in the contemplative state, even if it also involves an ACTION in which intelligence, *intellectus fidei*, has something to say. And the same must be true of catechesis . . .

Saturday, December 18, 1993
The "porch" of Vatican II

Christian lays out the objectives of Sacrosanctum Concilium *and the ways in which it contributes to catechesis within the broader aims of Vatican II by quoting at length from its first two articles. The liturgy forms and shapes the faithful: or at least that is one of its aims.*

The "porch" of Vatican II is thus the Constitution on the Sacred Liturgy, *Sacrosanctum Concilium*.[23] And here are the first words of the preamble:

23. Christian here writes *le porche*. We have decided to keep the architectural image while acknowledging that "entry point" or something similar might sound more idiomatic.

> This sacred Council has several aims in view: it desires to impart an ever increasing vigor to the Christian life of the faithful, to adapt more suitably to the needs of our own times those institutions that are subject to change, to foster whatever can promote union among all who believe in Christ, to strengthen whatever can help to call the whole of mankind into the household of the Church. The Council therefore sees particularly cogent reasons for undertaking the reform and promotion of the liturgy.[24]

And it continues immediately:

> For the LITURGY, "through which the work of our redemption is accomplished,"[25] most of all in the divine sacrifice of the Eucharist, is the outstanding means whereby the faithful may express in their lives and manifest to others the mystery of Christ and the real nature of the true Church.

This text is enlightening as regards the catechetical function of the liturgy: not only is the liturgy the privileged site of catechesis, but it contributes greatly to forming catechists. All the faithful draw from the liturgy, even if unconsciously, the aspects of their vocation as a lifelong witness (or disciple), an apostle of the teachings of Christ and of the church. We thus pass from cultic celebration to the celebration of a life that we know can be, in its entirety, the site of the presence of God, a site of adoration. And further on, the Council rightly recalls, "There is hardly any proper use of material things that cannot thus be directed toward the sanctification of men and the praise of God."[26] The admirable service of the simplest things in the

24. Constitution on the Sacred Liturgy (*Sacrosanctum Concilium*), https://www.vatican.va/archive/hist_councils/ii_vatican_council/documents/vat-ii_const_19631204_sacrosanctum-concilium_en.html.

25. Secret of the Ninth Sunday after Pentecost.

26. *Sacrosanctum Concilium* 61.

sacraments or in the sacramentals demonstrates, without saying a word about it, the aptitude of LIFE to be sanctified in its entirety and, at the very same time, to proclaim the sanctity of the Creator. Here we find something regrettable that perhaps marks the progress made since Vatican II; as you will have noticed, the definition of the liturgy is given in that text as dependent upon "the mystery of Christ and the real nature of the true Church." I think that nowadays we would immediately emphasize that the Church, in its cultic function, is nothing but the sacrament of the vast capacity for adoration of the whole of creation . . . and also that the mystery of Christ is accomplished everywhere God is served, honored, adored, or even simply sought "in spirit and in truth."[27] It was Jesus himself who said as much to the Samaritan woman.

Tuesday, December 21, 1993

Continuing from the previous conference, Christian articulates the ways in which Sacrosanctum Concilium *implies that the liturgy is not an inflexible monolith, but something that can be shaped and formed in its specifics. While the fixed forms of prayer in Christianity and Islam are essential and foundational, "the overflowing of the heart" necessitates a modicum of flexibility.*

It is perhaps interesting, still with the aim of better understanding the fundamental relationship between catechesis and the liturgy, to go over the four aims that the Second Vatican Council set for itself and that it expressed—and this is important—as early as the Constitution on the Sacred Liturgy, as if justifying the fact of the Council's having started

27. John 4:24.

its work of teaching and reform [*aggiornamento*] of the Church in that manner.[28] The holy Council thus proposed

> 1. "to impart an ever increasing vigor to the Christian life of the faithful." A life lived in faith, like faith itself, is susceptible to PROGRESS, and this progress relies upon time, in the regularity and succession of each day. The temptation to blink must be avoided. There is no rest in the life of faith merely because it is situated from the beginning in the grace of the seventh day, of the paschal Sabbath . . . because it needs to continue to do the daily work of creation.
>
> 2. "to adapt more suitably to the needs of our own times those institutions that are subject to change . . . ." This idea comes back frequently in the Constitution, every time it is suggested that the rites be revised, purged of outdated elements and of the additions of a former time. The liturgy is a LIVING being . . . and *vita in motu.*[29] Faith is also a LIVING being. Experience shows that when worship solidifies, so does belief, and its formulations, like the rubrics, come to seem almost absolute. There are here a freedom and a humility of expression that, understood properly, are the source of infinite enrichment. We know, we see that it is predominantly otherwise in Islam. It can seem reassuring to have a single, simple *shahâda*,[30] a *salât* whose details are regulated. We then surmise that the overflowing of the heart always needs to find a place on the margins of this ritualism, in the *dhikr*,[31] for example, or the different *'aqîda* (additional credos) with there, too, the temptation to formalize the bursting forth of spontaneity. When we prepare the Office or the Eucharist with the task of

28. Laid out in *Sacrosanctum Concilium* 1.
29. "Life in motion."
30. "testimony," the Islamic profession of faith.
31. "remembrance," repetitive phrases used to bring to mind the presence of God.

leading or presiding over them, we see clearly that it would be easier to stick to the ready-made expressions "that have been proven," as we say. But our labor[32] is in the service of the creativity that is inherent in faith. And our Office, composed of set elements and of others left to the freedom of the heart that believes and prays, is indeed that place where LIFE announces itself as a reality today.

Wednesday, January 19, 1994
Liturgy and UNITY . . .

Christian resumes with the third objective of Vatican II as articulated in Sacrosanctum Concilium, *namely union amongst Christians. This conference falls within the Week of Prayer for Christian Unity, an initiative of the World Council of Churches. The parenthetical observation at the start refers to the fact that on Christmas Eve a squad from the Armed Islamic Group (GIA) visited the monastery intent on compelling the brethren to contribute to their campaign. There began the deliberations over whether or not to leave the community.*

[After Christmas . . . and lots of other things!]

It is good in this Week of unity[33] to return to the aims that Vatican II put forward for itself and that can then be found enumerated in the first paragraph of its "precursory" text: the Constitution on the Sacred Liturgy. These aims are entrusted to all of us from the moment the Council sees them as inscribed in the worship of the Church, and they are valid

32. Christian writes "*notre travail d'accouchement*," a play on work and giving birth.

33. The Week of Prayer for Christian Unity.

for all the times of this worship, that is to say that they must be found to be very much alive and palpable in the present day of our liturgy. This is a way for us monks, who are so connected to the prayer of the Church, to be aware that we are at the heart of the mission and the progress of the Christian life in us and, step by step, in the whole world.

The holy Council thus proposed, following on 3. "to foster whatever can promote UNION among all who believe in Christ." Today it can seem obvious to us that the unity of those who believe in Christ comes through the prayer of Christ lived together. Ecumenism was reinvented when it became as if solicited in the course of a "week of prayer" open to all Christians and agreed to by all. Prayer once more became a prerequisite. The Holy Spirit was recognized by all as the teacher of unity—a unity already bestowed since, as we confessed, within all of us there arises the cry of *Abba! Father!* and this is the joy of our Christian faith. Saying the *Pater Noster* together: what an achievement!

However, let us be very aware that the liturgy is also the site where our divisions have managed and still manage to worsen, and even to excommunicate one another, in the most sacramental sense of the term. The Council itself only advised *communicatio in sacris* with much reservation, running into the question of knowing whether the sacrament should first of all signify an already common, shared faith, or whether it also has the effect of promoting this. . . . What is certain is that the churches in their *praxis* still remain divided with respect to "intercommunion," and even often to one same baptism, and a difference in rites that seems more and more to be a richness, an incalculable treasure in the service of a faith that is always greater than its expressions, is something else entirely.

Yet the sacrament, the Eucharist in particular, only has its full meaning as the signifier and bearer of a UNITY that is forever given, as present and as real as the unique body of the Savior behind the veil of the "elements." As long as we concede that there is only ONE House,[34] all the while specifying that the dinner table is not open to everybody, we really run the risk of getting the wrong house, or at any rate, as Saint Paul said to the Corinthians, of not celebrating the Passover of the Lord sacrificed for all in remission of sins, and first of all of the sin of our divisions that we all share. Confessing this sin in an undivided manner is already a step forward! The liturgy invites us every day to celebrate indivisible grace.

Saturday, January 29, 1994
Liturgy and mission *ad extra*

In embracing the notion of a People of God that incorporated everyone, Vatican II proposed that "at all times and in every race God has given welcome to whosoever fears Him and does what is right" (LG 9). The documents of the Council, especially the Decree on Ecumenism, Unitatis Redintegratio, *welcomed movement toward "the restoration of unity among all Christians." Christian reflects on the maxim* Extra ecclesia nulla salus, *a paraphrase of a passage in Letter LXII of Cyprian of Carthage (d. 258).*

Getting to the fourth aim that the Council proposed . . . an openness *ad extra*, towards those who belong to the modern world without being visibly incorporated into the Church. Vatican II thus proposed, from the outset, 4. "to strengthen whatever can help to call the whole of mankind into the household of the Church."

34. This seems like a pun on *οἰκουμένη* / *οἶκος*.

Just as the three previous objectives seem clear to us and still relevant to us in their formulation, including the one that aims at unity among Christians, since that unity is still in the making . . . so does the Council's last point seem to me to be marked by a theology of the Church and a conception of mission that one might think would have changed quite a bit over the last thirty years. It is clear that behind this expression there is a quite a strict, narrow interpretation, in the words of the saying borrowed from Saint Cyprian: "outside of the Church there is no salvation."[35] We have learned since to put this quotation back into its original context, which was essentially within the Church: there should be no divisions between Christians to the extent that each part would claim to be the agent of salvation to the exclusion of the others. But the Church has, in fact, got to the point of preaching the baptism as a necessary condition of salvation. The ending of Saint Matthew could be invoked in support.

The Church forgot that its vocation was to be itself, in the world, like the great SACRAMENT of the communion of saints and the encounter with the God of Jesus Christ, the sacrament of the kingdom and not the kingdom itself, to which, in fact, all people are called by universal redeeming grace. Our bishops recalled this in their document of 1979: "Nobody can know to what God is calling every person in his or her path in this world." It would be interesting to demonstrate that the Constitution *De Ecclesia*, dated one year after this text, already represents progress from this initial statement. And if the Council gave itself a pastoral Constitution on "the Church in the modern world," it was indeed in order better to express this absolutely necessary, dialogic relationship between Church and world: dialogic but neither possessive nor syncretist. "Inclusive," as Paul VI said, which is to say that it did not excom-

35. Letter LXXII of Cyprian of Carthage (d. 258): *Salus extra ecclesiam non est.*

municate, and that everything that makes up humanity interests and interpellates the Church as being of the order of grace linked to Creation as to Incarnation. Finally, it is clear that *concourir*, "to call," does not mean *succeeding* and that the Church, like its Master, has the experience of the sovereign freedom of each person, even if it is hard for the Church, as it is for Jesus, to see the rich young man apparently distancing himself from the riches of the kingdom.

But what is perhaps most surprising about the fourth objective of the Council is that it is placed here in direct relationship with the liturgy. How can people who are not within the Church feel themselves to be "called," interpellated, by the worship of the Church in which they are not supposed to participate? What wants to be said here is addressed first of all to the members of the Church, to us. It matters that the liturgy be an OPEN place. The liturgy is neither a conclave nor a ghetto. Pentecost opened wide the doors of the Cenacle. No locks on our churches, nor entry cards. They are generally public places. And the prayer that unfolds in them is designed to be public. And to demonstrate that this prayer is addressed to everyone, "for you and for many . . . ,"[36] it is expressed for everyone: "prayer of the faithful" or "universal prayer"; it's all the same thing.

We find here the image of the tree where all birds can come and make their nest or simply seek some shade, with this paradox linked to the parable: it requires time for a tree truly to rise in the direction of heaven. For birds, this movement is evident. And the Church here is a tree. It is the Holy Spirit, which is (rather) a sort of bird! A bell tower in the countryside (like a minaret . . .), bells (like the call of the muezzin) contribute to summon "all people to the heart of this place of worship that is realized by the Church of Jesus Christ present

36. A citation of the Institution Narrative in the Eucharistic Prayer.

amongst humankind." But also the word revealed at the heart of the liturgy and that is at once "call" and catechesis, human language and expression of faith, sign and credo. The signs themselves contribute to this call destined for everyone, because they belong to the life of each individual: water, bread, wine, oil, etc. . . . "In the liturgy, the sacrament and the symbol must reach as far as the public square and bring to that a new meaning," as Rembert Weakland said in a recent lecture,[37] and he also says, "The liturgy gives to the believers on the outside, in the world, the foundations which enable them to discern what belongs to the Spirit and what does not belong to the Spirit. . . . Thus the Eucharistic community becomes more aware of the broken body of Christ in the world." It is through this that the liturgy contributes to the Church's vocation to be catholic, and that it is in its entirety the living catechesis of this catholicity, addressed to all people, even if it needs, to reach the multitude, to go through the little core of the faithful who celebrate the liturgy in Church, like Christ reduced to confiding the Good News in twelve unlucky survivors of the crowds that followed him.

Saturday, February 26, 1994

ALMSGIVING, PRAYER, FASTING . . .

This conference was read on the first Saturday of Lent. The works of the Gospel referred to in this conference are given in Matthew 6. These may be compared with the tools for good works in the fourth chapter of the Rule of Saint Benedict and, indeed, with three of the five pillars of Islam: salât *(prayer);* zakat *(almsgiving);* sawm *(fasting). Each, for Christian, points*

37. Christian's reference is to Weakland's words quoted in the *Bulletin de l'Alliance Inter-Monastères* 55 (1993).

to God, self, or the other, in the context of the commandment of love for God and neighbor.

The three tools recommended for Lent, three "works" of the Gospel (given in this order), three pillars of Islam, three tools of Benedict . . . three that make just ONE. And yet they are three, like the three partners in the commandment of love: the other, God, myself. I am directed towards the other by CHARITY, or the other is directed towards me when it is I who am the recipient. PRAYER sends me towards God in a back-and-forth initiated by God. And I, this "me" that I find so hard to love, to confess, see how FASTING gives myself back to myself. A fasting of my mouth, and also of my lips, my ears, my senses, my thoughts . . . in order to find once more the path of the heart where God gives me the ability to love the one he loves in me.

The importance of fasting in its proper place—the difficulty, too, since it is easy to see that an excessive or exclusive love of oneself would mean instantly rejecting all forms of fasting, an anti-fasting that would lead to using one's sense gluttonously, in an internal, egocentric fashion, in ignorance of the other and of God. It is thus necessary to know how to make fasting specific in its own, primary aim—love, respecting "MYSELF"—in order better to include it, for fasting and charity are connected by sharing, just as prayer and charity join together in intercession, and all three are brought together in the EUCHARIST in order to celebrate the mystery that they must signify collectively, that of the communion of saints. And thus it is that these three, which Jesus gives back to us in the Sermon on the Mount and which the Church offers to us on the very threshold of Lent, are going to recreate the human being in its original newness, and reveal the image buried in God's secret.[38] If they have something to do

38. Perhaps an oblique reference to *You died, and your life is hidden with Christ in God* (Col 3:3).

with the resemblance that remains the highest destiny of humankind, it is because they fall within the jurisdiction of that which is enclosed in the Unique: in a word, before returning to this point, suggesting that charity means the Spirit, that prayer means the Son, and that fasting means the Father . . . and that it is even for this reason that it is so difficult to use these tools in spirit and truth.

Tuesday, March 1, 1994
. . . and TRINITY in GOD

The three tools of Lent are associated with the Persons of the Trinity: Christian suggests that alms may be aligned with the Spirit, prayer with the Son, and fasting with the Father.

ALMSGIVING is the work of the SPIRIT: the Spirit shares his gifts with us but is above all a GIFT, given from the Father to the Son, and from the Son to the Father in reciprocated love. The Spirit gives from one to the other. That reminds us that charity is rarely unidirectional, even if its content, on either side, differs. Who can say which of these is most valuable: the giving of money or the smile offered in exchange? The Spirit keeps us in a state of openness to welcome and to gift-giving. He does not keep anything for himself and has nothing of his own.

PRAYER is the work of the Son: offered through the Spirit, no doubt, but born from the very being of the Son that prayer expresses and accomplishes: *Abba! Father* . . . The Son is Prayer. He is this cry. And everything that he does is sustained by this cry. We can say of him that everything is "prayer," that his action is contemplation, that his work is thanks-"giving." . . .

As for FASTING, it is the work of the FATHER; it is even for this reason that it is so difficult for us to conceive of it and to live it . . . approaching it from this angle is perhaps new, but suggestive. And doing so can help, it seems to me, to give fasting its own specific, personal autonomy, without cutting it off from the other two "pillars" (charity and prayer) and turning it into something absolute. By definition, fasting is "hollow" . . . it is dispossession, self-forgetting, and also desire. It is the refusal to identify oneself with something relative, and even less with something superfluous: food, words, spectacle, any ordinary possession. . . . It means respecting the proper identity of every being, of bread as of stone (which must remain a stone and not become bread), of every creature placed here and considered to be GOOD.

Thus fasting is called CHASTITY when it concerns contemplating and loving a human partner without monopolizing him or her so as to take a selfish pleasure in them. Only the Son, the true Bread of God (John 6) can sate the expectations of such a fast, and only the Son can confirm that this fast is very relative, since it is in its entirety a RELATION desired with the other, while only the Absolute of the Other can fill the hollow of such an absence. The fasting of Mary, in the Qur'an, which involves not "speaking to anybody today"[39] in anticipation of the Word. A profound—and often lost—meaning of Ramadan, of Lent as well, with Jesus in the desert experiencing the Father after his baptism in the Jordan. In a word, fasting means the kenosis that pre-exists in the Father and within which the Son can be eternally begotten in the compassion of the Spirit.

39. A reference to Qur'an Surah 19.26: "Indeed, I have vowed to the Most Merciful abstention, so I will not speak today to man." In the chapter talk for June 19, 1993, Christian talks about it as a fast from speaking.

Saturday, March 12, 1994

CATECHISM: the celebration of the CHRISTIAN MYSTERY

Ordained in 1964, Christian was thoroughly grounded in the theology and thinking of the Second Vatican Council. The "mystery of salvation" of which Christian speaks is introduced in Lumen Gentium, *where the Church itself is also described as "a mystery." In making reference to creation and the "Mass on the world" he borrows from Pierre Teilhard de Chardin, SJ, the not uncontroversial palaeontologist and Jesuit who saw no contradictions among creation, evolution, and Christian faith. The "Symbol of the faith" mentioned in CCC 1066 is a reference to the Creeds.*

> **CCC 1066** *In the Symbol of the faith the Church confesses the mystery of the Holy Trinity and of the plan of God's "good pleasure" for all creation: the Father accomplishes the "mystery of his will" by giving his beloved Son and his Holy Spirit for the salvation of the world and for the glory of his name (Eph 1:9). Such is the mystery of Christ, revealed and fulfilled in history according to the wisely ordered plan that St. Paul calls the "plan of the mystery" (Eph 3:9) and the patristic tradition will call the "economy of the Word incarnate" or the "economy of salvation."*

Coming to the very text of the Catechism after a long introduction: the etymology of "liturgy and catechesis" in their mutual constitutive, historical connections; Vatican II and the mission of the Church. As a prelude, numbers 1066–1068 ponder, "Why the liturgy?" In number 1066, the liturgy is immediately situated at the heart of creation. It is as a part of creation that the liturgy appeals to me and draws me into its movement. The liturgy is the expression of the "mystery of SALVATION" in which I become part of the will of the Father offering his Son and the Holy Spirit: through the liturgy, I enter into the economy, that is to say, into the "laws of the house." I return, rather, to this admirable order that ought to govern the interior of the house-Creation so that the relationships that resonate within the Trinity might be established there between all.

It might perhaps have been necessary for it to be more evident, from this first number, that there could be no possible liturgy in the heart of creation were there not an eternal liturgy in the very heart of God. The liturgy is part of the image and of likeness. The Holy Spirit is there to bear witness to this. It is the Holy Spirit who, for all eternity, makes not only the angels and celestial beings sing joyful psalms, but especially and first of all the very Being of the Son in an uninterrupted thanksgiving, which did not need creation to have a concrete point of reference. It is this first mystery that enables us to imagine and to join with the hidden praise of all beings, even the most inanimate, and to celebrate this praise, particularly in the Psalms: praise of the earth and of stones, of the sea and the stars . . . If every creature bears within itself the trace of the divine, it is not in order to be idolized and erected into an absolute, but in order to be susceptible to sweep all the others up into this immense cosmic harmony.

Teilhard and so many others knew to celebrate this "Eucharist over the world," which is "thanksgiving of the world," the unique mystery of the Christ "revealed in history" from the beginning. This cosmic praise is Incarnation begun. It is revelation inscribed in the nature of things. There is a power that reveals the world that stems from this universal vocation towards divine worship. There is only one absolute rule in order that this native symphony does not become cacophony: the worship must remain ordered according to its Source. If the catechism situates us directly within the "economy of salvation," it is because it takes as its starting point the statement that the water has been polluted, that it no longer returns to the Source. The only worship possible is that of the PUBLICAN.[40]

40. The parable of the Pharisee and the Publican, Luke 18:9-14: *God be merciful to me, a sinner.*

Tuesday, March 15, 1994
nos. 1067–1068 the paschal mystery

Christian explains that the paschal mystery, a new passover in Christ, is the subject of the liturgy. He ties the worship of God to the history of God's people and their own concerns, since humanity is not "unscathed by sin."

> CCC 1067 *"The wonderful works of God among the people of the Old Testament were but a prelude to the work of Christ the Lord in redeeming mankind and giving perfect glory to God. He accomplished this work principally by the Paschal mystery of his blessed Passion, Resurrection from the dead, and glorious Ascension, whereby 'dying he destroyed our death, rising he restored our life.' For it was from the side of Christ as he slept the sleep of death upon the cross that there came forth 'the wondrous sacrament of the whole Church'" (SC 5). For this reason, the Church celebrates in the liturgy above all the Paschal mystery by which Christ accomplished the work of our salvation.*[41]
>
> CCC 1068 *It is this mystery of Christ that the Church proclaims and celebrates in her liturgy so that the faithful may live from it and bear witness to it in the world:*
>
> > *For it is in the liturgy, especially in the divine sacrifice of the Eucharist, that "the work of our redemption is accomplished," and it is through the liturgy especially that the faithful are enabled to express in their lives and manifest to others the mystery of Christ and the real nature of the true Church. (SC 2)*

41. Parenthetical notes in Christian's citations to the Catechism are footnotes in the published Vatican edition.

The liturgy is "principally celebration of the paschal mystery," that is, of the mystery "of the blessed Passion of our Lord Jesus Christ, his Resurrection from the dead, and his glorious Ascension." You might then wonder what the liturgy was before the manifestation of this mystery, before the Incarnation inscribed it in the course of events. Especially since humanity seems to be, almost to the same extent as God, at the origin of this "mystery" insofar as humanity took, in Christ's passion, an active part with which we are familiar. Is the liturgy tied to human sin and, instantaneously, to the most significant expression of this sin, which is the supreme injustice of the CROSS? The "wonderful works of God [. . .] of the Old Testament," evoked by the Catechism as a prelude to the paschal mystery, seem themselves to be tied to the evil that is prevalent amongst humankind, whether the flood, exodus, or exile.

And it is true that however far back in time you look, the worship human beings offer to God seems to stem directly from their consciousness of their own limits and of the power held by the spirit of evil over them, over their works, over their environment and the whole of creation. Undoubtedly, worship involves glorifying God, but with the confessed desire that he protect his faithful, deliver them, support them, preserve them from themselves and from misfortune. Human as I am I can only dream of a "pure nature," unscathed by sin; I need faith in order to affirm that such a nature exists. Likewise, we can only dream about "pure worship," worship prior to sin, which would be the gratuitous celebration of the Love of God, without reference to the salvific work made necessary by our shying away from love.

And yet, was humanity not CREATED in order to worship God, to praise him, to serve him, and in this way freely to merit eternal life? That was the definition of the old catechism. In this case, is it not to denature the liturgy to define it principally as a celebration of the paschal mystery, perceived as closely dependent on its denaturation by sin? It seems that this impasse can only be escaped by situating the paschal mystery, resolutely, in GOD, just as I have situated the liturgy at the heart of the mystery of the Trinity. There is an eternal PASSOVER in God. It is passover wherever there is will, gift, and love. The mystery of God is PASCHAL and it is this mystery that is "realized" in the most concrete sense of the word, first of all in creation, then by adapting itself to humanity in all its conditions, including that of the sinner.

Tuesday, March 22, 1994
The Passover in God

In this chapter Christian makes explicit the connection between the passover of Exodus 12 and the paschal mystery of Christ's death and resurrection. Beginning with the title, he uses similar language to describe passover, the paschal mystery of Christ's death and resurrection, and "passage." Christ passes from the Father to the world, allowing the world to return to the Father. In the liturgy, this passage from death to life is commemorated. There is also movement—or passage—between the Persons of the Trinity: "when the Son turned himself wholly towards the Father to give the Spirit back to him." In the liturgy, we can situate ourselves more readily in the divine economy, avoiding making the house of prayer of Luke 19 into a den of robbers.

So the great works of the Old Testament are tied to the "paschal mystery" because they are already to do with the "mystery of Christ." The same must be said of CREATION itself, which is cosmic liturgy presided over by the Spirit, celebration of the effective Word, passover, primordial passage from the Father to the world, setting in motion the return of the world to the Father. It is the detour in this return, due to sin, that gives to this paschal movement the meaning and value of a "work of redemption." It is significant for us that in history the passover of the people in the desert effectively anticipated the passover of Christ on the cross . . . and that the passage of humanity through God's creative hands can be recognized as the very first beginning, imprinting in human nature itself a predilection for abandoning itself into its Father's hands; when the time comes, this abandonment will find a way to express itself as the pinnacle of perfect worship, the greatest love, including all people in a filial liturgy in which the passage is accomplished.

The Last Supper and the cross take on a sense of celebration—a celebration that is unique and definitive—because human will, gift, and love find there, in unison, the will, gift, and love that express the paschal desire intimately experienced in God. Let's repeat this: Christ's "paschal mystery" only exists because there is passover in God. The trinitarian life is nothing other than this paschal mystery, shaping each Person in the obligatory passage that draws it towards the other two, each in its own way. The indivisible unity that is called God revealed itself to us in its unimaginable perfection when the Father's Voice celebrated the Son, in the cloud of the Spirit, and when the Son turned himself wholly towards the Father to give the Spirit back to him: this is the Passover.

The highest destiny of humanity is to enter into this liturgy, in which they can collaborate in their own right because they are themselves defined as capable of will, gift, and love, in the image and likeness, from the beginning. SALVATION, for humanity, means rediscovering God's very path of mystery by allowing themselves to be integrated once more into the divine economy, that is, by fitting better and better into the "laws of the house" that make this house "a house of prayer" and not what it has become, the "den of a robber"[42] who is ceaselessly tempted by "plundering the burnt offerings."[43]

Thursday, March 24, 1994
nos. 1069–1070
What does the word "liturgy" mean?

Christian is reacting here to the Catechism's dismissal of the popular but discredited etymology of λαός, ἔργον as "the work of the people," by suggesting that the liturgy is both work directed towards God and work accomplished by God. For monks (as indeed for the whole Church) it is worth remembering that a wide variety of activities fall under the remit of the Opus Dei and that they are worth holding together in unity, just as the liturgy of the Word and the liturgy of the Eucharist are distinct but united. Christ is the "one leitourgos, the unique minister," the true High Priest (see Heb 8:2-6). The reference to March 21 is to the founding, on the Feast of Saint Benedict in 1098, of the abbey at Cîteaux, the mother house of the Cistercians, where a more literal interpretation of the Rule of Saint Benedict meant a closer adherence to the parts of the Rule concerned with manual labor. For Christian's own community, hundreds of years later, this combination of prayer and work was also a reality.

> **CCC 1069** *The word "liturgy" originally meant a "public work" or a "service in the name of/on behalf of the people." In Christian tradition it means the participation of the People of God in "the work of God" (cf. John 17:4). Through the liturgy Christ, our redeemer*

42. Luke 19:46: *My house shall be called a house of prayer . . .*
43. Cf. Isa 61:8.

and high priest, continues the work of our redemption in, with, and through his Church.

CCC 1070 *In the New Testament the word "liturgy" refers not only to the celebration of divine worship but also to the proclamation of the Gospel. In a liturgical celebration the Church is servant in the image of her Lord, the one "leitourgos" (cf. Heb 8:2, 6); she shares in Christ's priesthood (worship), which is both prophetic (proclamation) and kingly (service of charity):*

> *The liturgy then is rightly seen as an exercise of the priestly office of Jesus Christ. It involves the presentation of man's sanctification under the guise of signs perceptible by the senses and its accomplishment in ways appropriate to each of these signs. In it full public worship is performed by the Mystical Body of Jesus Christ, that is, by the Head and his members. From this it follows that every liturgical celebration, because it is an action of Christ the priest and of his Body which is the Church, is a sacred action surpassing all others. No other action of the Church can equal its efficacy by the same title and to the same degree. (SC 7)*

We do not go back on this definition, having already said that the liturgy is a "public service," that is to say that it works on behalf of a people and with their participation. The liturgy is entirely work, the work of this people and Opus Dei, work, the work of God (that is to say, work directed towards God and work accomplished by God). In no. 1070, the Catechism usefully recalls that the Greek word λειτουργια is used in the New Testament to designate all at the same time things, works, and actions that are apparently as different as worship, proclamation, and the exercise of charity. The diaconal serving at tables (Acts 6), like the apostolic service of the word, are both in the order of the "liturgy."

This understanding of leitourgia is what helps us, as we well know, to welcome with a sense of the urgency of their unity the different obligations and observances of our monastic state. It was undoubtedly the grace of Cîteaux, on March 21, 1098, to restore the balance of this wholly liturgical vocation in the "house of God" that the monastery is, by defending this house better against the excrescence of the properly cultic function. Following the example of its Master and Lord, the one "leitourgos," the unique minister (Heb 8:2-6) of the new Covenant, the Church is wholly and at the same time priestly, prophetic, and royal. Its sacerdotal function is exercised most directly in worship, its prophetic function in proclaiming the Gospel, and its royal function in serving the poor. In fact, the unity of this mission is signified within the liturgical celebration itself, where the Word is proclaimed and where the manifest signs of the bread and the wine are given to be shared, thereby summoning and already making present at the eucharistic table all the members of the Body of Christ, in particular the most helpless, those whose hunger and destitution we must strive to relieve.

Tuesday, March 29, [1994]
nos. 1071–1072
The liturgy as source of LIFE

(Holy Tuesday)

As the previous chapter indicated, the action of Christ and the action of the Church are united, as in the Eucharist. The Church does not merely repeat the words of institution of the Eucharist, "she enables this word to be effective today." The reference to the day's Gospel (John 13:21-33, 36-38, in which Jesus foretells his betrayal and Peter's denial) well illustrates the fact that Christ's own action can be impeded by human obstacles. The bodily imagery, especially towards the end of this chapter, helps one to see the work of the Church as the work of a single organism (the body of Christ?), of which the liturgy acts as the "blood of the organism." Again, reference to the Rule of Saint Benedict reminds Christian's brothers of the primacy of the liturgy and of the love of Christ.

> CCC 1071 *As the work of Christ liturgy is also an action of his Church. It makes the Church present and manifests her as the visible sign of the communion in Christ between God and men. It engages the faithful in the new life of the community and involves the "conscious, active, and fruitful participation" of everyone. (SC 11)*

> CCC 1072 *"The sacred liturgy does not exhaust the entire activity of the Church" (SC 9): it must be preceded by evangelization, faith, and conversion. It can then produce its fruits in the lives of the faithful: new life in the Spirit, involvement in the mission of the Church, and service to her unity.*

The work of Christ "and" action of his Church. The one calls for the other. And this is evident since Jesus took into his hands, in a way, the worship of humankind, the liturgy of the multitude, in a visible, sensory, palpable, "sacramental" as we call it, manner. In the same place, at the same time, he calls his apostles to "DO" the same, in memory of him, as a connection to life with him. In fact, this is very much God's wont: to do *and* to give something to be done, so that human action is not simply imitation. This action is creation. It is life, that is to say, movement. When the Church repeats the words of its Master, she is not merely engaged in repetition; she enables this word to be effective today, she gives it life in a way, just as she gives Life to the elements that she takes into her hands at each Eucharist. It is this today that is the

Body of Christ, "the visible sign of the communion in Christ between God and men," the people of here and now. It is for this reason that the liturgy involves the "conscious, active, and fruitful" participation of everyone. [And today's Gospel, this last meal of Jesus with his friends as it is narrated by John, shows well, from Judas to Peter himself, the limits and obstacles that human beings can impose upon the liturgical "work" of Christ and therefore also of the Church.][44]

But just as "The sacred liturgy does not exhaust the entire activity of the Church," might it be said that it does not exhaust the entire activity of Christ? The question has been put forward. In fact, Christ's activity will continue beyond the meal. He too is going to go out into the night under whose cover Judas fled from the common table.[45] But what will follow then right up to the achievement of the cross is nothing other than the development in deeds of what has been signified in the offering of the bread and the cup, as in the service of the washing of the feet. It can be said that the entire activity of Christ is from then on as if gathered up in that which is celebrated in the Eucharist.

It seems to me that we ought to say, likewise, that if the liturgy does not exhaust the entire activity of the Church, the liturgy contains this activity entirely and gives it meaning, in the manner of the heart, which breathes in and holds back[46] and thus sees all the blood of the organism go round: evangelization, faith, and conversion lead to the liturgy; new life, mission, and unity ensue from the liturgy, and vice versa. Saint Benedict says this in his own way when he affirms both that the monk must hold nothing dearer than the Office (*Opus*

44. The brackets are Christian's.

45. John 13:30: *And it was night.*

46. Fr.: *qui aspire et refoule*—an example of Christian's use of embodied imagery.

Dei, RB 43) and nothing dearer than the love of Christ (RB 4) and Christ himself (RB 72).

Tuesday, April 12 (after Easter)
no. 1073
Prayer and liturgy

All heartfelt prayer, even when it is dismissed as pietistic, is a participation in the prayer of the Lord and finds its "source and goal" in the liturgy. Christian warns us that so-called paraliturgical prayer should not be so narrowly and dismissively categorized, even as liturgy itself should properly not be rigidly defined as that which is provided by the texts and rubrics of the authorized books. Rather, the Spirit inspires those who pray and those who worship, as part of the "filial respiration" of the people of God.

> CCC 1073 *The liturgy is also a participation in Christ's own prayer addressed to the Father in the Holy Spirit. In the liturgy, all Christian prayer finds its source and goal. Through the liturgy the inner man is rooted and grounded (cf. Eph 3:16-17) in "the great love with which [the Father] loved us" (Eph 2:4) in his beloved Son.*

All the activity of Christ is as if gathered up in that which is celebrated in the liturgy: not merely evoked, but offered, actualized, and signified beneath the veil of the sacrament. It is in this way that the liturgy is, utterly, direct participation in Christ's own prayer turned towards the Father in the welcome and offering (the inhalation and exhalation) of the Spirit. It is the filial respiration, in a way, that here becomes ours. The catechism strongly asserts that in the liturgy "all

Christian prayer finds its source and goal" . . . just like the whole of Paul's letter to the Ephesians, which is called as a witness to root the inner man therein. In this, we come to understand the whole tradition of the Church, which reminds the faithful of the vital necessity of immersing themselves again in the Sunday celebration of the mystery of Christ.

At the same time, we wonder: so many simple people, who are assiduous in praying, are a bit lost in a liturgical context that sometimes seems to them abstract or traditional. The most popular forms of piety are often conceived as paraliturgical: processions, pilgrimages, saying the rosary, etc. . . . Cults know this well. There was a time when the liturgy was identified with that which conformed to the rubrics, assuming the power to declare what "is," and is not, "liturgical." It is perhaps necessary to interpret this numbered point in the Catechism very broadly . . . and, on the side of the instinct of those who are simple, seek that filial respiration that is the liturgy of heaven and earth celebrated by Christ in the Spirit. It then becomes possible to decipher this same impetus in "all prayer" and "at all times," because it is always and everywhere that the Spirit inspires, through means and ways known to God alone, the worshipers of the Father in spirit and in truth.

The definition of the liturgy would seem too narrow to us if it had to situate the participation in Christ's own prayer exclusively in the Christian temple, on this particular mountain, in Rome or in Jerusalem. The worship of the Church, celebrated in our Christian sites, is wholly sacramental, that is to say that it expresses and contains all this movement of a return to God that animates humankind whatever the extent of their faith or their connection, conscious or not, to Christ and to his Church. Different rites have often imposed boundaries. We need to stick to a definition of the liturgy that integrates all legitimate boundaries in order to grant to these the expression of something of the ever-greater mystery of the love of Christ guiding every person towards his Father.

Ephesians 6:18: *In all your prayer and entreaty, keep praying in the Spirit on every possible occasion.*

Thursday, April 14, 1994
nos. 1074–1075
Catechesis and liturgy . . .

The maxim lex orandi, lex credendi *was already one of the subjects of Christian's chapter on December 14, 1993. Christian gives a couple of examples of liturgical catechesis from the life of Christ, which we now commemorate: the remembrance of not just the Last Supper but the whole passion and also the resurrection initiate us into the mystery of Christ. In the foot-washing of Maundy Thursday Christ "transforms the entirety of his life and ours into sacramental catechesis." There is a paraphrase of Exodus 12, referencing the future telling of the story of the passover. Having called the liturgy the lifeblood of the body of Christ, Christian chooses another simile: liturgy and catechesis are "two visible lungs that breathe in invisible air," nourishing the body.*

> CCC 1074 *"The liturgy is the summit toward which the activity of the Church is directed; it is also the font from which all her power flows" (SC 10). It is therefore the privileged place for catechizing the People of God. "Catechesis is intrinsically linked with the whole of liturgical and sacramental activity, for it is in the sacraments, especially in the Eucharist, that Christ Jesus works in fullness for the transformation of men" (John Paul II, CT 23).*
>
> CCC 1075 *Liturgical catechesis aims to initiate people into the mystery of Christ (It is "mystagogy.") by*

> *proceeding from the visible to the invisible, from the sign to the thing signified, from the "sacraments" to the "mysteries." Such catechesis is to be presented by local and regional catechisms.*

At the beginning of this series of mini-chapters, much has already been made of the intrinsic connection between catechesis and the liturgy, in particular by recalling and commenting upon the old saying *lex orandi, lex credendi.* If the catechesis "aims to initiate people into the mystery of Christ," its antecedents can be sought in the very context of the passion and resurrection of Christ as they have come down to us through the gospels: the Last Supper is a liturgical celebration . . . and it is the ultimate pedagogical scene. According to the fourth gospel, Jesus both celebrates Passover with his disciples, that is to say he yet again maintains his links with the principal rite of his people, which was thanksgiving and catechesis (if your children ask you . . . you will tell them!)[47] . . . , and at the same time he inaugurates a new sacramental gesture that integrates the whole of his humanity and ours. In fact, through the washing of feet, he transforms the entirety of his life and ours into sacramental catechesis. And then he takes up and re-sumes (that is, he assumes once again) all his Word: assimilating it means allowing himself to be caught up in the movement that leads him to the Father and that constitutes both his own mystery and that of the whole of the liturgy on earth as in heaven.

And after the resurrection, the apparitions of the Living Christ connect these two aspects even more closely, particularly since Christ's presence is then entirely about the "signified" and no longer only about the signifier. This fact is confirmed beautifully on the road to Emmaus, where the old Word makes himself a living catechesis but above all sets

47. Exod 12:26: a reference to the telling of the story of the Passover.

"hearts on fire" (it is the only thing that has been transcribed from this for us!), and where the Presence steps aside faced with the "signifier," the broken bread, as soon as this Presence is recognized as the mystery that is signified by the bread. Catechesis and the liturgy are rather like the two visible lungs that breathe in invisible air so that this air breathes life into the whole organism, all of the Body of Christ in his Life, which is Spirit. The two "Tables" of the Eucharist have not ceased to make them function together . . . .

Saturday, April 16, 1994
no. 1076
The paschal mystery in the age of the Church

"Le temps de l'Église" *is occasionally shorthand in French for the history of Christ's apostles after Pentecost. "The Paschal Mystery in the Age of the Church," the title of Chapter One of Section One (The Sacramental Economy) of Part Two (The Celebration of the Christian Mystery) of the Catechism shows us that the life and the practice of the Church on earth, yesterday and today, is the subject of these reflections. There is a continuity between the events of salvation history and the life and death and resurrection of Christ, and between those events and an age where God acts in Christ "in a new way appropriate to this new age," through the Church.*

> CCC 1076 *The Church was made manifest to the world on the day of Pentecost by the outpouring of the Holy Spirit (cf. SC 6; LG 2). The gift of the Spirit ushers in a new era in the "dispensation of the mystery"—the age of the Church, during which Christ manifests, makes present, and communicates his work of salvation through the liturgy of his Church, "until he comes" (1 Cor 11:26).*

> *In this age of the Church Christ now lives and acts in and with his Church, in a new way appropriate to this new age. He acts through the sacraments in what the common Tradition of the East and the West calls "the sacramental economy"; this is the communication (or "dispensation") of the fruits of Christ's Paschal mystery in the celebration of the Church's "sacramental" liturgy.*

This is a pivotal paragraph in its presentation of the "sacramental economy" as the "implosion" of the paschal mystery in the age of the Church. In fact, the CHURCH already belongs entirely to the mystery of Christ Victorious over death and our partner in glory. The catechism underscores this reality of the faith, which is invisible, by describing Pentecost as a manifestation, an EPIPHANY of the Church, answering the first epiphany, which celebrated the mutual visitation of the Messiah and the "nations" at Bethlehem.[48] At Pentecost, "all the nations under heaven"[49] are represented in a symbolic fashion in Jerusalem and, in the context of a liturgy, of an expression of worship. The Holy Spirit takes over this celebration in order to enliven it in its entirety, to show that he is its inspiration, and to re-establish it in the paschal sequence of events: wind, fire, word, and "piety" too, are summoned in order to be the elements of this "epiphany" . . . and most of all, this sampling of humanity that will make manifest the vocation of each individual, and of all people, which is participation in the Paschal SACRAMENT.

It is the humanity of the Word made flesh that made a sacramental economy possible . . . likewise, from that time forward, every person can receive through the Church this same sacramental vocation, destined to "make manifest," "over time,"[50] the grace of eternity in which humanity is

48. I.e., the various Magi.

49. Acts 2:5.

50. The same phrase as the title (*dans le temps*).

fulfilled. There is no sacrament-Church without Christ, who says, "this is my Body," and without the individual (even if all alone!), who is there to say, "here I am," a member of your Body, "flesh of your flesh": and it is the Spirit who from henceforth establishes a connection between the two. In fact, the elements of human life—water, bread, and wine—are called upon as reinforcements, in the sacramental economy, only so that human beings may themselves each become a SACRAMENT. The liturgical service to which these elements are appointed does not erase the fact that they were created for humankind and not the other way round. If they become a sacrament, it is so that humans MAY BE a sacrament, the sacrament of Christ the Son, and sacrament of the communion of all people in Christ. This is why the charity that moves directly between individuals will always take precedence over the sacrament. This is precisely the message of the washing of the feet. Participating in the paschal sacrament of humanity in Jesus Christ, each of us is able to say, *it is not I who* LIVE *but Christ who lives in me.*[51]

Tuesday, April 19, 1994
no. 1077
The liturgy, work of the Trinity

The first paragraph of this chapter of the Catechism, which introduces "The Father—Source and Goal of the Liturgy," is a citation of four verses from the beginning of the Letter to the Ephesians (vv. 3-6, not 1-3 as Christian writes). If liturgy is an action of the Trinity (cf. March 12, 1994), it is also a work of the Trinity. The introduction of Mary, who in her Magnificat both worships God in Trinity and gives us words with which to do the same, "give[s] birth to us in the liturgy."

51. Gal 2:20.

N.B. The liturgy can be called "work of the Trinity." *Opus Dei*, work accomplished by the triune God, because there is, as I have already said, "some" liturgy in God. God "works" outside himself, so to speak, in the way that he exists and works in the very intimacy of his own interior life. We know that God's BEING, which is "impenetrable" to our eyes, has been revealed to us as LIFE: the divine milieu is one of living relations. Here "the original" of all liturgy is expressed, in the worship in the Spirit of the Word who is the very Truth of the Father.

That said, we can enter into the workings of the Catechism, which tries to specify the action, the work proper to each of the divine Persons in the liturgy of the people of God. It is evident that each of them will thus "work" in the same way as they "work" at the heart of the trinitarian mystery. It is also evident that these different modalities are inseparable and indissociable, and that they contribute to reinforcing the trinitarian life, since they have the aim of integrating humankind into that life, to bring humankind back to that life as to their place of origin. Humanity already participates fully in the eternal worship in the Glorious Body of Jesus Christ and in that of Mary, wholly assumed by the plenitude of a *MAGNIFICAT* that never ceases to give thanks to the Father through the Son in the Spirit. Mary remains the sanctuary awaiting all the holy people destined for the heavenly liturgy (cf. Apocalypse), the temple of a visitation in which the worship of heaven and earth meet and unite.

Every time the Eucharist is celebrated down here under the mode and veil of the sacrament, it seems to me that Mary has only to resume her *magnificat* in order to join in; in her, we are in communion with the real Presence, which no longer needs the sacrament. She proclaims, "My soul glorifies the Father in God my 'JESUS,' and the Spirit trembles with joy at this."[52] With all the instinct of the Son whom she bore, she knows that the

52. A paraphrase of the *Magnificat*.

Father is the source and goal of the liturgy. With her, we can read the start of Ephesians 1:1-3, which by itself constitutes the whole of no. 1077 of the catechism. In her entirety, she is pure praise of the glory of the Father, and this as a mother. Her role in this liturgy is to give birth to us in the liturgy and to connect us to the liturgy in our FILIAL way.

Thursday, April 21, 1994
no. 1078
BLESSED *be God the Father . . .*

Remaining with Ephesians 1, Christian shows that blessing can be found both descending from the Father as word and gift and also in the ascent of humanity's "saying-well" (Christian uses "bien-dire," which picks up bene + dicere *in Latin). The* Opus Dei *that Saint Benedict commends ascends from humanity, but, as we have seen, it is also an action of God. "God's action" here is contrasted to "action de grâce," thanksgiving.*

> *CCC 1078 Blessing is a divine and life-giving action, the source of which is the Father; his blessing is both word and gift (eu-logia, bene-dictio). When applied to man, the word "blessing" means adoration and surrender to his Creator in thanksgiving.*

Blessed be God the Father who has BLESSED *us with all kinds of* BLESSINGS *. . . .* The Father's approach in the liturgy happens here in the specific manner of BLESSING. The quotation from Ephesians 1:1-3 gives back to the blessing its dual movement, which proclaims both image and relation. An ASCENDING movement: humanity is invited to BLESS God (humanity is the subject), and a DESCENDING movement: God who bends over humanity in order to fulfill them (God is the subject), in such a way that all God's gifts can be interpreted as "blessings." To stay with the Latin term whence our French word directly stems, there is God's "saying-well" towards humanity, which summons humanity's "saying-well" towards God.[53] This is what the Catechism develops in this article on the Father.

Let's look at no. 1078 . . . "Blessing is a divine [. . .] action . . . ." This means that it is God who is the first to bless, who says what is WELL. In Greek, ευ-λογειν. There is a good λόγος, a good WORD about humanity. This Word has revealed itself in the end times, and we have known that it was GOOD because it did the work of the Father (John 6). "To say WELL," when it has to do with God, is the same as taking action. God's action is in keeping with another form of action undertaken by humanity, and which is thanksgiving, adoration, and praise.[54] Benedict, once again, is right to call our office of praise an *Opus Dei*, one of God's actions.

Another reflection based on the simple Greek etymology, ευλογια. It is notable that this word includes the root of WELL, the GOOD, like the other two words that are the heart of the Christian faith: ευαγγελιος, GOSPEL and ευχαριστειν, EUCHARIST. These three words are directly linked to Christ's Person and his Action: he is the Gospel of God, he is the EUCHARIST. He is BLESSING, EULOGY . . . But it is the Father who is called, properly speaking, the BLESSED One. In Mark 14:61, the high priest interrogates Jesus: *Are you the Christ, the Son of the Blessed One?* (eight times in the New Testament). Εὐλογητός, ἀγαπητὸς, παράκλητος: only the third word has been transposed into French:[55] the Spirit is the Paraclete. The Son is the Agapete (*Agapit*, a Latin first name) and the Father is the

53. Fr.: *bien-dire*. As Christian says, this comes from the Latin meaning of benediction (*bene-dictio*).

54. More satisfying in French, because thanksgiving is "*action de grâce*."

55. Or indeed into English.

Eulogete of the Trinity, he who blesses for all eternity because he has a good λόγος, and everything follows on from that . . .

Saturday, April 23, 1994
no. 1079
The whole of God's work is a BLESSING . . .

*Christian uses both the prologue of John's gospel and the account of creation in Genesis to illustrate God's work as a blessing, a "speaking-well" of the created order: God said that it was good. The end of Luke's gospel offers another bookend: after Jesus raised up his hands and blessed (*εὐλόγησεν*) the apostles on the road to Bethany, they spent their time "continually in the Temple praising (*εὐλογοῦντες*) God."*

> CCC 1079 *From the beginning until the end of time the whole of God's work is a blessing. From the liturgical poem of the first creation to the canticles of the heavenly Jerusalem, the inspired authors proclaim the plan of salvation as one vast divine blessing.*

No. 1079, which is very succinct, emphasizes God's work as a BLESSING. The articles that follow go over (and relate in detail) the events in the history of salvation as being as many concrete blessings of a BLESSED God who bestows blessings, who is, in his very being, a BLESSING. The matter is indeed that of the first, DESCENDING motion of BLESSING. God has the initiative. "In the beginning was a BLESSING . . . ," God's "saying-well." It's another way to explain the first verse of John, *In the beginning was the Word*. In the story of creation, God BLESSES the living creatures on the fifth day. A blessing that is linked to fecundity: *God blessed them, saying, "Be fruitful, multiply, and fill the waters . . . let the birds multiply*

. . . ."[56] The note in the TOB[57] presents God's blessing as "a power that is LIFE-giving" (*the words of eternal life*).

This blessing reaches its moment of greatest intensity after the creation of man: *God* BLESSED *them, saying to them, "Be fruitful, multiply, fill the earth and* SUBDUE *it. Be* MASTERS *of the fish of the sea, the birds of heaven and all the living creatures that move on earth."*[58] It will be noticed that, for the first time, God addresses somebody. Until then, it might even be said that he was SPEAKING "into thin air"! Now he speaks to THEM. His "saying-well" has an interlocutor, a partner. From that moment on, man endowed with speech, with λόγος will, likewise, become capable of "saying-well," of "saying something good."

It might be thought that this first word would be turned towards God. According to Genesis 2:23, man's first blessing is addressed directly to the woman, and the compliment rebounds indirectly onto God, who has created a being who is so appropriate for man. This is not original sin! Note, however, that in this article the Catechism interprets the whole of the story of creation as a "liturgical poem" and thus as a word of God, undoubtedly, but a word that is received by humanity and given back by humanity as worship in homage to its Creator. The precise moment at which the interlocutor of the blessing returns to its source and turns towards its "benefactor" in order to BLESS him and give thanks to him for what he has done, by "MAKING memory." This first "poem" and the canticles of the heavenly Jerusalem are assimilated to one another. In passing, you will recognize[59] the apostles in the temple at Jerusalem, there where the old man Simeon BLESSED the child . . . the last word of the Gospel of Luke

56. Gen 1:22.
57. *Traduction œcuménique de la Bible.*
58. Gen 1:28.
59. Fr.: *recuperez.*

. . . *in the Temple* BLESSING *God* (in the Vulgate: *laudentes et benedicentes*: Luke 24:53), a direct response to[60] Jesus' final gesture on the road to Bethany: *raising his hands he* BLESSED *them. Now as he* BLESSED *them, he withdrew from them and was carried up to heaven* . . . . By this point Jesus has said everything about God's creative blessing and also about the thanksgiving of humanity to its Father: both are entrusted to the Church.

Tuesday, April 26, 1994
no. 1080
A history of blessing . . .

Christian continues the story of God's blessing resounding through creation and throughout human history. God's blessing, "berakhah" *(בְּרָכָה),* "baraka" *(بركة) of the children of Abraham (cf. Gen 12; Gen 17) is offered in spite of human "saying-badly," (Fr.* "mau-dire"*).*

> **CCC 1080** *From the very beginning God blessed all living beings, especially man and woman. The covenant with Noah and with all living things renewed this blessing of fruitfulness despite man's sin which had brought a curse on the ground. But with Abraham, the divine blessing entered into human history which was moving toward death, to redirect it toward life, toward its source. By the faith of "the father of all believers," who embraced the blessing, the history of salvation is inaugurated.*

Saying that "in the beginning was the blessing" . . . means inserting God's blessing, his saying-well, into history as well

60. Error in French text: *ou*. Recte *au*.

as into eternity. The day will come when the blessing will be made "flesh," revealing to us the FILIAL face of the Father's blessing. A way of entering into history will very quickly be that of following the succession of generations. This is the meaning of the promise made to Abraham: God's blessing, his "baraka," given from age to age, "to his descendants forever."[61] From now on, the father blessed by God knows that there is a blessing for his son. Abraham blesses Isaac, and Isaac blesses Jacob . . . there is, however, one doubt: God has blessed all his creatures.

Man does not know how to reconcile God's unique blessing and the multiplicity of his children. Abraham does not believe that he is able to bless Ishmael himself. He asks God to do it, and, strangely, God's words to Ishmael will be the same as those to Abraham, and to Isaac next: *He too will walk in my presence.*[62] Living in God's presence, praising him, BLESSING him, this is what defines the content of the BLESSING, more than land or even posterity. Isaac will try not to exclude Esau after Jacob's usurpation, his secretly inheriting the blessing. But the lesson seems to have caught on, for the dying Jacob will have a particular blessing for each of his children.

Strangely, between Adam and Abraham, man believed himself capable only of "saying-badly," that is, of cursing:[63] it is the ground that will "curse" Adam, and Noah will curse Ham, all the while blessing God for his other two sons. God, for his part, does not curse: he drives Adam and Eve out, but without speaking badly of them; God marks Cain so as to protect him; he saves Noah so as not to fail in his blessing . . . It is very clear that since the very beginnings of this history of salvation, God's blessing is the key to understanding

61. See the *Magnificat.*

62. See Gen 17.

63. Christian plays here on the contrast between "*bien-dire*" (to say well or bless) and "*mau-dire*" (to say badly or curse).

succession, connecting the generations to one another, step by step, from the origin to the endpoint, a key that will function when humanity inscribes in its own becoming the praise and BLESSING of God, creating in this way, unwittingly, a fully FILIAL behavior of which Abel is the prototype.

It is here that the Semitic root of "blessing," בָּרַךְ, reveals all its concrete richness: *barak*. God is the first SUBJECT of this verb, notably in its intensive form, *bârak*. But the original meaning is, as we know (*Allâh ibârak, bârak Allâh fîk*), to make the camel's knee bend. We kneel to receive a blessing and to BLESS. Paul will say, *This, then, is what I pray, kneeling before the Father, from whom every fatherhood, in heaven or on earth, takes its name . . .* (Eph 3:14).

Thursday, April 28, 1994
no. 1081
From blessing to blessing . . .

This paragraph in the Catechism lists important moments in salvation history that culminate in the cross, "the meeting-place of all blessings, the mysterious place where God's will is made explicit."

> **CCC 1081** *The divine blessings were made manifest in astonishing and saving events: the birth of Isaac, the escape from Egypt (Passover and Exodus), the gift of the promised land, the election of David, the presence of God in the Temple, the purifying exile, and return of a "small remnant." The Law, the Prophets, and the Psalms, interwoven in the liturgy of the Chosen People, recall these divine blessings and at the same time respond to them with blessings of praise and thanksgiving.*

Here we have the start of a list of God's "blessings" on his people: a Covenant counted out[64] in salvific actions. And the Catechism only inscribes itself in a long line of evocations, where we find, for example, Paul in his speech to the synagogue of Antioch in Pisidia (Acts 13: today's first reading): *Men of Israel, and fearers of God, listen! The God of our nation Israel,* etc.[65] The promise made to Isaac is always there: *I shall be with you and* BLESS *you!* (Gen 26:3). Everything is a blessing, even "the purifying exile." And it has often come to pass that what is initially understood as an ordeal—exodus and its stages, for example—may later establish itself in memory as the site of a particular watchfulness on the part of God . . . all that path that was preparing to welcome the cross, the gallows of the damned, as the meeting-place of all blessings, the mysterious place where God's WILL is made explicit, his WILL that is to BLESS and to give once and for all the pledge of this "will," his Only Son who is his very own BLESSING.

But the verticality of the CROSS also perfectly expresses humanity's response to all God's attentive acts: *I bless you, Father* . . . Jesus is the "blessing of God made flesh," but also "man made BLESSING," returning entirely to the Father in glorious praise. The blessings of God and humanity intersect and intertwine (the BERAKÔT): at the heart of the People of God, humanity has held onto this crossing of paths, finding in this their lookout post: "recall[ing] these divine blessings and at the same time respond[ing] to them with blessings of praise and thanksgiving." Moses and the PROPHETS in succession. But also the whole of the small people who express themselves in the Psalms and who have never done with asking and thanking, with welcoming and giving thanks. Is not the best way to say "again" to say "thank you"? BLESSING God means confessing from whom we hold the GOOD that we have and that we are. Some examples:

64. Fr.: *monnayée.*

65. Acts 13:16-17. The full reading is Acts 13:13-25.

in Psalm 27 (28) v. 6 *BLESSED be the Lord, for he hears the sound of my prayer.*
v. 9 *Save your people, BLESS your heritage, shepherd them and carry them for ever . . .*

in Psalm 113B v. 12 *The Lord will keep us in mind, he will bless . . .*
he will bless the House of Israel . . . the House of Aaron, those who fear . . .
v. 18 *we, the living, shall BLESS the Lord.*

Tuesday, May 3, 1994
no. 1082
God from whom all blessing descends . . .

*Christian refers here to the Roman Ritual and its second section, "the new ritual of blessings" (*De benedictionibus*), which was separately published in 1987. In its General Introduction, it states,*

> *The source from whom every good gift comes is God, who is above all, blessed for ever. He who is all good has made all things good, so that he might fill his creatures with blessings and even after the Fall he has continued his blessings as a sign of his merciful love . . .*
> *Scripture attests that all the beings God has created and keeps in existence by his gracious goodness declare themselves to be blessings from him and should move us to bless him in return. This is above all true after the Word made flesh came to make all things holy by the mystery of his Incarnation.*[66]

66. See *Shorter Book of Blessings* [from the *Roman Ritual*] (New York: Catholic Book Publishing Co., 1990), general introduction, 18–20.

> **CCC 1082** *In the Church's liturgy the divine blessing is fully revealed and communicated. The Father is acknowledged and adored as the source and the end of all the blessings of creation and salvation. In his Word who became incarnate, died, and rose for us, he fills us with his blessings. Through his Word, he pours into our hearts the Gift that contains all gifts, the Holy Spirit.*

The last two points of this article on the Father, source and goal of every liturgy, situate blessing in the liturgy of the Church, and likewise the liturgy of the Church in an economy of BLESSING. It is first of all the DESCENDING aspect that is evoked in no. 1082: "the divine blessing is fully revealed" as a trinitarian work, as a GIFT of the LIVING God, whose intimate language is that of mutual BLESSING. God is ready to BLESS everything, on earth as in heaven. It is his primary task, and it is infinitely creative and re-creative. Saint Basil defined blessing as "the imparting of holiness" (Letter 199 to Amphilocius).[67] This communication appears to the Church all the more urgent since the redemptive mystery with which it culminates teaches the Church to what extent people and things have been able to be blessed in their usage and/or in their destination as well as being diverted from this participation in the sanctity of God that was their common vocation.

The imaginativeness of the Church when she solicits God's blessings may come as a surprise! Every situation (travel, sickness, ordeal, exam, birth, seasons, etc.), every event, and every element of daily life can give rise to a special blessing. We must refer to the new ritual of blessings, which starts with the blessing of individuals and goes on to comprise human activities, objects (including the sea! . . . and in order not to forget any-

67. Fr.: *la communication de la sanctification*. See Saint Basil, Letter 199, to Amphilocius, concerning the canons: https://www.newadvent.org/fathers/3202199.htm.

thing, there is also the "blessing of other things"); it ends with the blessings of thanksgivings, which incorporate to a greater extent, perhaps, the ascendant aspect that is always present.

The Preliminaries of this Ritual, too, start by situating in God the source and the end of all the blessings. God wants all creatures to be filled with his blessings, and he has kept these blessings even after the first human fault, as a sign of his mercy, which is itself also a blessing since it comes from the same Heart that adapts to poverty in order to proclaim the GOOD more loudly and first. Christ is presented as the "supreme blessing of the Father."[68] After his Ascension, he sends the Holy Spirit, through whom "the blessing of Abraham in Christ is accomplished more and more when it passes to his children."[69] Our God is thus a God who blesses, who proclaims *mubârak*. We will forever say of God only that he is *mubârak*. Everything happens in the liturgy as if to answer more fully Jesus' promise (reread in today's Gospel): *Whatever you ask in my name I will do, so that the Father may be glorified in the Son . . . I will* DO *it* (John 14:13-14).

Saturday, May 7, 1994
no. 1083
The dual dimension of the liturgy . . .

At the end of the section of the Catechism entitled The Father—Source and Goal *comes this culminating paragraph. Christian sees the dialogue between God and the Church as an* admirabile commercium, *an "admirable exchange," in the words of the antiphon (at Vespers on the Octave of Christmas):*

68. The Father's supreme blessing upon us. *Shorter Book of Blessings*, 19.
69. See Gal 3.

"O wonderful gift: the creator of the human race, taking our flesh upon him, deigns to be born of a virgin; and, coming forth without seed of man, bestows his Divinity upon us." Having mentioned the numerous berakhot *of the Jewish tradition, Christian points out some of the innovations of Vatican II: the introduction (or perhaps re-introduction) of blessings (with an introduction very similar to the* berakhot*) over the bread and wine at the offertory and the introduction of solemn blessings over the people, to say nothing of all the occasions of blessing throughout the Mass and throughout the year.*

> CCC 1083 *The dual dimension of the Christian liturgy as a response of faith and love to the spiritual blessings the Father bestows on us is thus evident. On the one hand, the Church, united with her Lord and "in the Holy Spirit" (Luke 10:21), blesses the Father "for his inexpressible gift" (2 Cor 9:15) in her adoration, praise, and thanksgiving. On the other hand, until the consummation of God's plan, the Church never ceases to present to the Father the offering of his own gifts and to beg him to send the Holy Spirit upon that offering, upon herself, upon the faithful, and upon the whole world.*

This last paragraph nicely brings the two movements together. That of the Church who BLESSES God, *benedicare Deum = laudare*, that is to say, who praises and gives thanks. And that of a Church who invokes God's blessing in order to *bene-dicere aliquid = consecrare*, in order to set apart, consecrate, bind all people and all things to God. This is an *admirabile commercium*[70] that asks to take root in the life of every person signed in their baptism by this dual dimension, situated within this back-and-forth. Saint Augustine makes all this clear in his commentary on Psalm 66 (cited in the entry on "Bénédiction" in volume one of the *Dict. Enc. Lit.*):

70. "Admirable exchange."

"Let our soul bless the Lord, and let God bless us. When God blesses us, we grow, and when we bless the Lord, we grow; to us both BLESSINGS are profitable. [. . .] First, there is in us the blessing of the Lord, and the consequence is that we also bless the Lord."[71] In fact, not blessing God for his gifts is a sign of ingratitude—even a THEFT. The rabbinical tradition on the *Berakhot* was clear: "it is *forbidden* for a *man to enjoy* anything of this world *without* saying a *blessing, and if anyone enjoys anything of this world without a blessing, he has profaned the sacred.*"[72]

With this in mind, we will notice two new elements that are (re)introduced into the eucharistic liturgy inherited from Vatican II. First of all, the two blessings for the bread and the wine, marking the presentation of the gifts. This text takes up that of the traditional Jewish *beraka*, which Jesus made his own by incorporating it quite naturally in the actions and words of the Last Supper: Blessed are you, Lord God of all creation, for. . . . And then, we make our supplication. This blessing introduces a request that sheds light on the depths of all God's gifts. Each person, by welcoming these gifts, knows that they must give meaning to everything that this person is, must nourish their life, and guide them towards the kingdom. There is also, as an annex to the new Missal, a whole series of "solemn blessings" and of prayers over the people, whose distant origins are to be found in Aaron's blessing (Num 6:24-26). The grace bestowed in the solemnity or celebration is evoked in order to call for the grace to live sustainably,[73] like a token of the salvation to come, toward which all divine blessings point. We should see in the same way the blessing of water on Sundays, or of the ashes or of the palms, or all those of the

71. Augustine, commentary on Psalm 66: https://www.newadvent.org/fathers/1801067.htm. The identity of the source Christian cites here as *Dict. Enc. Lit.* is unknown.

72. Berakhot 35a: https://www.sefaria.org/Berakhot.35a.2?lang=bi.

73. Fr.: *den vivre durablement.*

Easter vigil: fire, water . . . , recapitulated in the proclamation of the Easter news, of the EXULTET, which reappears in that key gesture of every eucharistic prayer: *it is right and just, equitable, salutary, to* BLESS *you . . . but above all . . . .*

Tuesday, May 10, 1994
She who is "blessed" among women

Christian offers a digression from the trinitarian sequence of the Catechism in devoting a chapter to the Blessed Virgin Mary, who is "blessed" among women and the fruit of whose womb is also "blessed." Here her cousin Elizabeth both proclaims and gives thanks for the blessing of God. Elizabeth, in Christian's words, restores human language and the human gaze, which are both created for praise but are often distracted with other objects. Having had this blessing proclaimed, Mary's own "eucharist" or thanksgiving ("son chant de bénédiction, son eucharistie"*) is proclaimed too.*

"She is BLESSED Virgin . . . woman . . . mother . . . queen." We sing this at each one of our Little Hours. It is impossible not to dwell for a moment (in the month of May!) on this living link in a long back-and-forth of BLESSING: MARY! Mary is truly at the crossroads of blessing, the point at which the "saying-well" of God and of humanity come together, "congratulate" each other, in a way. *Blessed among women* . . . This appellation is not bestowed upon Mary by the angel but rather by Elizabeth in her response to the greeting of the Visitation. And this appellation is indissociable from that which follows immediately and which is addressed to the still hidden child in the Virgin's womb: *BLESSED is the fruit of thy womb* (Luke 1:42).

Elizabeth proclaims the special blessing of God that rests on Mary, and at the same time she gives thanks—in the name of all of us, the first to do so—thanks to God for this GIFT given by God to the human race. In a movement of the Spirit, she is the first to join in God's reaction faced with his virgin creation brought forth from his hands. God SAW that everything was GOOD . . . and Elizabeth confirms as much. She is able to do so because everything is reborn in Mary. But in so doing, she contributes to the ATONEMENT of humankind, to the restoration of human language and of the human gaze, both created for PRAISE but diverted from their object by the cupidity and pride of people who seek their own gratification. Humanity wanted to monopolize what is good . . . and also thought they were able to declare themselves to be GOOD independently from their Creator.

Elizabeth finds once more the path of humility without which no BLESSING is possible in either direction. A woman herself, she BLESSES another woman and declares this woman to be more "blessed" than all other women—more blessed, then, than herself. And upon the child whom Mary bears there rests a blessing that is even greater than that which rests on the child she herself bears. Mary can then burst into her song of BLESSING, her own EUCHARIST: *My soul glorifies the Lord . . . the Almighty works marvels for me.* Mary, God's "blessing" over all the human race, is not numbered with the Son, who is the BLESSING in God, God's BLESSED one. Mary's *BARAKA* will be able to be passed on to all those who from generation to generation will call her BLESSED.

In the Qur'an, things happen differently. Mary is accused (of adultery) by her relations, and it is her Child who defends her: "Indeed, I am the servant of Allah. He has given me the Scripture and made me a prophet. And He has made me blessed wherever I am [. . .] And [made me] dutiful to my mother."[74] The only man who is proclaimed "God's BLESSED one" in the Qur'an knows himself that he must BLESS his own mother . . .

74. Surah 19:30–32.

Saturday, May 14, 1994
nos. 1084–1085
CHRIST'S work in the liturgy: ABIDE

The Catechism now moves to the participation of the second Person in the liturgy, and Christian uses its heading here, with the added word "Abide" ("demeurer"*). When Christ abides with us, all those who are present in the sacramental economy are also there. There is a poignancy to this assertion, owing to the deaths six days before this chapter of Henri Vergès, a Marist Brother, and of Sister Paul-Hélène Saint-Raymond, the first two of the nineteen Martyrs of Algeria. Both were working in the archidiocesan library in Algiers and were assassinated by radicals posing as policemen. Their funeral, which Christian mentions took place at the basilica of Notre-Dame d'Afrique, was held on May 12. He notes that the same Gospel (John 15:9-17,* No one has greater love than this, to lay down one's life for one's friends*) was read on the day of their death (the Sixth Sunday of Easter, year B), at their funeral, and on this day, the feast of Saint Matthias. Christian says that the liturgy of Eastertide, which culminates in the feast of the Ascension, is all the commentary that is needed, as the paschal mystery can only be contemplated by celebrating it.*

> CCC 1084 *"Seated at the right hand of the Father" and pouring out the Holy Spirit on his Body which is the Church, Christ now acts through the sacraments he instituted to communicate his grace. The sacraments are perceptible signs (words and actions) accessible to our human nature. By the action of Christ and the power of the Holy Spirit they make present efficaciously the grace that they signify.*
>
> CCC 1085 *In the liturgy of the Church, it is principally his own Paschal mystery that Christ signifies and*

> *makes present. During his earthly life Jesus announced his Paschal mystery by his teaching and anticipated it by his actions. . . . His Paschal mystery is a real event that occurred in our history, but it is unique: all other historical events happen once, and then they pass away, swallowed up in the past. The Paschal mystery of Christ, by contrast, cannot remain only in the past, because by his death he destroyed death, and all that Christ is—all that he did and suffered for all men—participates in the divine eternity, and so transcends all times while being made present in them all. The event of the Cross and Resurrection abides and draws everything toward life.*

- Nos. 1084–1085: no other commentary than that of the liturgy of all these days since Easter and the Incarnate Word's consummation into glory that we celebrated with the Ascension on Thursday.

- Perhaps state more forcefully that everything, in Christ, is "Paschal mystery," . . . "all" the mysteries of Christ from his conception up to his resurrection, stem from the Hour of his Passing from this world to the Father . . . and that from henceforth, all the events in our history, steeped in this mystery through baptism, stem from this same Hour. This is what we express when we do not separate the deaths of Henri and of Paul-Hélène from everything that happened before in their lives . . . and also, when we reread what they lived through and their at once tragic and glorious end in the light of the unique Event of the CROSS and the RESURRECTION. They too, as it has been said, have become henceforth "grains of wheat sown in the earth."[75] And from now on they have a mysterious connection not only to the worship of the glorious Christ, but also to the worship of the church. They have become part of the

75. John 12:24-26, the Parable of the Grain of Wheat.

sacramental economy that makes us believe that when Christ signifies himself, he also signifies "them" in him . . . when Christ abides, they ABIDE . . . when Christ continues to COMMUNICATE his life "to his friends," at the same time he also communicates the fullness of life of all the members of his Body, connected to his glory as they have been through the liturgy of his presence in the world, of his sufferings, and of his death. An eloquent sign of this is, of course, the fact that the same eucharistic sacrifice enables us to CELEBRATE these different events in the life of Christ and of his Church. In very concrete terms, we have encountered the same Gospel (John 15:9-17) from last Sunday (6th Sunday of Easter B) . . . this Thursday at Notre-Dame d'Afrique in relation to Henri and to Paul-Hélène (*No greater love than . . .*), and today for the feast of Saint Matthias.

Tuesday, May 17, 1994
nos. 1086–1087
From the church of the apostles . . .

Christian sees these paragraphs as helpfully connected to the Johannine High Priestly Prayer (paraphrased below), which begins to be read on this day (May 17: John 17:1-11; May 18, vv. 11-19). This prayer is "eucharistic" and "consecratory." He refers surprisingly to the "New World" Symphony (Op. 95, B. 178) of the composer Antonin Dvořák (composed in 1893), which seems to be a metaphor for unity. The liturgy is seen as a privileged site of unity, celebrated in communion with the apostles and saints through the ages, with the pope and other "concelebrants" of the one liturgy of the ages.

> **CCC 1086** *"Accordingly, just as Christ was sent by the Father so also he sent the apostles, filled with the*

Holy Spirit. This he did so that they might preach the Gospel to every creature and proclaim that the Son of God by his death and resurrection had freed us from the power of Satan and from death and brought us into the Kingdom of his Father. But he also willed that the work of salvation which they preached should be set in train through the sacrifice and sacraments, around which the entire liturgical life revolves" (SC 6).

CCC 1087 *Thus the risen Christ, by giving the Holy Spirit to the apostles, entrusted to them his power of sanctifying (cf. John 20:21-23): they became sacramental signs of Christ. By the power of the same Holy Spirit they entrusted this power to their successors.*

- These two points are a direct commentary on the seventeenth chapter of Saint John's gospel, which we are reading over these days: *Father . . . just as you have sent me, I too, I have sent them . . . .*[76] And the context of this sending forth is liturgical: not only the feast of the Jewish Passover, but also this solemn prayer, said to be "sacerdotal," and at once "eucharistic" and consecratory.
- This prayer is "exorcizing": *protect them from the Evil One*!
- It is sanctifying: *Sanctify them in the Truth.*
- It is the gift of the Word: every Christian liturgy will be the site of this transmitted Word, the privileged site of the announcement of the Word incarnate in the words and language of its apostles.
- It is the gift of unity: every Christian liturgy will be the privileged site of this transmitted communion, the site

76. John 17:21.

of the gathering together of a "portion" of the multitude offering itself as a sign of the "New World symphony."

- We think we may state—*a contrario*—that communal liturgy is no longer possible:
  - when the Word is no longer received and interpreted as the expression of unity given unrepentantly;
  - when the sacraments no longer proclaim sanctification in Christ open to all in the name of the reality of a salvation that is even greater than the sign by which it is celebrated.
- The "apostles" are the vanguard in a long succession of liturgists: they have been constituted "sacramental signs of Christ." "Constituted," that is to say, "established TOGETHER," connected to one another by their faithfulness to this worshipful ministry that cannot be exercised estranged from intimate communion with all the other "concelebrants" around the world. The link to the liturgical ministry of the bishop of Rome (through the breaking of bread) could seem to guarantee this vital harmony from one to another that everyone is tasked with celebrating, wherever they are sent, both as an offering of oneself and as a welcome to others.

Thursday, May 19, 1994
nos. 1088–1089
The glorified Christ . . .
(Dedication of the cathedral of Algiers)
. . . present in the earthly liturgy

Christian continues, as the High Priestly Prayer continues in the Gospel at Mass this day, with the language of the high priest "who continues to offer himself to the Father for all eternity," with whom our liturgical unity is an expression of ecclesial unity. When anyone baptizes, as the Catechism reminds us, it is really Christ himself who is the minister. On this anniversary of the consecration of the diocesan cathedral (the Cathédrale du Sacré-Cœur d'Alger) in 1963, Christian notes that this feast is also an occasion of "reconstituting . . . the edifice of living stones," the people of God of the diocese, and especially the unity of the clergy under their bishop (as happens at the Chrism Mass on Maundy Thursday). If the sacramental privileges of priests stem from their bishop, so too there is a greater descent from Christ himself, even (and perhaps especially) when the sacraments are celebrated among the humble and meek.

> CCC 1088 *"To accomplish so great a work"—the dispensation or communication of his work of salvation—"Christ is always present in his Church, especially in her liturgical celebrations. He is present in the Sacrifice of the Mass not only in the person of his minister, 'the same now offering, through the ministry of priests, who formerly offered himself on the cross,' but especially in the Eucharistic species. By his power he is present in the sacraments so that when anybody baptizes, it is really Christ himself who baptizes. He is present in his word since it is he himself who speaks when the holy Scriptures are read in the Church. Lastly, he is present when the Church prays and sings, for he has promised 'where two or three are gathered together in my name there am I in the midst of them'" (SC 7; Matt 18:20).*

> CCC 1089 *"Christ, indeed, always associates the Church with himself in this great work in which God is perfectly glorified and men are sanctified. The Church is his beloved Bride who calls to her Lord and through him offers worship to the eternal Father" (SC 7).*

Two points that are ideally suited to today's celebration: commemorating the dedication of a church means reconstituting in prayer the edifice of living stones that has constituted and constitutes this part of the people of God since the moment the church gave herself this place of worship. When this concerns a cathedral church, this SIGN must be extended to all those who come under the same pastoral task, as well as to every aspect of the life of faith that turn a diocese into an Incarnation of the kingdom. It also means recapitulating to an even greater extent all the sacraments, since to those that are celebrated in an ordinary church must be added those of confirmation and especially of ORDINATION, all of which depend directly upon the priesthood of the bishop. The Chrism Mass of Maundy Thursday, usually celebrated in the cathedral, indeed embodies the worshipful task that is that of a specific church dedicated to be a complete sign of the universal Church. If there is a place that must be "consecrated," it is without doubt the cathedral . . . and the liturgical anniversary of this consecration is an opportunity to join together, in prayer, all the faithful who want to appear as interested parties in the visible sign that the Church wishes to show forth of its invisible unity. If it is possible to speak of the unity of the Church signified in the liturgy, this is indeed because all the sacraments celebrated by the Church point to the unique high priest who continues to offer himself to the Father for all eternity, just as he never ceases to intercede on our behalf.

Of course, the Christ in glory is also PRESENT in the diversity of all humanity, and most particularly in those of the poor and the small: every person is CHRIST in gestation. But the liturgy is the privileged place in which this gestation is welcomed, supported, and brought to term day after day. The place, too, in which this gestation is realized not only in those who consent to it, but also for the multitude who are unaware that their cry is the cry of birth pangs. The prayer of the PSALMS which is entrusted to us expresses this reality of the Church: two or three suffice to sing these Psalms in his Name, and the WHOLE Christ is there in all his members whose cries and faces are reiterated by the Psalms.

Saturday, May 21, 1994
no. 1090
A foretaste of the heavenly liturgy (*'îd al-'Adha*) (on the vigil of Pentecost)

Christian's chapter reminds us that Eid al-Adha (the feast of Sacrifice) was celebrated the previous day. He reflects on the similarities of the Christian pilgrimage of life towards the New Jerusalem with the Hajj *or Islamic pilgrimage towards the* Kaaba *in Mecca (which began a few days earlier). The Christian* Kaaba *(the House of God, towards which all prayer is directed) is Christ in glory, whose own direction leads us to worship to the Father and sing a hymn of glory (there is no God but God, the* ilah'a illa Allâh, *or Holy, holy, holy Lord God of hosts).*

> CCC *1090* *"In the earthly liturgy we share in a foretaste of that heavenly liturgy which is celebrated in the Holy City of Jerusalem toward which we journey as pilgrims, where Christ is sitting at the right hand of God, Minister of the sanctuary and of the true tabernacle. With all the warriors of the heavenly army we sing a hymn of glory to the Lord; venerating the memory of the saints, we hope for some part and fellowship with them; we eagerly await the Savior, our Lord Jesus Christ, until he, our life, shall appear and we too will appear with him in glory" (SC 8; cf. LG 50).*

- This point comes round while our ears are full of the earthly liturgy, which is connected to the great celebrations of the Feast of Sacrifice at Mecca. The liturgy turns us into travelers, into "pilgrims." It sets us in motion in space and time, *hic et nunc*, towards that which is beyond space and time.[77]

- Our *Kaaba* is not a specific corner of the world, not even Calvary or the Holy Sepulchre . . . it is Christ in glory, who also indicates to us our *qibla* to the extent that, like him, with him, we turn ourselves towards the Father. It is in this way, as we can sense, that all prayer can join and merge with his to sing the hymn of glory: the *ilah'a illa Allâh* or SANCTUS!

- One day everything will be made manifest . . . for the time being, to accept that this[78] may sound to us like "discordant shouts."

- What is certain is that in the name of how we conceptualize the liturgy and the unique Liturgist, we should let ourselves be interpellated by all worship and adoration that comes from a sincere heart. It is in all places, in every language, culture, and religion, that the Father seeks and finds worshipers in spirit and in truth.

- Once prayer is understood as a pilgrimage inviting us to reach God, or to go out of ourselves, or to fumble in search of that intimate point of our being where we no longer belong to ourselves, or to join the immense crowd of those seeking God so as to become no more than poor and modest members of that communion, it seems to me that here is where all boundaries are blurred. Not only should it be possible to "pray together," but we should also feel ourselves to be called HERE to be Christ made present, to be He who comes running when two

77. Introductory symbols in the text such as • are reproduced without further comment from the French edition.

78. Fr.: *cela*: possibly the earthly liturgy mentioned in the previous point?

or three are gathered in his Name, which is the Name of the great Supplicant[79] of all humanity, there to unite ourselves with the one who takes these humble forms[80] of our imperfect prayer in order to imbue them with his Spirit and offer them to the Father transfigured in his Prayer. Is he not the Only One who knows how to pray in the proper way?

Tuesday, May 24, 1994
nos. 1091–1092
The HOLY SPIRIT and the Church in the liturgy . . .

Christian's title picks up the new heading at CCC 1091. He compares the activity of the Holy Spirit in the liturgy to a "micro-climate" in which human actors are also "in theory . . . more available," more receptive to the Spirit's actions.

> CCC 1091 *In the liturgy the Holy Spirit is teacher of the faith of the People of God and artisan of "God's masterpieces," the sacraments of the New Covenant. . . . When the Spirit encounters in us the response of faith which he has aroused in us, he brings about genuine cooperation. Through it, the liturgy becomes the common work of the Holy Spirit and the Church.*

> CCC 1092 *In this sacramental dispensation of Christ's mystery the Holy Spirit acts in the same way as at other times in the economy of salvation: he prepares the Church to encounter her Lord; he recalls and makes Christ manifest to the faith of the assembly. By his*

79. Fr.: *priant.*
80. Fr.: *especes.*

transforming power, he makes the mystery of Christ present here and now. Finally the Spirit of communion unites the Church to the life and mission of Christ.

- No. 1091 already read on the eve of Pentecost: reread it alongside no. 1092.
- Two points entirely new in their wording; they give back to us a tradition much better conserved by the Eastern Churches.
- Cf. the felicitous expressions:
    - The Holy Spirit, in the liturgy, teacher of the faith for all the people of God.
    - Artisan of "God's masterpieces," that is, the sacraments.
    - The Holy Spirit comes to meet / moves towards what it has inspired in us: in this way the cooperation that enables the liturgy to be the "common work" of the Spirit and the Church is established.

The LITURGY creates something like a "micro-climate" in which all the ordinary activity of the Holy Spirit spread across the world is condensed and concentrated. Here the mystery of salvation, which is at work always and everywhere, is expressed. Here the Spirit reveals itself to be more effective because, in theory, here the Spirit finds us to be more available. There are basically four different temporal parts to this ACTION:

- Prepare the Church for the ENCOUNTER with her Lord: one thinks of the old man Simeon to whom the Holy Spirit had spoken for a long time . . .
- Recall and make CHRIST manifest to the faith of the assembly: Jesus announced this to us, and it is he who will repeat all this to us. He will bear witness to it. He

will unveil. The apostles remembered. The memorial "is" revelation.

- Make the dynamism of conversion included in the message and sacrifice of Christ present and current. This is the accomplishment of the promise to "CALL everything to him," to renew everything, to forgive and ease, to confirm, heal, and unite, to feed and quench thirst, to give increase and freedom to those who adore the Father in spirit and in truth.
- The Spirit is the Spirit of COMMUNION . . . and it is in this respect that the Spirit gathers the members of the Church together so that together they may be the LIVING Christ continuing his mission. The Spirit who delivered the message of Pentecost is also the Spirit who kept the apostles at prayer so that the UNITY necessary to their sending out could be established.

Thursday, May 26, 1994
no. 1093
The Holy Spirit PREPARES us to welcome Christ

Of all people, Christian thinks, monks should keenly understand the "back-and-forth of Scripture" shared by the First / Old and New Covenants, since they spend a vast amount of time in the prayer of the Psalms. There is a close bond between all of God's people, as the account of salvation history in Eucharistic Prayer IV makes plain:

> *You are the one God living and true, existing before all ages and abiding for all eternity, dwelling in unapproachable light; yet you, who alone are good, the source of life, have made all that is, so that you*

might fill your creatures with blessings and bring joy to many of them by the glory of your light.

CCC 1093 *In the sacramental economy the Holy Spirit fulfills what was prefigured in the Old Covenant. Since Christ's Church was "prepared in marvellous fashion in the history of the people of Israel and in the Old Covenant" (LG 2), the Church's liturgy has retained certain elements of the worship of the Old Covenant as integral and irreplaceable, adopting them as her own:*
— notably, reading the Old Testament;
— praying the Psalms;
— above all, recalling the saving events and significant realities which have found their fulfillment in the mystery of Christ (promise and covenant, Exodus and Passover, kingdom and temple, exile and return).

- We will stick to this point especially so as to note the responsibility that is incumbent upon us—most particularly upon us who are monks—to be the witnesses and the living "memory" of these preparations of the Holy Spirit in and through what we call "the Old Testament," that is, the First Covenant.

- THE HOLY SPIRIT who "accomplishes" that which has been prefigured . . . is also the one who PREPARED this fulfillment over a long period of time. And the work of preparation is no more finished than is the work of fulfillment. We can say that from henceforth the two are intertwined, not only because most people remain in concrete terms outside of the Church, but also because in each of the baptized, in each of us, our turn to the Gospel must always be renewed. Come what may, the Holy Spirit carries out its work in the world and completes all sanctification. The fourth Eucharistic Prayer summarizes well this historical development from the first to the second Covenant, which resonates unceasingly in all of our stories of faithfulness.

- The liturgical reform of Vatican II has involved an admirable rehabilitation of the First Testament. From now on most of the books of the Bible have become food for the people of God, and the care taken in connecting the first reading and the Gospel, on Sundays and on feast days, enables us better to appreciate the continuity of inspiration, the presence of one same Spirit veiled in the old letter[81] and more open in the Gospel message. Personally, I am truly sorry that this connection is not offered to us in the Easter period, during which the first reading is always taken from Acts; it is, all the same, this paschal reality that has occasioned Jesus' two lessons of catechism through the Law, the Prophets, and the Psalms, to the disciples on the road to Emmaus and then to the other apostles gathered together (cf. Saint Peter in today's reading).[82]
- As MONKS, we are dedicated to the back-and-forth of Scripture:
    - Because the most important part of our prayer remains the Psalms, in which we seek Christ's voice, which the Spirit helps us to recognize.
    - Because our vocation comes under the prophetic function of the church and is gladly expressed in the images and style of Isaiah, Jeremiah, Hosea, and the Song of Songs, doubtless with much greater spontaneity than in Saint Paul's pastoral style.
    - Because we do not consider ourselves to be "square" with the Old Law while we feel ourselves to be far from being truly at ease in the freedom given by the

81. E.g., the Old Testament.
82. 1 Pet 2:2-5, 9-12.

Gospel. "Thou shalt not kill" and the other of the Ten Commandments are part of the chapter on Benedict's Good Works![83]

Saturday, May 28, 1994
no. 1094
Liturgical "typology" from the Old to the New

Christian reminds us that the harmony of Scripture is well treated in the Catechism as well as in the theological tradition of the Church. The Catechism remarks that "The Church . . . has illuminated the unity of the divine plan in the two testaments through typology, which discerns in God's works of the Old Covenant prefigurations of what he accomplished in the fullness of time in the person of his incarnate Son" (CCC 128); "the Old Testament retains its own intrinsic value as Revelation reaffirmed by our Lord himself" (CCC 129).

> **CCC 1094** *It is on this harmony of the two Testaments that the Paschal catechesis of the Lord is built (cf. DV 14–16; Luke 24:13-49), and then, that of the Apostles and the Fathers of the Church. This catechesis unveils what lay hidden under the letter of the Old Testament: the mystery of Christ. It is called "typological" because it reveals the newness of Christ on the basis of the "figures" (types) which announce him in the deeds, words, and symbols of the first covenant.*

- The harmony of the two Testaments is the subject of numbers 128–30 of the Catechism, discussing the Canon of Scripture.

83. RB 4 (the Tools for Good Works) mentions each of the Ten Commandments.

- It will be recalled here that this harmony has also explicitly been the subject of the paschal catechesis of the Lord, then of that of the apostles and of the church fathers.
- This "typological" re-reading essentially takes place henceforth in a liturgical context, even though the "figure" could have no precise connection to worship. Like the flood, it is its re-reading as a "type" of baptism that consecrates and sanctifies it, in a way . . . the earlier event serves as an announcement of and a support to an approach to faith whose nature is radically different. Only the Holy Spirit can make the connection. Without the Holy Spirit, the Flood only involves the rescuing of a family permitted by Providence during a natural disaster. Without the Holy Spirit, baptism would only involve a one-off intervention by Christ in a specific life, and water would be an element, arbitrarily chosen, of this demonstration. The flood offers a completely different perspective on baptism: the water that engulfs is also the water that sustains and saves; the individual who emerges is also connected to the whole of humanity, who are called to be reborn through that individual; the individual becomes the promise of life, the rainbow of a universal Covenant . . . because the whole of creation is involved in every baptism, just as it was fully involved in the flood.
- We might therefore go back in detail over all the "signs" of the Old Testament listed here . . . and still others, in order to resituate them in the light of the Gospel and the life of the Church. Instinctively, we will seek the "meaning" in that which constitutes the new people of God and makes them a "communion" of a sacramental nature. Another typical example can be read in the passage—which has become so "natural" because it has been emphasized and announced by Christ so often (including a whole speech in John 6)—between manna, ordinary bread not directly related to worship, and the

eucharistic table. One sole mystery of INCARNATION enables us to pass from one to the other, and while the Eucharist gives us to celebrate continued Incarnation (as in the passage from the late Philippe Ferlay read this evening), it also permits us to read manna as an anticipated Incarnation. In the liturgy the activity of everything that makes up our daily life (like manna) is able to be done to the praise of the Father's glory, through the celebrated sign of a nourishing and efficacious Presence (as in the Eucharist). "Thus the whole of creation is fulfilled as God's dwelling place" (Philippe Ferlay).

Saturday, June 4, 1994
no. 1096
Jewish sources of Christian liturgy

Christian here omits CCC 1095, which speaks of Advent, Lent, and the Easter Vigil as moments at which salvation history is rehearsed in the liturgy of today. He says that these are opportunities for catechesis. He points out some of the similarities and difference between Jewish and Christian worship, and indeed echoes with Muslim ritual prayer, pilgrimage, and the sacrifice (qurbani) *of a fine animal.*

> **CCC 1096** *Jewish liturgy and Christian liturgy. A better knowledge of the Jewish people's faith and religious life as professed and lived even now can help our better understanding of certain aspects of Christian liturgy. For both Jews and Christians Sacred Scripture is an essential part of their respective liturgies: in the proclamation of the Word of God, the response to this word, prayer of praise and intercession for the living and the dead, invocation of God's mercy. In its characteristic*

structure the Liturgy of the Word originates in Jewish prayer. . . . The relationship between Jewish liturgy and Christian liturgy, but also their differences in content, are particularly evident in the great feasts of the liturgical year, such as Passover. Christians and Jews both celebrate the Passover. For Jews, it is the Passover of history, tending toward the future; for Christians, it is the Passover fulfilled in the death and Resurrection of Christ, though always in expectation of its definitive consummation.

- Cf. the last issue of *Feasts and Seasons*[84] "on the Jewish sources of the Eucharist."
- Cf. the "schemas" inherited from the Old Testament
  - For the liturgy of the word: the penitential liturgy, the solemn proclamation, psalms, homily.
  - For the Eucharistic liturgy: some progression[85] was necessary from the Last Supper itself, linked to the paschal meal, and it follows that passover has become quotidian in order better to highlight that it has been accomplished and is henceforth permanent.
  - For the Office and the liturgy of the Hours: the sanctification of the Hours through praise and the Psalms.
- Here, it would also be necessary to consider the Jewish sources of Muslim liturgy (*salât*, five times a day, and Friday prayers, not to mention the Pilgrimage with the ritual sacrifice of the lamb).
- Finally, continue to be sensitive to the key words of this passage and to this continuity that the Church has

84. This is the periodical *Fêtes et Saisons* 484 (January 1994), entitled *Au sources juives de l'Eucharistie.*

85. The passage about the Passover?

disseminated in all its successive liturgical languages (Greek, Latin, eruption into vernaculars), without translating them from their Semitic original. These key words act, incidentally, as witnesses to unity, to communion between the churches: *AMEN! ALLELUIA! HOSANNA!* (there is a further example which has not survived Vatican II: *SABAOTH!*).

Tuesday, June 7, 1994
nos. 1097–1098
A people well disposed . . .

Christian speaks here of a liturgy of "communal preparation" of people "who do not approach [God or Christ] in the same way." "Assisi" probably refers to the gathering of world religions at Assisi on October 27, 1986, when Pope John Paul II invited faith leaders to come together to pray for the common intention of peace. Assisi, of course, also brings to mind the so-called Assisi Network, which by invitation of the future Pope Paul VI and through the work of Fr. Aldo Brunacci used Catholic institutions and networks in and around the town to protect several hundred Jews from attack and deportation from 1943 to 1944. During that time, Yom Kippur was kept in 1943 by those being protected, with the preparations for the meal for the end of the fast being done by nuns in a local monastery . . .

> CCC 1097 *The liturgical assembly derives its unity from the "communion of the Holy Spirit" who gathers the children of God into the one Body of Christ. This assembly transcends racial, cultural, social—indeed all human affinities.*

> CCC 1098 *The assembly should prepare itself to encounter its Lord and to become "a people well disposed." The preparation of hearts is the joint work of the Holy Spirit and the assembly, especially of its ministers. The grace of the Holy Spirit seeks to awaken faith, conversion of heart, and adherence to the Father's will.*

- Every liturgical action is an encounter between Christ and the Church. Christ who prays and the Church who prays. There is a movement from one to the other. It is the Holy Spirit who guarantees the freedom of this encounter and its openness; as Christ cannot suffer himself to be enclosed within the limits of time and place, neither can the Church. There is no excommunication that might be either Christ's doing or that of the Church. Both are always greater than "racial, cultural, social—indeed all human affinities". . . to which doubtless ought to be added "doctrinal and even religious affinities."
- The liturgy is undoubtedly the site of meaning and celebration of the realized, agreed communion between Christians confirmed in one same faith. But it is also, usually, a site within which there must be able to be expressed both the Church's waiting for the other members of Christ who do not know him or who do not approach him in the same way, and the search of those people who, in all good faith and all good will, honor God in different ways. Jesus recognized himself in the faithfulness of non-Jews and pagans, of those who did not worship in Jerusalem . . . Something like this was expressed at ASSISI when everyone came together for a liturgy that was the communal PREPARATION for an encounter with a different other and with a "greater" God.
- There is always, in every liturgy, something of the already there and of the not yet . . . this is why, regardless

of the good disposition of people's hearts, it is wise to start by a stage of preparation. The Abbé Pierre[86] begins the Eucharist with the *gloria* . . . I'm not sure. It is said here that you must make space for the Holy Spirit, who "awaken[s] faith, conversion of heart, and adherence to the Father's will." This is undoubtedly wise. And this can happen without letting oneself be impeded by the terminology "have mercy!" . . . and also by granting the required space to the opening song, which is designed to gather people together in order to welcome everything from God. Make way for John the Baptist, who precedes the Christmas *Gloria*!

Thursday, June 9, 1994
no. 1099
The Holy Spirit and the Church cooperate . . .

The Muslim dhikr *("remembrance"), phrases or prayers habitually repeated in order to bring God to mind spiritually (e.g.* Allahu akbar*), is compared with the Christian practice of the rosary. If Christ's very function is to "remember himself," the Holy Spirit helps to connect us to this practice in bringing the mystery of God to mind.*

> **CCC 1099** *The Spirit and the Church cooperate to manifest Christ and his work of salvation in the liturgy. Primarily in the Eucharist, and by analogy in the other sacraments, the liturgy is the memorial of the mystery*

86. Fr. Henri Grouès (1912–2007), a French priest well known for his work with homeless people and refugees; he held views that were often at odds with those of the hierarchy.

of salvation. The Holy Spirit is the Church's living memory (cf. John 14:26).

- The Holy Spirit PREPARES . . . here, the Spirit RECALLS . . . and then REALIZES . . .
- This short no. 1099 is very contained. It says a lot . . .
- It states first of all and once again the cooperation of the Spirit and the Church: "us and the Holy Spirit," in the words of the apostles![87] And this cooperation is a kind of "epiphany" of Christ, Christ made manifest.
- The liturgy is a site of this manifestation. It is not the only one (we need to remember this), just as the liturgy is not the only site of cooperation between the Holy Spirit and the Church. MARY is there as a witness to this. There are sites of life and passion like the manger, Cana, Calvary, where this manifestation of salvation in Christ "is enacted." Places and times that are in themselves "profane," that is, "on the threshold of the Temple" . . . but here, too, the Holy Spirit and the Church cooperate (through Mary!) just as much and even more so than inside the Temple.
- The liturgy is in its entirety MEMORIAL . . . this is true "primarily in the Eucharist" but also "by analogy in the other sacraments," and, it ought to be added, in every expression of worship. The *Opus Dei*, our "Office," is memorial, not only in the memory of the (Jewish) prayer that Jesus made his own, throughout his life, but also because it is Jesus who remains the great Supplicant of every celebration. Patronage of Saint Ephrem of whom it has been said that he was the "harp of the Holy Spirit." And the Spirit is there to keep alive our memory of

87. Acts 5:32. Fr.: *nous et l'Esprit Saint.*

Christ's prayer that Christ himself remembers for us in front of his Father. We remember then that Christ's very function is to REMEMBER HIMSELF . . . and the Holy Spirit connects us to this function, which is at once filial and fraternal. The *dhikr* of Muslims, like the rosary of Christians, seems to me to have to do with the same function that the Holy Spirit seeks to awaken in people of good will.

- This is why we can say that the Holy Spirit is the Church's living memory, as Jesus himself proclaimed: *But the Advocate, the Holy Spirit, whom the Father will send in my name, will teach you everything, and* REMIND *you of all that I have said to you* (John 14:26). The Church's "living" memory, because it is enriched, at every stage of "remembering," by an ever-greater perception of the mysteries of Christ that never cease to enrich our memory if we do not fix them in the only "memory" that we have of them.

Tuesday, June 14, 1994
no. 1100
The Word of God recalled . . .

Monks under the Rule of Saint Benedict devote time to prayerful reading (RB 48). Christian reminds us that lectio divina can help to "make [the] Word our own," allowing it to be "the word of life" rather than a "dead letter." In lectio, Christian says that even if we allow the reflections of others to guide our reading, study, and preaching, in order for the word to live it must be "the fruit of our [own] experience and . . . mingled with some of our own lifeblood." It is important for our experience of the liturgy, too, not to ossify.

> **CCC 1100** *The Word of God. The Holy Spirit first recalls the meaning of the salvation event to the liturgical assembly by giving life to the Word of God, which is proclaimed so that it may be received and lived:*
>
> > *In the celebration of the liturgy, Sacred Scripture is extremely important. From it comes the lessons that are read and explained in the homily and the psalms that are sung. . . . (SC 24)*

- The Holy Spirit is the life of God and the life of the Word. It is thus the Spirit who "gives life" to the Word of God . . . who supports the life of this human language entrusted to the faith of the Church so that it may continually reveal God's speech. Like all life, this life is made to be given, to be received, and to be lived. It is up to us to make this Word our own, and to make it, in today's world, either "the Word of life"[88] or, in contrast, a "dead letter." You will notice that the Psalms are mentioned explicitly.

- The Word of God is "extremely important" in the liturgy: it is at its center, at its very heart. It is the reference point of the acts and symbols, the gestures and the things shared. And it is a challenging reference point: it is sometimes easier to comment on the life of a saint than to comment on the Word of the day. Now the Church of Vatican II wanted in a way to exorcize this temptation, to which it has so often succumbed (e.g., the second readings in the Office of Readings on saints' days, which are no longer hagiographical). Returning to the Word is an onerous task. It involves "lectio," that is, welcoming the Holy Spirit with, at the outset, that attitude of poverty, attentiveness, and inner silence that alone can make

88. See 1 John 1.

of "this" Word our "life" today. Brother Henri[89] used to say to Brother Michel, what we expect from you are texts, words that have been meditated over (whether these are the Psalms, readings, or the intentions of the Office, introductions or homilies at Mass). This also means that if it is legitimate to draw on what others have written, preached, and thought about the texts that we have to comment on (and I do not deny myself this), in order for our word to be living and to give life it is always necessary that it be the fruit of our experience and that it be mingled with some of our own lifeblood. It is said here that the Church has done precisely this when composing prayers, orations, hymns . . . We are lucky to live at a time when this great liturgical laboratory has had to function anew in order to give "vernacular" languages their rightful place. Everyone can participate in this effort of continual translation of the Word. On the one hand, there is the dogma that is necessary in order to mark out the stages of interpretation, but there is also the risk of immobilizing the Word . . . a little like the way a photograph IMMOBILIZES a person. The liturgy is not a photo album to be leafed through, at the risk of forgetting that the Life of the album is there and offers itself to be seen, heard, and deciphered. We will never be able to take a photo of the Holy Spirit. In the diversity of our different temperaments and cultures, each one of us has something to say about this Word who is its Life.

89. [Henri Vergès, e.g., the Abbé Pierre].

Tuesday, June 21, 1994
no. 1102
Communion in FAITH . . .

*"Simple people" is a phrase that Christian uses (*les simples*) on several occasions. It is not used pejoratively, but seems to refer rather to the many faithful people who, not being monks or intellectuals, practice their faith genuinely and devotedly, and perhaps with a focus on elements of popular piety. Here, for instance, he cites the day's Gospel (Matt 22:34-40). To love God and to love one's neighbor is to receive the Spirit and to foster the appearance of God's grace in the wider community. Christian skips CCC 1101, which explains that the Spirit puts worshipers "into a living relationship with Christ."*

> CCC 1102 *"By the saving word of God, faith . . . is nourished in the hearts of believers. By this faith then the congregation of the faithful begins and grows" (PO 4). The proclamation of the Word of God does not stop with a teaching: it elicits the response of faith as consent and commitment, directed at the covenant between God and his people. Once again it is the Holy Spirit who gives the grace of faith, strengthens it and makes it grow in the community. The liturgical assembly is first of all a communion in faith.*

- The Word as the nourishment of faith: there is a sort of back-and-forth between the Word and faith, both of which are gifts from God calling to one another. The Word remains unrooted and without fruit unless it finds a ground prepared to welcome it . . . and this ground will return to a state of wilderness if it does not allow itself to be worked, flooded, moved by the Word. That said, the faith of simple people often relies upon a simple Word that inhabits them entirely and which, for them, contains all the Law and the Prophets. Thus the Golden Rule (see today's Gospel).[90]

- Within this point, we move, without any warning, imperceptibly from personal faith, working within the heart of every believer (described in the French as Christian rather than as "Catholic," happily so!) to community faith, through which "the congregation of the faithful begins and grows."[91] Now community faith is neither a reaction to personal faith nor the sum of all the personal faiths represented in the congregation . . . no more than the air in nature is the sum of the air that we breathe. The air includes the air we breathe, but it is also much more than that. The faith of the church is enriched by the faith of each believer without identifying itself with any individual faith: faith includes the faith of each believer but is also much more than this.

- The proclamation of the Word is not a simple teaching . . . it calls for a RESPONSE that is at once consent and commitment. Mary's *FIAT* contains within itself alone this dual sense of YES to the principle and of cooperation in its implementation. But committing oneself means setting out on a journey . . . , and the journey may be a long one. The teaching itself is constant. It is a continual formation. The very nature of the Word—infinite, inscrutable—demands as much. We are never finished with the Word. Who can claim to "know" it? Who, moreover, can claim to contemplate it fully? In this sense, there is no "Muslim" in Christianity,[92] except the Word itself, who is at once both Word and Response, unique Word and perfect Response.

90. Matt 22:34-40.
91. Fr.: *"communion des chrétiens."*
92. E.g., one who submits?

- This is why we should be wary of isolating, in this context of growth and of what is unfinished, the conclusion to this point, which asserts that "The liturgical assembly is first of all a communion in faith." It is this type of statement that, throughout the Church's history, has resulted in people being "excommunicated." Because it is a question of becoming a communion, all stages of FAITH, all approaches have their own place within that, people of little faith just like any others. They too can be apostles! The Christian communion is a pluralist, open assembly formed by mutual welcome and shared expectation . . .

Thursday, June 23, 1994
no. 1103
Anamnesis . . .

"Anamnesis" means recollection or reminiscence. Christian reminds the listener of the frequent recollection in Christian worship and practice of historical acts (the priest, especially, is a "man of memorial"), and one must "make memory" of those acts, for which task "language is necessary"; an act must be done. Yet the Church has not always been "infallible in its discernment" of the nature of righteous people or the right side of a war. The Arabic phrase kun *(the imperative "be")* + fayakun *means "be, and it is."*

> **CCC 1103** *Anamnesis. The liturgical celebration always refers to God's saving interventions in history. "The economy of Revelation is realized by deeds and words which are intrinsically bound up with each other. [. . .] [T]he words for their part proclaim the works and bring to light the mystery they contain" (DV 2). In the liturgy*

of the Word the Holy Spirit "recalls" to the assembly all that Christ has done for us. . . . The Holy Spirit who thus awakens the memory of the Church then inspires thanksgiving and praise (doxology).

- A constant reference to the interventions of God in history. It is necessary for there to have been an act of God, authenticated by a word. This is why the Church cannot give itself over to any "cult." The Church has, in the past, lent its support to questionable celebrations. Cf. the *Te Deum* on the occasion of the victory of a people (over another, needless to say!). The cult of the saints is thus subject to official recognition. The Church deploys its authority to discern whether a particular "righteous person" was indeed "the word of God" addressed to the community of the present day. The Church has not been infallible in its discernment.

- The economy of Revelation works through DEEDS "and" WORDS . . . for humans, words do not suffice. *It is not enough to say to me "Lord! Lord!," you must also DO!* As it says in today's Gospel (Matt 7:21-29).[93] For God, we might almost say that works do not suffice. Language is necessary, the Word who authenticates the works. Even if this is simply "so be it!" *kun (fayakun)*. The sacrament is at once symbol and word, "sign of an accompanying word." The Word "reveals" the mystery . . . it always leads further than appearances.

- It must be reiterated that ANAMNESIS is a vital function of the church. There is no church without "memorial." This mission was willed by Christ and directly entrusted

93. Matt 7:21: *"Not everyone who says to me, Lord, Lord, will enter the kingdom of heaven, but only the one who does the will of my Father in heaven."*

by him to his apostles. The priest is only a priest to the extent that he is a man of memorial. He is there to fertilize . . . the praise and thanksgiving (the doxology) of God's people. If monasteries represent, embody, a people "devoted to praise," this is a visible and meaningful connection with a Church who celebrates the memory of her Lord and who, on SUNDAYS at a minimum, calls herself to keep this paschal mystery alive. Anamnesis "and" doxology together make up a living Church, a Church that is at once sacerdotal and prophetic. History shows that a Church that is not fully committed to memorial, and to its mystery of presence in action, risks no longer feeling the need for monasteries, no longer being able to inspire monastic vocations. More generally, religious vocations consecrate in Church the indissoluble covenant between saying and doing. The Word is never simply recitation (*qur'an*); the Word is action. But this action must itself refer continually to the Word by whom it is called and authorized.

Tuesday, June 28, 1994
no. 1104
The Holy Spirit ACTUALIZES . . .

Even if liturgical celebrations follow the same form every day, in a true celebration actualized by the Holy Spirit there should be no "weariness and boredom." Christian goes on to compliment the possibility of variation in prayers and texts after the Council but reminds us of the longevity and value of fixed forms in which, "under the veil of repetition, something absolutely unique to each occurrence was, and continues to be, celebrated."

CCC 1104 *Christian liturgy not only recalls the events that saved us but actualizes them, makes them present. The Paschal mystery of Christ is celebrated, not repeated. It is the celebrations that are repeated, and in each celebration there is an outpouring of the Holy Spirit that makes the unique mystery present.*

- The Holy Spirit PREPARES . . . RECALLS . . . and also, as it is said here, ACTUALIZES the mystery of Christ.
- It is one and the same mystery then that has been prepared, for a long time, that is recalled, and that, in being recalled, in this memorial, is made present both at a particular time and in a particular place.
- This mystery is CELEBRATED and not REPEATED . . . the celebrations are repeated . . . externally, the form remains more or less the same, from day to day, from celebration to celebration. Here there is the risk of causing weariness and boredom. Then we tell ourselves that, happily, it is not a matter of simple repetition since the word changes every day . . . and also because a certain amount of variety can occur in the rites and in the prayers. This was a fortunate innovation of Vatican II. But, in fact, there have been centuries during which the daily form of the Eucharist remained almost unchanged and unchanging. The Sunday liturgy of the Word varied, but the eucharistic liturgy itself, in which the mystery is signified, never did. There, under the veil of repetition, something absolutely unique to each occurrence was and continues to be celebrated. The mystery prepared throughout the ages and still today, recalled by generations of believers including our own, here assumes present meaning and significance. It is our most real reality . . . "real presence," the reality of the present.

- It is fundamentally quite simple: Try telling a married couple that they are repeating themselves when they say to each other, today, "I love you," those utterly ordinary, first-date sort of words. If they say these words to one another, it is not only to remind themselves that they have said them to each other, but because, today, this "is" still true, this remains born in a particular way.
- "An outpouring of the Holy Spirit" is necessary, one that captures all the elements of the mystery in order to establish the connection, the binding force: Christ and I, both of us connected to the present day by this "bread," which is precisely daily bread, new manna given by God for this day. I may miss the invitation of the Holy Spirit, and then the actualization of the mystery will still take place, but without me . . . a little like the manna that was there, rejected by a people who were sick and tired of this food. By making himself present God has taken the risk of seeing other present things be preferred to him. Until the day when we will be weary like Kohelet, discovering that everything repeats itself, except for God.

Thursday, June 30, 1994
no. 1105

EPICLESIS . . .

The "sending down" or "invoking upon" refers to the Holy Spirit, whether on the gifts prepared for consecration or on the people gathered. Eucharistic Prayer II (cited below) is cited as inspired by "Hippolytus," for many years the unchallenged author of the "Apostolic Tradition," an important paradigm for the liturgy of the early church, which contains a recognizable Eucharistic Prayer.[94] *("The Cardinal" is presumably Léon-Étienne Cardinal Duval [d. 1996]).*

> **CCC 1105** *The Epiclesis ("invocation upon") is the intercession in which the priest begs the Father to send the Holy Spirit, the Sanctifier, so that the offerings may become the body and blood of Christ and that the faithful, by receiving them, may themselves become a living offering to God (cf. Rom 12:1).*

- επι καλειν: to call upon, invoke upon. . .
- In the structure of the eucharistic prayer, the epiclesis is the prayer that takes place immediately before the institution narrative. In the second Eucharistic Prayer, the oldest of those provided to us by the Vatican II Missal (following the tradition of Hippolytus around 215): *Make holy, therefore, these gifts, we pray, by sending down your* SPIRIT *upon them, so that they may become for us the Body and Blood of our Lord, Jesus Christ.*
- In the third Eucharistic Prayer, we find very clearly something like a double epiclesis, one over the offerings and one over the faithful: *by the same* SPIRIT *graciously make holy these gifts we have brought to you for consecration, that they may become the Body and Blood of your Son our Lord Jesus Christ.* And after the consecration: *May he [the* HOLY SPIRIT*] make of us an eternal offering to you, so that we may obtain . . .*
- Same invocation of the Holy Spirit in the fourth Eucharistic Prayer with a note afterwards that all those who are going to share this bread and this cup may be gathered together into one body, *that they may truly become a living sacrifice in Christ to the praise of your glory.*

94. See Paul F. Bradshaw, *Apostolic Tradition: A New Commentary* (Collegeville, MN: Liturgical Press, 2023), for the reception history of the text "Apostolic Tradition."

- In the tradition of the Eastern Church, the epiclesis is consecratory. In the West, it has become customary to consider only the words of the eucharistic institution itself as consecratory, thereby running the risk of turning these into a magic spell! We may think that this reduction is linked to the absence of epiclesis in the formulation that has become, since the sixth or seventh century, the only eucharistic prayer of the Roman Church and that we preserve under the form of the first canon, relieved of some of the many repetitions present in the old version. I have heard the Cardinal tell me that he never used the first Eucharistic Prayer because it does not mention the Holy Spirit. Doubtless the Holy Spirit must be sought there where it has been hidden (providing it has been put there!): *bless, acknowledge, and approve this offering in every respect; make it spiritual and acceptable, so that it may become for us the Body and Blood of your most beloved Son* (at the end we pick up the words of all the other eucharistic prayers). One same GESTURE "over" the offerings emphasizes the invocation. Finally, you will notice that the structure of the epiclesis is the same as that of any prayer: to the Father so that he REALIZES the Son[95] through the Holy Spirit.

Saturday, July 2, 1994
nos. 1106–1107
Epiclesis and MARY . . .

The coming of the Spirit upon the bread and wine does seem consecratory in this paragraph. The comparison of the visitation of the Spirit upon Mary at the conception of Christ and

95. Fr.: *réalise le Fils.*

the epiclesis in the Eucharist remind one that in saying "Amen" at the end of the eucharistic prayer, we are also adding our own "Fiat."

> **CCC 1106** *Together with the anamnesis, the epiclesis is at the heart of each sacramental celebration, most especially of the Eucharist:*
>
> > *You ask how the bread becomes the Body of Christ, and the wine . . . the Blood of Christ. I shall tell you: the Holy Spirit comes upon them and accomplishes what surpasses every word and thought. . . . Let it be enough for you to understand that it is by the Holy Spirit, just as it was of the Holy Virgin and by the Holy Spirit that the Lord, through and in himself, took flesh. (St. John Damascene, De fide orth. 4.13)*

> **CCC 1107** *The Holy Spirit's transforming power in the liturgy hastens the coming of the kingdom and the consummation of the mystery of salvation.*

- The epiclesis at the HEART of each sacramental celebration (of the Eucharist especially). There is then, in every sacrament, a calling down of the Spirit, which most often accompanies the gesture of the laying on of hands: consecratory words and gesture that express the free compliance of each person with the creative and transforming mission of the Holy Spirit. The Spirit, from its very beginnings, is UPON[96] humanity, not in order to weigh on humanity in a domineering fashion, but rather in order to envelop humanity in its protective and fecund shadow, like Mary.
- The quotation from John of Damascus makes a comparison between what happens in the Eucharist and what

96. Fr.: *sur*.

happened in Mary. See how the Spirit who SURPASSES (every word and thought) OVER-COMES.[97] He overflows. But he must be called, because he does not impose himself. No more than the sun can impose itself upon a house with closed shutters. Of course, closing the shutters does not change anything about the existence or the heat of the sun. In so doing, the sun is simply avoided. We can avoid the Holy Spirit. The church is that seed of humanity that does not want to avoid the Holy Spirit and that rather calls upon the Spirit whole-heartedly so that in and through herself the real presence of the Body and Blood of Christ may be accomplished. As happened in Mary. There is a whole poor and God-fearing people who, in the Old Testament, fervently called upon the Holy Spirit . . . thus expressing the epiclesis that was necessary for the consecration of the Virgin. And Mary's *Fiat* was the expression of her free participation in the epiclesis of her people calling for the fulfillment of salvation. It seems to me that the solemn AMEN that concludes every eucharistic prayer corresponds to Mary's *Fiat*. All of God's people thereby recognize the prayer of epiclesis that the celebrant has expressed in their name and that the Father has granted by letting the Spirit accomplish over the bread and wine that which he accomplished once and for all in Mary: giving humanity to the Son so that the Son can give back to the Father this humanity that freely gave itself to him. The *PER IPSUM* . . . seems to me to be the joyous, eucharistic affirmation (eucharistic here in its fullest sense) of the successful, fulfilled epiclesis of the church. If we interpret it in this way, it seems to me to belong to those who complete it with a triumphant AMEN, rather as the *Magnificat* belongs to the one who said *Fiat*.

97. Fr.: *sur-vient.*

Saturday, July 9, 1994
no. 1108
The communion of the Holy Spirit

[There is a gap of a week between this and the previous chapter.]

Here, the English text confirms Christian's point. While the French text describes the mission of the Holy Spirit "de **se** *mettre en communion avec le Christ" (to bring itself into communion with Christ), the English text has the correct pronoun: "to bring* **us** *into communion with Christ" (emphasis added).*

> **CCC 1108** *In every liturgical action the Holy Spirit is sent in order to bring us into communion with Christ and so to form his Body. The Holy Spirit is like the sap of the Father's vine which bears fruit on its branches (cf. John 15:1-17; Gal 5:22). The most intimate cooperation of the Holy Spirit and the Church is achieved in the liturgy. The Spirit, who is the Spirit of communion, abides indefectibly in the Church. For this reason the Church is the great sacrament of divine communion which gathers God's scattered children together. Communion with the Holy Trinity and fraternal communion are inseparably the fruit of the Spirit in the liturgy.*

- "Se mettre en communion avec le Christ": it would be essential to consult the original text. Here, the phrasing is awkward. Surely it must read: in order to bring "us" into communion. Moreover, if the Holy Spirit forms the Body of Christ, in the Church as in Mary, can the Spirit be said to be one "body" with Christ, just like each of us or the Virgin herself? The Spirit is the soul of this

Body. It is not itself "body." It is the sap of the vine. It is itself neither vine shoot nor even "vine stock."

- In the liturgy, the most intimate COOPERATION of the Holy Spirit and the church. The church constituted by the Holy Spirit as a SACRAMENT of what the Spirit is itself, that is, communion of the Son with the Father. In this sense, Mary's cooperation with the Holy Spirit belongs both to reality and to the sacramental: at work in Mary was the mystery of presence and communion, Incarnation and salvation in the Eucharist, which will become the great sacrament for humanity. In her, this invisible reality took on flesh and a filial face. But this real presence of the Son in Jesus, which means that we cannot, for example, describe Jesus as a "sacrament" in the way that the Church understands this term, was nonetheless in Mary the visible sign, finally unveiled to human eyes, of the Father's desire to gather all his scattered children together. And Mary with Child was already cooperating with this even greater work, which never ceases to continue from age to age. Since the fruit of the Spirit is not only communion with the Holy Trinity but also fraternal communion, it will reach maturity only in the fullness of time, when "the number of the elect" will be fulfilled. And the liturgy keeps us in suspense: "participating" wholeheartedly—despite our weaknesses—in the worship of the Trinity, and "working" wholeheartedly so that all persons yesterday, today, and forever may find their human place and fraternal vocation in the liturgical symphony of the church, which is the sacrament of the kingdom entrusted to us in the here and now.

Tuesday, July 12, 1994
no. 1109
Epiclesis and mission . . .

Christian mentions the expression "praise of glory," attributed to Elizabeth of the Trinity, a French Carmelite (d. 1906, canonized 2016) who late in life called herself "Laudem Gloriae" and who hoped that her objective in heaven would be to lead other souls to encounter with God in Trinity.

> CCC 1109 *The epiclesis is also a prayer for the full effect of the assembly's communion with the mystery of Christ. "The grace of the Lord Jesus Christ and the love of God and the fellowship of the Holy Spirit" (2 Cor 13:13) have to remain with us always and bear fruit beyond the Eucharistic celebration. The Church therefore asks the Father to send the Holy Spirit to make the lives of the faithful a living sacrifice to God by their spiritual transformation into the image of Christ, by concern for the Church's unity, and by taking part in her mission through the witness and service of charity.*

- Epiclesis, which is thus invocation of the Holy Spirit at once over the offerings and over the faithful, enables us to measure what the action of the Holy Spirit will be in the congregation. Becoming the "Body of Christ," the congregation finds itself, like Christ, dedicated to the salvation of the world, sent, one step at a time, to the multitude. All of the faithful are called to consent to their personal vocation, which is to be in their own way "praise of glory" (Elizabeth of the Trinity), to take their place in the people of God and in the whole of humanity that participates in the same vocation: offering to the praise of glory of the Father, in the Son.
- The fruits of the Spirit cannot be limited to the eucharistic communion . . . if they come through this com-

munion, it is not in it that they most frequently offer themselves to be tasted. The eucharistic communion must remain what it is: *mysterium fidei*, the mystery of faith . . . faith in God, faith in humankind, whom God wants to use to accomplish in them what has been given, as a promise, in the humanity of Jesus.

- These fruits are enumerated here: "spiritual transformation into the image of Christ," "concern for the Church's unity," "taking part in her mission through the witness and service of charity." Each of us can feel called to these four levels[98] every time we participate sacramentally in the Eucharist. If anyone is lukewarm in these areas, they need to ask themselves about the quality of their eucharistic commitment.

- In contrast, we are indeed compelled to note that some of these fruits, which are at times cruelly lacking in "regular churchgoers," are striking in non-churchgoers, in non-Christians (see Jean-Marie Huet's book). Is this not scandalous for the faith? Personally, I connect all these "fruits" (more or less untamed in relation to the church)[99] to Christ's offering of himself, an offering made once and for all and perpetuated in church. THIS is what Christ wanted to be accomplished in everyone. I see here what Jesus himself stated when he marveled at the beauty of the humble and lowly (Matt 11): it will be noticed that he gave thanks over this, he made a eucharist, epiclesis to the glory of the Father. I happily repeat the profound words of Jean Sullivan: "Jesus is what happens when God speaks (and acts) without

98. Including eucharistic communion, mentioned above.

99. The adjective Christian uses here is *sauvage*: wild, uncivilized. He clarifies that he means this from the point of view of the Church, rather than from his own perspective, and he affirms later in this chapter that for him those who are outside the Church can also be Christ-like.

obstacles in a person's heart." The difference does not lie in being baptized or not, in being part of the sacramental communion or not, even if all this HELPS a great deal . . . the difference lies in the "without obstacles."

Saturday, July 16, 1994
nos. 1113–1114
Sacraments . . . of Christ, Mary, and monks

Christian notes that Saint Benedict does not speak of the sacraments (the editors of RB 1980 say that "the scarcity of references to the Eucharist in the RB may seem scandalous").[100] *The Rule sees priests who enter as taking their place in precedence in order of their entry into the community. In speaking of priests in the monastery (see RB 60), Christian says, "the priest cannot be given the 'right' to celebrate Mass." In other words, this faculty to celebrate Mass is at the discretion of the abbot, rather than by virtue of what in modern terms one would call his* celebret.

CCC 1113 *The whole liturgical life of the Church revolves around the Eucharistic sacrifice and the sacraments (cf. SC 6). There are seven sacraments in the Church: Baptism, Confirmation or Chrismation, Eucharist, Penance, Anointing of the Sick, Holy Orders, and Matrimony (cf. DS 860; DS 1310; DS 1601).*

CCC 1114 *"Adhering to the teaching of the Holy Scriptures, to the apostolic traditions, and to the consensus [. . .] of the Fathers," we profess that "the sacra-*

100. *RB 1980: The Rule of St. Benedict in Latin and English with Notes*, ed. Timothy Fry et al. (Collegeville, MN: Liturgical Press, 1981), 410.

ments of the new law were all instituted by Jesus Christ our Lord" (DS 1600–1601).

- All this is less simple than it seems: sacraments "all instituted."[101] The great quarrel with Protestantism, which only recognized baptism and the Eucharist (then . . . penance a little bit . . . and Holy Orders a bit too).[102] Here the phrase is general; nothing is said about form. Nothing is enumerated.
- "The whole liturgical life of the Church revolves around . . .": is there not here a harmful reduction? The monastic tradition remains here the point of reference of an internal liturgical life that stands apart, in all likelihood, from that which is celebrated in the Eucharist, but which broadens the sacramental horizon and bears witness to a MEANING, a SIGN of the Church outside of directly sacramental celebrations. It is characteristic that Saint Benedict does not speak about the sacraments as such. Mass and communion are evoked by him but only accidentally . . . resituated within the framework of the life of the monk (it is clear for a priest who enters the monastery that he cannot be given the "right" to celebrate Mass). Typical too that the Mass is called *MISSAE* . . . and that this name equally designates the sending out of the whole celebration.
- The liturgical life of a MONK takes place, for the most part, in what is called *Opus Dei*. This office of the Psalms is linked to the Eucharist by JESUS himself, in a way, on Maundy Thursday. But it is an open office, in which all those who, for different reasons, do not have access to the sacramental life are able to participate: sinners, non-Catholics, non-Christians. This office enables us to say

101. Fr.: *tous institués.*

102. The punctuation in this sentence is Christian's marks of suspension rather than representing a textual ellipsis.

that there is a sacramentality of the Body of Christ that is wider and more diffuse than that which is expressed in participation in the sacraments.

- And it is here that the patronage of Mary, Virgin of Carmel, is invaluable for us: Mother of the contemplative life and of worship in spirit and truth, Mary is not directly connected to any sacrament. It may even be said that she approaches all the sacraments obliquely since she receives what they signify not through them but otherwise. Which proves, incidentally, that we cannot lean on this example in order to exclude women from the presbyterate . . .

Tuesday, July 19, 1994
nos. 1115–1116
Easter sacraments

Christian speaks of "masterworks." The French term in both cases is "chef-d'œuvre," although the English translation varies in fact between "masterwork" (here, in no. 1116) and "masterpiece" (in no. 1091). Christian goes on to play on both parts of the French term, œuvre *(work, and therefore action) and* chef *(head, and thus capital).The notion that Jesus himself "in his entirety" was a sacrament, "the sacrament of the encounter with God" is a reference to* Le Christ: sacrament de la rencontre de Dieu *by Edward Schillebeeckx, and the aforementioned essay "The Mass on the World," by Pierre Teilhard de Chardin, is also mentioned.*

> CCC 1115 *Jesus' words and actions during his hidden life and public ministry were already salvific, for they anticipate the power of his Paschal mystery. They an-*

nounced and prepared what he was going to give the Church when all was accomplished. The mysteries of Christ's life are the foundations of what he would henceforth dispense in the sacraments, through the ministers of his Church, for "what was visible in our Savior has passed over into his mysteries" (Saint Leo the Great, Sermo 74.2).

CCC 1116 *Sacraments are "powers that come forth" from the Body of Christ (cf. Luke 5:17; 6:19; 8:46), which is ever-living and life-giving. They are actions of the Holy Spirit at work in his Body, the Church. They are "the masterworks of God" in the new and everlasting covenant.*

- Saint Leo: "what was visible in our Savior has passed over into his mysteries . . ." Sacraments = the continued Incarnation, an Incarnation that remains in its paschal movement. For the end and meaning even of the Incarnation is not first of all that the Word becomes flesh, but that our flesh is introduced into the divine world of the Word.

- The sacraments are thus these "living powers" that come from the glorious Body of Christ in order to bring back all those whom they touch. They are powers that come from the Head to bring together, unite, all the members with the Head.

- The masterwork of God: it is the second time that this phrase appears (no. 1091: the Holy Spirit as the artisan of "God's masterworks," which are the sacraments of the New Covenant). The word is revealing. These are the "works" of God. It is God who ACTS. These works are "capital," in the sense that their action is essential . . . and also in that they come from the head, from the boss (in French, *chef*; in Latin, *caput*); works that come from the head and lead back to the same.

- To be linked to the words and actions of Jesus "during his hidden life and public ministry." This means that Jesus in his entirety was then a SACRAMENT, "the sacrament of the encounter with God" (Schillebeckx), but also that each sacrament points to JESUS in his entirety, even if for each of them, the angle of approach differs. On close consideration, in each sacrament there is something of all the others. Each of them proclaims the work of the Spirit that unites us with Christ, at each stage as in all acts of life . . . , but the encounter with the sacrament is not exhausted by the sacraments by which it is signified. This encounter is offered to all, at every moment. Whoever experiences this encounter outside of the sacraments understands, if one is a Christian, that what is accomplished in this case had already been GIVEN in the sacrament. If one is not a Christian, this is how one is introduced and led, unconsciously, into the paschal mystery. One of the great texts that sets out this universal sacramental dynamism seems to me to be the "Mass on the World" by Teilhard. Vocation of the whole of creation and the whole of humanity to become a filial SACRAMENT.

Thursday, July 21, 1994
no. 1117
The sacraments of the Church . . .

Ribat refers to a kind of retreat or hostel on the frontier, originally for military use; later, the term was applied to Sufi houses of study or centers in which to learn from a great teacher.

> CCC 1117 *As she has done for the canon of Sacred Scripture and for the doctrine of the faith, the Church, by the power of the Spirit who guides her "into all*

> *truth" has gradually recognized the treasure received from Christ and, as the faithful steward of God's mysteries, has determined its "dispensation" (John 16:13; cf. Matt 13:52; 1 Cor 4:1). Thus the Church has discerned over the centuries that among liturgical celebrations there are seven that are, in the strict sense of the term, sacraments instituted by the Lord.*

- The Spirit guides us "into all Truth" . . . : in other words, the Truth is at once the way and the endpoint. We are on the way (thus "into all Truth"), but we have not reached our target. Thinking we had would mean stopping on the way . . . recalling the subject of the Ribat, the first to be formulated as a prayer: "Lead us into all Truth . . ."[103]
- The Church has recognized this "treasure" . . . The sacraments are a treasure, but a "relative" treasure. Humanity is the great treasure received by the Church, and humanity itself is the very treasure of God that Jesus has helped us to recognize as such by inscribing himself in that treasure. Cf. Jeremiah's wonderful expression in today's first reading (Jer 2:1-13): *Israel was holy to the LORD, the first fruits of his harvest.*[104] The treasure of the sacraments, to the extent that it is destined for Christians alone, can lead the church to have too narrow a vision of herself. Because the Church is naturally "ecstatic" (Paul VI), she will never be able to be satisfied by that which is conceived for her internal use, even if this is already great riches. These "riches" of the sacraments are not absolute for anyone, neither for the Church, nor for the faithful, nor for God—not even baptism or the Eucharist . . . , precisely because they are signs of the

103. John 16:13.
104. Thursday of week 16 in Ordinary Time.

Absolute, which goes beyond them and in front of which they fade away.

- Steward of "God's mysteries": the three areas evoked (the Canon of the Scripture, Doctrine, Sacraments) have been extended in different ways depending on the churches. It is a fact that there is an abiding unity as regards the existence of the Scriptures, articles of Christian faith, and the sacramental economy. In the widest sense, it is the Church herself that is a "sacrament," unique in its kind. The Evangelists have no other . . .
- SEVEN . . . this figure is "definite." It designates associated rites and words that have a precise ecclesiastical efficacy, linked to the FAITH. It does not exhaust either the rites or the words. The "sacramentals" are there to widen the field of sacramentality. And, once more, each of the SEVEN conveys something of all the others. At the center, the "HOLY" Sacrament . . .[105]

Tuesday, July 26, 1994
nos. 1118–1119
By and through the Church . . .

It is not easy in some circles to say extra Ecclesiam nulla salus, *but Christian helpfully observes here that although the sacraments have become attached to Christ, "he remains independent, and his grace can make use of other channels." Yet the sacraments (and the sharing of the sacraments) are means by which the unity of the Church is made plain, and "every*

105. Fr.: *le "SAINT" Sacrement.*

church recognises her own by the way they participate in the sacraments."

> **CCC 1118** *The sacraments are "of the Church" in the double sense that they are "by her" and "for her." They are "by the Church," for she is the sacrament of Christ's action at work in her through the mission of the Holy Spirit. They are "for the Church" in the sense that "the sacraments make the Church" (St. Augustine, De civ. Dei, 22, 17; cf. St. Thomas Aquinas, STh III, 64, 2 ad 3), since they manifest and communicate to men, above all in the Eucharist, the mystery of communion with the God who is love, One in three persons.*

> **CCC 1119** *Forming "as it were, one mystical person" with Christ the head, the Church acts in the sacraments as "an organically structured priestly community" (LG 11; cf. Pius XII, Mystici Corporis [1943]). Through Baptism and Confirmation the priestly people is enabled to celebrate the liturgy, while those of the faithful "who have received Holy Orders, are appointed to nourish the Church with the word and grace of God in the name of Christ" (LG 11).*

- The sacraments are THROUGH and FOR the Church (no. 1119: IN the church): *per ipsam et in ipsam et ad ipsam* . . .
- Modeling this phrase in this way on Christ indicates where to locate an important distinction: the sacraments are of Christ, that is to say, they are through Christ, with him, in him . . . but they are not FOR Christ, except insofar as they are for his Body, which is the Church. They do not "make" Christ. Christ has attached himself to them, but he remains independent, and his grace can make use of other channels. In contrast, the Church as sacrament needs the sacraments in order to signify

herself as such in her own, visible mission of sanctifying a world that is moving ahead.[106]

- "outside of the Church, no sacraments" . . .[107] and it is easy to understand why, in the very administering of the sacraments, the Church remains highly sensitive to the extent to which the faithful who call upon her belong to her (investigations for baptism, marriage . . .). Every separation, every schism has immediate consequences for the sacraments. Each Church recognizes her own by the way it participates in the sacraments. From this perspective, the sacraments have multiplied as much as the churches.

- It is right to say that the sacraments are FOR the Church, providing, once again, that it is not forgotten that the Church herself is FOR the world. The sacraments only maintain the inner life of the Church in order that the Church may be the life of the world, the living yeast of the human dough. The pot may indeed be made of clay, but it is not sealed. Ever since the creation, the mystery of communion in God has been an OPEN mystery, and the Church can only be herself by signifying this openness, which is at the very heart of the most intimate communion.

- The Church that acts in the sacraments as a "priestly community" continues to act outside of the sacraments as a "prophetic community" . . . and this is why she is also prophetic in the sacraments, a fact that enables her to celebrate ALONE knowing herself to be UNITED with the multitude (and not only with the community).

106. Fr.: *en marche.*
107. Another gesture to the maxim *extra Ecclesiam nulla salus.*

Thursday, July 28, 1994
no. 1120
Ministerial priesthood . . .

In this chapter Christian is indebted to the ecclesiology of the People of God, which has influenced discourse on the hierarchy of the Church since the Council. All the baptized are, of course, part of the royal priesthood of all Christian people, the baptismal priesthood. Christian holds that all three orders of ministry (deacon, priest, bishop) are participating in diakonia *or service to the whole People of God—he may be making a pun on* ordonné, *which can mean both "ordained" and "organized." The 1971 Synod, mentioned in passing, was the Second Ordinary Assembly of the Synod of Bishops (erected by the Council), which studied the Ministerial Priesthood. The Arabic term* ribat *here may refer to the act (by ordained ministers) of standing watch over a frontier post (*ribat*).*

> CCC 1120 *The ordained ministry or ministerial priesthood is at the service of the baptismal priesthood (LG 10). The ordained priesthood guarantees that it really is Christ who acts in the sacraments through the Holy Spirit for the Church. The saving mission entrusted by the Father to his incarnate Son was committed to the apostles and through them to their successors: they receive the Spirit of Jesus to act in his name and in his person (cf. John 20:21-23; Luke 24:47; Matt 28:18-20). The ordained minister is the sacramental bond that ties the liturgical action to what the apostles said and did and, through them, to the words and actions of Christ, the source and foundation of the sacraments.*

- Ordained ministry is at the SERVICE of the baptismal "priesthood." It is a "diakonia"; recall that it has at least three degrees and is thus organized on three levels, with three forms of "service."

- Its only direct MEANING lies in its being for and dependent upon the faithful (Augustine: "With you, I am a Christian; for you, I am a bishop"),[108] and yet people have also spoken of the "priest of non-Christians."[109] For the faithful, the priest is a sacrament of the Church in its plenitude, of the Head and the Body both together. Cf. the 1971 Synod: the Church is never as certain of her presence in a particular place as when she is present through a priest who is there *in persona Christi et in persona Ecclesiae.*

- The ordained ministry is a "LINK": it is a *ribat*. It signifies continuity, uninterrupted succession. It bears witness to what Christ said and did, to what the apostles said and did following Christ, and to what the Holy Spirit, today, says and does in order that the faith may live. It has a catalyzing function, meaning that it contributes to establishing contact, often without its knowledge. It grants coherence and consistency to God's people. It is the sign of being WITH, of God being WITH (neither above, nor close by or apart).

- Even churches that do not recognize ordained ministry have felt the need to vary and to authenticate the functions of their members, and to delegate or bestow authority on particular individuals, thereby granting to them a more important mission in relation to the Word or to the congregation.

- The concept of ordained ministry depends greatly on how the Eucharist is conceptualized: whoever says and

108. Cf. Office of Readings, 24th Sunday in Ordinary Time. But this is not a direct quotation. Correctly Augustine reads: "I must distinguish carefully between the aspects of the role the Lord has given me."

109. See Serge de Beurecueil, OP, *Prêtre des non-chrétiens* [*Priest of Non-Christians*] (Paris: Cerf, 1968).

creates[110] the real presence in the sacrament participates directly in this presence and its reality in the world.

Saturday, July 30, 1994
no. 1121
Sacramental character

The reference to Catholicism is to Catholicisme: hier, aujourd'hui, demain *(Paris: Letouzey et Ané), editions of which were published in (among other years) 1950 and 1991 (in seven volumes). Christian is emphasizing here that the Church seems to be losing the idea of sacramental character, as evidenced by its absence in this reference text.*

> CCC 1121 *The three sacraments of Baptism, Confirmation, and Holy Orders confer, in addition to grace, a sacramental character or "seal" by which the Christian shares in Christ's priesthood and is made a member of the Church according to different states and functions. This configuration to Christ and to the Church, brought about by the Spirit, is indelible (DS 1609); it remains for ever in the Christian as a positive disposition for grace, a promise and guarantee of divine protection, and as a vocation to divine worship and to the service of the Church. Therefore these sacraments can never be repeated.*

- N.B. The *Catholicism* of 1950 in which the article "CHARACTER" refers to "sacramental character"; in the *Catholicism* of 1991 in which the article "SACRAMENT" is published, this idea has completely disappeared!

110. Fr.: *dit et fait la présence réele.*

- There are therefore "indelible" sacraments, permanent signs. We are within our rights to wonder, "Is this not on the part of the Church a way to appropriate and control time, to bind God's unforeseeable grace?" The answer: Signs of God must also be able to express that God is not bound to time . . . that when he gives himself, it is with this character of the eternal that is proper to him, that his GIFTS are without repentance, that in this Covenant between God and humanity, there is first of all and before all else this great indelible sign of the CROSS on which all the other "signs" of the Church depend. In fact, every sacrament has something to do with eternity, whether we think of the indissoluble nature of marriage . . ., of the permanent presence behind the eucharistic species, or even of the PARDON that is given once and for all, etc.

- There are, however, the Church tells us, three sacraments that have "character." They are remarkable. They pertain not only to God's eternity but also to his UNIQUENESS. They signify what is UNIQUE about the encounter with Christ: "it" leaves a trace, perhaps even first of all a trace in God! God, too, is himself marked. He does not forget. It is pointless to remind him of the special Covenant: "You belong to me! I have made you for my own!" God says to Moses (Qur'an).[111] So the sacraments cannot be repeated (no more than marriage between the same two spouses can be repeated. It's a question of Love): that's what this means. As a result, everything gets complicated when the Church herself ceases to be conscious of her own UNIQUENESS, when she divides herself. This harms the indelible character: where to find it? In this or that baptism? Are these ordinations valid? Have these or-

111. Surah 20.41?

dained women received the character? That is why people are also reticent about the expression "baptism of the Spirit," which simply means that the seal is there, but unrecognized; that the GIFT has been given but not received, that it has not been FRUITFUL (Augustine).[112]

- Do not forget however that it is a matter of SACRAMENTS, which are therefore linked to this existence here. Permanence is not the same as eternity. *Sacerdos in aeternum*, has it not been said? This is true of JESUS . . . and therefore of ALL the members of his Body. What is signified there in time and for all time leaves a trace that will be the striking "sign" of "all" the elect. Let's not envisage those who have been baptized in the front row, or the priests at the right-hand side in the Kingdom . . .

Tuesday, August 2, 1994
nos. 1122–1123
The "sacramental mission"

"Moubarac" is Youakim Moubarac, a Maronite priest and scholar who taught at the Institut Catholique de Paris and the Sorbonne, who was particularly interested in dialogue between faiths. The words attributed to him here speak volumes.

> **CCC 1122** *Christ sent his apostles so that "repentance and forgiveness of sins should be preached in his name to all nations" (Luke 24:47). "Go therefore and make disciples of all nations, baptizing them in the name of the Father and of the Son and of the Holy Spirit" (Matt 28:19). The mission to baptize, and so the sacramental*

112. *On Baptism, Against the Donatists* (Book VI).

mission, is implied in the mission to evangelize, because the sacrament is prepared for by the word of God and by the faith which is assent to this word:

> *The People of God is formed into one in the first place by the Word of the living God. . . . The preaching of the Word is required for the sacramental ministry itself, since the sacraments are sacraments of faith, drawing their origin and nourishment from the Word (PO 4).*

CCC 1123 *"The purpose of the sacraments is to sanctify men, to build up the Body of Christ and, finally, to give worship to God. Because they are signs they also instruct. They not only presuppose faith, but by words and objects they also nourish, strengthen, and express it. That is why they are called 'sacraments of faith'" (SC 59).*

- Commenting upon the whole of this part of "the sacraments of faith" is quite a delicate matter. It expresses the essential link between faith and the sacrament.
- The mission of the disciples is expressed here in very traditional terms. It is a definition that cannot satisfy us completely, since it does not leave any space for monastic vocation. The great missionary centuries (the seventeenth or nineteenth centuries) were not very monastic.
- If mission is a work of LOVE, the fact that it is freely given must absolutely be preserved. The flame that "urges" missionaries to leave their homes is first of all a consequence of the Gospel. It is because of the Gospel, in order to obey the Gospel, that I left . . . and one of the first signs of the Gospel is this way of living it wholly gratuitously and in a gift of myself that is as pure as possible. It is mine in my baptism and not initially for baptizing others.
- The Word of God, in fact, comes first in the sacrament, in all the sacraments. Its place is re-established very

clearly by the liturgical reform; even when the sacrament is celebrated outside of the Mass, it is first of all a liturgy of the Word.

- Likewise, the Word of God comes first in mission; not only is it prior to the sacrament, but it makes us believe that it is also prior to the annunciation itself by the disciple who is himself sacramental. The Word is spread to the multitude, and it is the work of the Spirit to watch over this seed burgeoning in every heart. Thus the word of the disciple is pre-empted, preceded, by the Word itself, and it is for this reason that it can be recognized and, God willing, be confessed in faith. I can be lukewarm or indifferent when I receive the Eucharist: how would my presence be sufficient to make someone else less lukewarm or indifferent?
- The mission of the contemplative in a non-Christian land, somewhere that has not been evangelized (in the active sense of the word), is "urged on by the LOVE of Christ to recognize and honor in the multitudes where his Presence is the catalyst of history" (Moubarac).[113] SEE the spirit at work and confess it. The monk's response to his call is "more evangelical than evangelizing," or evangelizing, if this is what God wants, because it strives, with the grace of God, to be evangelical. Discovering that Jesus pre-empted us on "the other side of the lake,"[114] amongst "the nations" . . . for those of us who are not called by the Church to baptize means that we need to recognize and encourage the grace of the Spirit that enables us to seek God tirelessly in listening

113. Presumably Youakim Moubarak, cf. Christian Salenson, *Christian de Chergé: A Theology of Hope*, trans. Nada Conic, Cistercian Studies 247 (Collegeville, MN: Cistercian Publications, 2012).

114. E.g., John 6:25—part of the Gospel of the day.

silently, in prayers from the heart, in conversion of life and joyful obedience . . .

Tuesday, August 9, 1994
no. 1124
Lex orandi, lex credendi

What comes first: prayer or faith? It is the Holy Spirit who comes "so that [we] may believe." Neither monasteries nor "the ghettos of intelligence or of science" in academia have an exclusive claim on grasping the mystery of faith. Indeed, there are those in monasteries who say, "Lord, Lord," but who will not enter the kingdom of heaven (see Matt 7:21) because of what they believe in deed. Secrets can be revealed to children.

> **CCC 1124** *The Church's faith precedes the faith of the believer who is invited to adhere to it. When the Church celebrates the sacraments, she confesses the faith received from the apostles—whence the ancient saying:* lex orandi, lex credendi *(or:* legem credendi lex statuat supplicandi, *according to Prosper of Aquitaine [5th cent.], ep. 8). The law of prayer is the law of faith: the Church believes as she prays. Liturgy is a constitutive element of the holy and living Tradition (cf. DV 8).*

- A point that is strangely presented around that famous saying, which can have two noticeably different meanings depending on the order in which the mutual dependence of the two laws of PRAYER and FAITH is understood. Which of the two comes first? Which of the two is the source? Can it be said that one stems wholly from the other, so that faith would come under prayer or prayer would be subject to the statements of faith?

- It must undoubtably be remembered that the Holy Spirit infused in our hearts is the "witness" of prayer. The Spirit alone prays properly. What is true of individuals is also true of the Church. The faith of Pentecost sprang forth from prayer. Here TRUST must be placed in the One who asks us to PRAY.

- And the Holy Spirit, given "so that you may believe,"[115] also bears witness to the faith. In receiving the Spirit, the apostles developed the symbol of the faith. And the Church assisted by the Holy Spirit knows that she has an "instinct of faith" that can be infallible, so long as she goes "through" the faithful.

- Finally, it is significant that the heart of the PRAYER of the Church is *mysterium fidei*, that very heart where she knows how to reach her Lord in the gift of himself and in his unceasing intercession, where she contents herself with re-saying and re-doing.

- History shows that monasteries have been home to heresies . . . that it is not enough to cry *Lord! Lord!* in order to be in the truth.[116] History has also shown that theology can become entirely dry and abstract and finally go astray if it confines itself to the ghettos of intelligence or of science, or to the blinders of a period, to the rigidity of a definition that swiftly turns to condemnation. Try to offer a prayer over the anathemas of the Council of Trent, or over the Syllabus.

- The Gospel is always there to honor Christ's PRAYER by giving thanks, making a Eucharist, for the secrets revealed to children. This reality reflects today's Gospel

115. John 20:31.
116. Matt 7:21.

and Psalm 8: *You have set your glory above the heavens. Out of the mouths of babes and infants!*[117]

- The Church believes as she prays . . . but the Church as guardian of the faith must remain attentive to that which arises in the heart of the one who prays. The Church would then see that the CREDO that she proposes (imposes?) is no longer a prayer except in its first word, while the GLORIA continues to bear witness to the happy Covenant between praise and faith. We should have the courage to get rid of words that no longer "sing"!

Thursday, August 11, 1994
Lex orandi, lex credendi: a few examples

The Alawiyya are a Sufi confraternity that invited the monastery into dialogue. In his biography, Salenson cites this chapter and Christian's account of the Alawites' invitation:

> *We do not want to get involved in a theological dialogue with you, because this has often erected barriers which are of human handiwork. But we feel called by God to unity. So we must allow God to invent something new between us. This can only be done in prayer. There is doubtless only a small number of Muslims who could understand this, and doubtless also a very small number of Christians who will believe in it. But this is what we feel called to do with you.*[118]

117. Ps 8.

118. Talk given by Christian to the General Chapter of the Cistercians (OCSO), 1993, cited in Salenson, *Christian de Chergé*, 184.

Christian hints that religious people of different faiths are only too tempted to reason and think, rather than to pray.

- There are "ages of the faith" . . . just as there are "expressions that succeed one another and are diverse, different even, from personal and liturgical PRAYER."
- There has been "progress in the development of the faith": this progress is often deeply rooted in personal prayer or in certain Christian groups. It is important that this progress reverberate through the whole of the Body. It can happen that the Body is invited to pray in ways that no longer correspond to what it "feels," nor even to what it professes. We have here a great responsibility that Saint Benedict demarcates well when he calls for voices and hearts to "agree."[119]
- The amazing question put by the apostles to Jesus: *TEACH US to pray!* Nonetheless, all they had done at rabbinical school was pray. The apostles clearly realize that Jesus changes something in the way they look with FAITH on God, and this new vision must allow itself to be tamed. This happens in prayer. The very first words, which are already very simple, change EVERYTHING: *OUR FATHER* . . .
- The instinct of the Alawiyya invites us to prayer and not[120] to dialogue about the faith. "God wants to create something new among us: give him the possibility of so doing. This can only happen through prayer." Then we go back down the mountain, but our mutual relations have changed; we can no longer describe ourselves as

119. *ut mens nostra concordet voci nostrae* (RB 19).

120. The translation in Salenson (*Christian de Chergé*, 184) omits this negation, which makes this passage make less sense in the context: prayer rather than discussion is the desired outcome.

strangers to one another, nor *a fortiori* excommunicate each other. It will even become necessary to take account of what has happened between us in order to "expand the space of faith." What is often a tragedy:[121] this inability to include what is real, lived, GIVEN in our wording. For example: the multiplying of votive Masses. In the past, there was a votive Mass to ask for protection against the pagans, which has now become partly on behalf of persecuted Christians. A votive Mass for the evangelization of the nations (formerly: promulgation of the *faith*): *ut hoc perpetuae salutis auxilio, fides semper vera proficiat* (cf. the two expressions on p. 944).[122] A votive Mass for Christian unity: *that they may be united under the true shepherd of your Church . . .* and the wording, on p. 937, calling for charity. A votive Mass for the Dead: there are "translated" phrases, some of which are applicable only to Christians, and some of which are more open (see p. 1061).

Saturday, August 13, 1994
nos. 1125–1126

The Church's sacramental rites cannot be altered, even by the "supreme authority in the Church," the Catechism observes, because (cf. CCC 1124) the sacraments allow the church to confess the apostolic faith. Christian points out the way he

121. Fr.: *drame.*

122. "That through this help to eternal salvation true faith may ever increase." Given by Christian in Latin. Prayer after Communion in the first Mass *pro evangelizatione populorum* in the 1970 Missal, now translated. The page numbers (given here by Christian) may refer to the pagination of an unspecified Missal.

thinks this should be interpreted: in principle, but with suitable accommodations and in the spirit of rubrics that "are only pointers in the right direction" and that leave much "up to the minister's initiative."

Christian makes mention of the "adjustments to Holy Week," referring to the amendments authorized by Pope Pius XII in the 1950s that restructured the Easter Vigil and added new rites for Palm Sunday, Holy Thursday, and Good Friday.

> **CCC 1125** *For this reason no sacramental rite may be modified or manipulated at the will of the minister or the community. Even the supreme authority in the Church may not change the liturgy arbitrarily, but only in the obedience of faith and with religious respect for the mystery of the liturgy.*

> **CCC 1126** *Likewise, since the sacraments express and develop the communion of faith in the Church, the* lex orandi *is one of the essential criteria of the dialogue that seeks to restore the unity of Christians (cf. UR 2; 15).*

- I think that the idea of a "sacramental rite" must be understood in a broad sense. A sacrament's validity has always been linked to the intention of the minister(s) to do what the Church wants. This intention prevails in all the adjustments that can seem essential according to the circumstances. Because it is important for the sign to be meaningful for those for whom it is destined. At the same time, it must always be remembered that the sign should lead to the mystery and then get out of its way. The sign cannot claim to explain or unveil everything. The spoken word, even in the vernacular, is still addressed to the faith. But it would be absurd today to insist that these words be in Latin on the pretext that they would then be better able to express the mystery. These words are also and above all words addressed to a specific man and a specific woman. Even in the institution of the Eucharist, Jesus spoke the language of his audience, an Aramaic dialect . . .

- "Sacramental rites" in a broad sense, therefore . . . and this interpretation is allowed by the "rubrics" of the Missal or of the ritual. Very often, they indicate the prayers and even the gestures and signs, all the while specifying that these can be adjusted . . . that these are only pointers in the right direction. Much is therefore left up to the minister's initiative. And we have often said to each other that it was essential to respect this margin of freedom in the choices of our liturgical community. It is also very evident that it would be extremely dangerous to open this door too wide. Many approximations, whims, and misinterpretations (counter-signs) would rush in.[123] It is sometimes necessary to have recourse to the *sensus Ecclesiae* that the community more rightly embodies. This is what has been done in the adjustments to Holy Week, for example. And we have reached some good results that serve the celebration of the paschal mystery . . . with one exception, I think, for Good Friday, where we are still fumbling around with different sensibilities.
- As for the connection between the *lex orandi* and Christian unity, I have already noted what a delicate matter this is . . . There have been so many wounds, so much rigidity, so many instances of mutual excommunication proclaimed at the heart of Prayer . . .

123. Christian is playing here on *contre-sens* as misinterpretation or error, but also more literally "against meaning/direction," which he follows by *contre-signes* in parentheses.

Tuesday, August 16, 1994
nos. 1127–1128
The sacraments of SALVATION . . .

This chapter observes that the sacraments in principle confer the grace they signify, but those who receive them must be properly disposed to receive it. Christian gives the examples of the sacraments of confirmation, which may not be very efficacious if a desire for the Spirit is not felt, and marriage, which may not be validly contracted if there is a diriment impediment (a "separating" impediment, which means that the marriage could not have taken place, for instance, a prior bond).

God INTERVENES: Christian writes here "INTER-VIENT," playing on the etymology of intervene *as "inter" (between) + "venire" (to come), although it works better in French (since "vient" is also the third person singular present tense form of "venir").*

> **CCC 1127** *Celebrated worthily in faith, the sacraments confer the grace that they signify (cf. DS 1605; DS 1606). They are* efficacious *because in them Christ himself is at work: it is he who baptizes, he who acts in his sacraments in order to communicate the grace that each sacrament signifies. The Father always hears the prayer of his Son's Church which, in the epiclesis of each sacrament, expresses her faith in the power of the Spirit. As fire transforms into itself everything it touches, so the Holy Spirit transforms into the divine life whatever is subjected to his power.*

> **CCC 1128** *This is the meaning of the Church's affirmation (cf. DS 1608) that the sacraments act* ex opere operato *(literally: "by the very fact of the action's being performed"), i.e., by virtue of the saving work of Christ, accomplished once for all. It follows that "the sacrament is not wrought by the righteousness of either the*

celebrant or the recipient, but by the power of God" (St. Thomas Aquinas, STh III 68, 8). From the moment that a sacrament is celebrated in accordance with the intention of the Church, the power of Christ and his Spirit acts in and through it, independently of the personal holiness of the minister. Nevertheless, the fruits of the sacraments also depend on the disposition of the one who receives them.

- The sacraments are the interventions of God "through, with, and in Christ": when God INTERVENES, something happens that is in the order of Salvation.
- Christ is at work: he is always working. The sacraments are inscribed in the logic of this work; they are his tools. Jesus bound himself to the sacraments with the same impulsion with which he bound himself to the life of all people. What happens through the sacrament, as regards the believer, finds a way to express itself in the life of the non-believer as well, so that access to faith is for the non-believer adherence to the sacraments, the recognition that the sacraments provide, directly, what had appealed to non-believers for a long time. In this way, the instinct of union with God will be "illuminated" by access to the eucharistic communion (just as for forgiveness[124] . . .).
- What is necessary here is that prayer of faith that, in church, confesses and solicits the power of the Spirit (*epiclesis*). Beautiful image of the FIRE that transforms into itself everything that it touches.
- *Ex opere operato*: there is nothing magical about this . . . It is Christ who has already accomplished what is asked of him, already, to realize in deeds, in the present day, such an existence. Whether the minister is more or less holy has nothing to do with the effectiveness of the

124. Fr.: *pardon.*

sacrament (except in that the minister himself derives little or less benefit for himself if he is not able to administer . . .).

- Nor is there anything magical in the fact that grace cannot ordinarily do anything to overcome the barrier erected against it by someone who does not have the necessary welcoming disposition. This is why it is possible to imagine the effectiveness of the sacrament of confirmation to be extremely limited in the case of someone who does not feel the need of the Spirit: the gift is left hanging. The gift has been given, placed at the door; one day, the door may be opened, and then "confirmation" will take place fully. The Church can therefore pronounce a sacramental marriage to be null and void if the dispositions of the ministers (the spouses) are clearly at odds with what the sacrament expects of them. *Listen! I am standing at the door, knocking . . .* [125]

Thursday, August 18, 1994
no. 1129
Necessary for salvation . . .

The Declaration of the Council Nostra Aetate on the Relation of the Church to Non-Christian Religions notes, "One is the community of all peoples, one their origin, for God made the whole human race to live over the face of the earth. One also is their final goal, God" (NA 1). It speaks relatively warmly of the Jewish and Islamic faiths. Christian is even more enthusiastic when he says that the necessity of sacraments for salvation does not mean that there is no salvation outside the Christian sacramental economy.

125. Rev 3:20.

CCC 1129 *The Church affirms that for believers the sacraments of the New Covenant are necessary for salvation (cf. DS 1604). "Sacramental grace" is the grace of the Holy Spirit, given by Christ and proper to each sacrament. The Spirit heals and transforms those who receive him by conforming them to the Son of God. The fruit of the sacramental life is that the Spirit of adoption makes the faithful partakers in the divine nature (cf. 2 Pet 1:4) by uniting them in a living union with the only Son, the Savior.*

- "for believers . . . :" in our own context, we have learned to become more strict about terminology. The distinction between "believers" and "Muslims" is vital to our neighbors, our friends, including in their interpretation of the Qur'an. It would be good for us to be attentive in drawing a distinction between "believers" and "Christians" . . . , and in the context of no. 1129, it would even be necessary to speak only in the name of "Catholics" in the institutional sense that this word has assumed in recent history.

- The "necessity" of the sacraments for salvation does not mean that there is no salvation for anyone outside of the sacramental economy. Just as Saint Cyprian's saying "outside the church there is no salvation" does not mean that only those who belong to the Church are saved. Cyprian was addressing Christians who were already tempted to draw a distinction between Christ and the Church, between faith in Christ and membership of the Church. He preached the union of the Church and of Christ founding one single category of membership. It is said here, likewise, that a Covenant of faith with Christ in the heart of the Catholic Church is mediated by a vital need for those means that Christ has chosen, we confess as much, to sustain this faith. We should be able to ask our Church, "To whom would we go, you have the sacraments of eternal life?"

- The Holy Spirit is thus bound to the sacraments. The Spirit channels through them its own work, which is that of making humanity conform to the likeness of the Beloved Son. Once more, this work of the Holy Spirit can take other routes . . . but experience shows that it then encounters strong competition and many parasites. The specific grace of the sacrament is to inspire, through word and deed, the realigning of one's own heart and one's own desire to what the Spirit wants to do. The sacrament then becomes a site of complicity. When what is at stake is recovering from an illness, nothing is more helpful than complete collaboration between patients and their doctor. When it is a matter of growing up, it is generally better for the child to receive gratefully the food prepared for them by their parents.

- Thus, as it is written in the second Letter of Peter: *he has given us, through these things, his precious and very great promises, so that through them you may escape from the corruption that is in the world because of lust, and may become participants of the divine nature* (2 Pet 1:4).

Tuesday, August 23, 1994
no. 1130
The sacraments of ETERNAL life

CCC 1130 The Church celebrates the mystery of her Lord "until he comes," when God will be "everything to everyone" (1 Cor 11:26; 15:28). Since the apostolic age the liturgy has been drawn toward its goal by the

> *Spirit's groaning in the Church:* Marana tha*! (1 Cor 16:22). The liturgy thus shares in Jesus' desire: "I have earnestly desired to eat this Passover with you [. . .] until it is fulfilled in the kingdom of God" (Luke 22:15). In the sacraments of Christ the Church already receives the guarantee of her inheritance and even now shares in everlasting life, while "awaiting our blessed hope, the appearing of the glory of our great God and Savior Christ Jesus" (Titus 2:13). The "Spirit and the Bride say, 'Come [. . .] Come, Lord Jesus!'" (Rev 22:17, 20).*
>
> *St. Thomas sums up the various aspects of sacramental signs: "Therefore a sacrament is a sign that commemorates what precedes it—Christ's Passion; demonstrates what is accomplished in us through Christ's Passion—grace; and prefigures what that Passion pledges to us—future glory." (St. Thomas Aquinas, STh III, 60, 3)*

- The sacraments then as a visible sign of an invisible reality: this reality concerns what has been accomplished to the extent that it re-presents what has been said and done through Jesus of Nazareth, born of Mary in the shadow of the Spirit, dead and risen to new life . . . and, more generally, everything that comes before and after, since Jesus accomplishes all the Scriptures and sums up in himself the creation and history of humanity. In his incarnate Person, he takes on all the "sacraments," all the while being himself the greatest "SACRAMENT" of God.

- This reality also concerns what has not yet been accomplished to the extent that it announces in advance the end, the goal, which is at once the end of time and the end of the sacraments. Christ in glory is no longer a sacrament. In him, all the sacraments fade away. This is why they can only ever be a "means" (cf. what has been said above).

- And we experience this sacramental reality today, that is, in a type of *no man's land* that concerns both the incomplete past and the future that has begun: it is, it was, and it is to come. The sacrament enables a DIAGNOSIS, which is a diagnosis of health, salvation, and life. In support of this diagnosis, the sacrament always presents itself as a remedy, as a fortifier, even as a successful surgical intervention, the grafting of a new heart onto a heart that is forever open, with a transfusion of the Holy Spirit.

- And with Saint Thomas Aquinas, we need to confirm this diagnosis with a PROGNOSIS . . . since the sacrament is also presented in this way: "it prefigures future glory!"[126] Accessing the sacraments means adhering to this prognosis. And here, one member of the Body drawing near to the sacraments suffices for the whole Body to be as if seized by what the sacraments signify. By participating in the sacraments, we invite ourselves to signify more by ourselves what they represent and what they announce: we become sacraments of salvation and of life for all those who do not have access to the sacraments of the Church and who are nonetheless included in the REALITY that the sacraments "prefigure," namely that Christ is EVERYTHING to everyone. We need to hold on very tightly to this reality, since it is for this reason that the profession of consecrated life is not a particular sacrament (unlike marriage, for example).

126. The French verb here is *pronostiquer* (to prognosticate, to predict), hence Christian's play on the idea of prognosis.

PART 2

In the Church, Here and Now.

January 17, 1995–April 6, 1995

Tuesday, January 17, 1995
Solitude and communion

Christian chooses the feast day of Saint Antony, who was an early model for the monastic life, to speak of the changing vocation of religious communities in Algeria. Many of the communities he mentions were small, or indeed had only one member remaining; at first glance this seems to be an attitude contrary to the typical religious vocation to community life. However, as Christian observes, sometimes a personal, exceptional vocation (for instance, that of Trappist hermits) means that a balance is struck between the mission of the Church, the charism of a religious community, and an individual's personal vocation.

The reference to a "core" around the bishop identifies the fact that Archbishop Henri Teissier had asked religious communities to consider the possibility of a rapid departure from Algeria while maintaining a "core" around the bishop to allow the Algerian church to continue in its mission.

The Poor Clares (Franciscan sisters) mentioned here had recently left their monastery to go to Nîmes. In his journal entry for January 7, Christophe mentions that one of their sisters had died in her sleep before they departed. He reports Jean-Pierre saying, "It's sad, everybody's leaving." It is into this atmosphere that Christian gives this chapter.

Under the patronage of Saint Antony (and on the eve of the start of the Week for Christian UNITY on the theme of κοινονια: communion with God, and communion with one another), we return to the idea of the "permanent" CORE[1] of the Church around the bishop. It is true that there are congregations that have left as a whole (the Poor Clares, the Sisters of Prado, Constantine, the Sisters of Bon Secours). There are also, already, congregations that are by now represented by only one member: the Sisters of the Sacred Heart, the Sisters of Charity, the Dominican Sisters of the Fields, the Little Sisters of the Assumption, at least for the moment, and for a long time the Franciscans (F. Didier), for six years the Marists (F. Henri). There are also congregations that have two members but in two different places, often far apart: the Sisters of Saint Augustine, the Sisters of Saint Joseph of Annecy, and also the Sisters of Grandchamp . . . without counting the White Fathers who live alone, here or there, and often for a long time (El Golea . . .), and now the Little Brothers: Yahya, Marcel . . . The Spiritans . . .

We may be surprised at these choices, which seem to contradict the vocation of these institutes to community life. In certain cases, the decisions may be the result of a personal vocation recognized by the institute but more or less exceptional. Our Order has its hermits. Most often, that has to do with an arrangement reached by mutual agreement that claims a connection, desired by the Holy Spirit, between the personal call, the charism of an institute, and the mission of the Church as a sacrament of God's people . . . the religious

1. Fr.: *noyau.*

community then finding its subordinate place in order to signify communion in the Church. A brother, a sister, bound by a charism that is recognized and lived out in a congregation, can, with the agreement of the congregation and in the freedom of their personal faithfulness to God's call, contribute to bringing this charism to a specific church so that the face of Christ shown by the Church may be more complete . . . The COMMUNITY is not dissolved but is instead lived out in a different way: first of all, as a connection to the Church and to all people, a connection that will not fade! And, moreover, as a spiritual connection of communion with the institute, and this is the only expression of this connection to the institute that will not fade.

Thursday, January 19, 1995
Community and communion

The mission of any religious community, says Christian, is to be a sign of communion with the whole Church, living and departed. Sometimes communities can become distracted by internal concerns or see their work as an end in itself, getting "stuck in a muddy pool" rather than a stream emptying into the ocean of the communion of saints. He refers to the ability to "change [one's] stability," that is, to move permanently from one monastery to another within a religious congregation, to continue along one's vocational journey. This was a familiar experience for some of the brethren, who had begun religious life in other communities and had subsequently come, following God's call, to Tibhirine.

A consecrated community is through its vocation a sign of communion . . . of communion with the Church, of the communion of all of God's people dedicated, in Christ, to appearing as an unfolding mystery, that of the communion of the saints, in which the community will be dispersed just as a stream is dispersed in the ocean. The stream may happen to get lost or run dry on its way, its impulsion may get caught up in a more or less artificial lake, or it may get stuck in a muddy pool. It is also possible that a community should cease to function save in a vacuum, believing itself to be an end in itself, weighing down on its members like something absolute that cannot be left without doing a U-turn and/or betraying God and the church, a little as in a marriage.

Now the covenant involved in the consecrated life must always be read as a permanent, definitive tie, uniting us to Christ, within the Church, through a congregation and a specific community that may disappear or evolve without this tie being changed substantially. A good number of us have already been through this experience, believing that we can change our stability and therefore our community, remaining faithful to our original call, parts of which may have taken shape over the course of a personal journey discerned in conscience and in obedience to human mediations in the ecclesial communion. On the basis of this discussion, which I consider to be quite clear, a few examples that may raise some questions:

- The Poor Clares: my mother asked me yesterday, "How could they all have left?" A good question. Just one example: Sister Élisabeth, the only temporary professed Daughter of Charity in Tangier. A contemplative vocation in these countries (no other location in the Maghreb except Tazert) at three months from solemn profession. She wanted to stay, said as much . . . she followed. It's exile . . . but, around her, the idea of a "return" has been able to be expressed (the Spanish Poor Clares).

- The Little Sisters of the Assumption: four of them remained, with one absent; two of them are afraid and want to lead the third in their departure, in the name of obedience . . . to whom? To what?
- The sisters in the south: the specific vocation of the White Sisters; all of them go back; they stay at Ghardaïa, El Golea. They are laywomen, without a community life: but what about their church life?

Saturday, January 28, 1995
Community and Church

Christian continues to reflect on the connection between the vocation to a particular form of the religious life and participation in the mission of the universal Church. Christian reminds the brethren that Saint Thérèse of Lisieux had volunteered to go on a mission to the Carmelite community established in Saigon in 1861. The mission of the Church is for ever, but particular expressions of religious life are "mortal," even the first four daughter houses of the Cistercians (La Ferté, Pontigny, Clairvaux, Morimond).

Of their own situation, Christian comments that even though it might be "unreasonable" to remain in Tibhirine, it is always "unreasonable" to be a monk!

"The Church will never say that you must leave." This is what the bishops confirmed on the occasion of the most recent meeting of the Regional Episcopal Conference of North Africa (CERNA).[2] And they said this addressing themselves to

2. Translator's note: the acronym CERNA stands for the French Conférence des Évêques de la Région Nord de l'Afrique.

religious and to their congregations. At this moment when our Algerian bishops are meeting with the pope in order to present our situation to him, it is good to return to the Church, and to the link that our community has with our Church, as to the link between our personal call and the mission entrusted to the universal Church. In fact, here we have two fundamental reference points: the individual and the Church. To both of these, promises of eternal life have been made.

We know that communities, congregations as such, are mortal. The four first daughters of Cîteaux are "dead." History also shows us that particular churches, even flourishing ones such as those of North Africa in the early centuries, can be swept away . . . can disappear as a constituted body. This can happen, all the while allowing the Church's vocation to exist everywhere . . . and there was a time when the Church was only represented here by slaves of Barbary pirates, just as it is represented in Saudi Arabia by those modern-day slaves, migrant workers (who are mainly Filipinos, as it happens). The vocation to leave for a place where the Church has not yet been established can also persist in the heart of someone who is baptized . . . this is sometimes a genuine, violent desire, but one that cannot be realized, as was the case for Saint Thérèse of the Child Jesus (in Vietnam).

So it's clear: the pope will never tell our bishops, "You need to leave Algeria." The local churches are sufficiently autonomous, and there is, above all, such a strong call for the church to be present everywhere, in specific localities, that this presence is respected and even desired for as long as those who ensure it believe that they are able to continue to maintain it.[3] We are also lucky, as a community, to have very concrete autonomy in relation to the Cistercian Order, an autonomy

3. In referring to "local churches" Christian is speaking of "particular churches" as defined by c. 368 of the 1983 Code of Canon Law, meaning dioceses or equivalent jurisdictions, each of which is a *portio populi Dei*, a portion of the people of God.

that most communities do not have in relation to their own congregation. The abbot general will not tell us, "you must leave," nor will the father immediate.[4] Unless there is an on-site investigation, the testing of each person's will, and ears other than our own to listen to the local church and the surroundings, resulting in the conclusion that "You are not able to stay: you are not sufficiently unanimous among yourselves, it is not safe enough, that is to say that there is not enough agreement about what you are, around you." Even then it would still be necessary to hold a vote that would make clear without a doubt what the members of the community might have "felt." We cannot simply be told "it is unreasonable for you to remain." Because we are in league with that which is "unreasonable," in the sense that it is always "unreasonable" to be a monk . . . this is always true, and it is even truer here and now!

Tuesday, January 31, 1995
Our community and our church

An underlying tension remains, despite the votes taken in mid-December during a time of discernment with the bishop—votes to remain part of the "core." In the face of a possible departure to Algiers or Fez (where there was already a small community), there was unrest; Christophe remarks (in his journal entry for December 13) about the possibility of a single member of the community breaking ranks to stay. He wrote, "It seems to me we cannot exclude possible separations among us if there is a compulsory departure. Perhaps we ought to discuss that."

4. The term for the superior of a Cistercian community's mother house.

Before continuing to reflect upon the motivations, conditions, and new demands of the presence of a church such as ours in this place and at such a challenging time for everyone, it seems good to me to go back over the votes that we made (or remade) in December and that have contributed to clarifying the relationship between our community and our Church. I said that these votes expressed a degree of common sense, that they were a sign of health and of realistic coherence. I still believe this. What was first of all made manifest was our desire to survive as a COMMUNITY. On this point we are unanimous. And this unanimity lends itself as well to staying here, for as long as circumstances allow, as it does to retreating to another location in the country if this seems possible and desirable.

We encounter this unanimity in the desire to take stock of a possible diaspora in a year's time. We would then provide ourselves with the means for a stable gathering whose defining features in terms of place and environment have been specified, as far as is possible, according to the mission that we recognize in ourselves at the present time here and that has united us from so many different backgrounds. It is the logic of our vow of STABILITY—which seems to me to be found both in this unanimity and in the permanence of this mission —that each one of us senses will now be difficult to assume in Morocco, as in Tunisia and in any other Muslim country.

As for our participation in the "CORE" of the Church around the bishops, this question did not come from us, and it may have been surprising particularly because it seemed to contradict our unanimous desire for a community future. And yet the question in principle about our community's participation in this core through one or another of its members received a large majority (five in favor; one against; one abstained). We can ask ourselves what the result of this vote means since the two subsequent votes saw a majority against or abstaining regarding a personal choice of individual participation (two in favor) or in pairs (three against). Especially since the brothers who voted IN FAVOR know themselves to be at risk of not receiving the support of the community, especially on account of the duties that are theirs in the community. I interpret these votes taken altogether as a desire on the part of the majority for communal belonging to this permanent CORE, in which we should be incorporated for as long as the Church and our surroundings allow us to. We know how rare these signs of hope in the future are going to become. We also know that no one could be entitled to such signs without a greater call from God and the Church.

Saturday, February 4, 1995
Our community as such *hic et nunc*

Christian reflects that the community has not been "suicidal" in its bid to remain, as the Algerian prefect of Medea had suggested; rather, it has been obedient. Jesus, who was obedient even to death on a cross, had not been "suicidal" in freely giving his life, and there were immediate consequences that signaled the significance of that act in the conversions of the Good Thief and of the Centurion. The reference to La Trappe may be literally to the original home of the Trappists near Alençon, France, which was reconstituted and rebuilt after the Revolution, or indeed (as Christian implies) to their own monastery.

The desire of the majority for community belonging has thus been expressed by us to the permanent CORE, who will inform our bishops of the Church's wish to remain in this country and to share the ordeal of this people who are its own by birth, adoption, or, in certain cases, the grace of baptism. This desire is not suicidal, even if it increases our exposure to the dangers of the moment, which, for sure, include a violent death. It will undoubtedly be necessary to go over the fact that the gift of death is included in the gift of life. But if it is not "collective suicide," as the old wali[5] used to say, this is first of all concretely because the risk does not seem to us inescapable. There is still room, in this clash with those who threaten us as strangers and/or as Christians, for a conversion of hearts.

Saying this, let us not forget the price that Jesus paid for the immediate conversion of the thief or of the centurion, and, more distantly but just as directly, for our own conversion. In Jesus' case, it was not a matter of suicide. Even if he freely chose to give his own life, he did not kill himself. Moreover, for us as for him, an attitude of OBEDIENCE was being lived out that made him receive this cup from the Father. No one, not even the Son, can claim this loving madness alone. The consent of the trinitarian community is necessary. For us, for each of us, the community's consent is likewise necessary. And for the community as such, what is required is something like an increased call from the Order and/or from the local church. Whence the importance of the dialogue into which we have entered with our bishop. And we cannot hear without gravity what this last said recently at the meeting of the Presbyterium: "What a joy it would be for us, and what a promise for the future of our church in Algerian society, if we could get through this crisis with our friends and then rebuild with them in a partnership endowed with new legitimacy. Think, as a symbolic example, of the situation of LA TRAPPE, in its surroundings, if the monastery's community can survive the crisis."

It must be said straight away that such a partnership in this risky venture would also draw its legitimacy from the gratuitous sacrifice of our eight brothers and sisters who have

5. Provincial governor.

already paid with their lives for the faithfulness that we are trying to express. But we need to be sensitive to this sign that the Church is seeking instinctively in a community. Saint Bernard[6] said plenty of times that a monastery is a little church, an *ECCLESIOLA*. This sign of herself that our church can no longer provide in constituted parishes, that diocesan priests without followers can no longer embody in a directly legible fashion—who will show this sign if not communities such as ours, which are at one with the shared mission that remains the same today as it was yesterday: offering up one's LIFE as Jesus did?

Tuesday, February 7, 1995
The gift of community presence

Christian repeats the last sentence of the previous chapter here, continuing the same train of thought. The sacrifice of Jesus is not just his, but that of the whole Trinity, and that individual sacrifice became that of the Christian community through his command to "do this in memory of me." The bishop, here, in having desired a "core" to support the mission of the Church, recognizes that he alone cannot be the representative of the work of the Church. There is a familiar pun in "Pierre . . . pierre," the given name that also means "stone" or "rock." The same pun works in Latin and Greek, but not in English. All members of the Church are called to be "living stones" (see 1 Pet 2:4-12). The community is called to be part of the "core" (Fr. noyau, *which also means "pit"*

6. Bernard of Clairvaux (1090–1153), abbot of the Abbey of Clairvaux, was a significant figure in the expansion of the Cistercian Order and an author of widely circulated sermons and treatises on Christian life and thought.

or "kernel" or, more attractively, "seed"); it was Tertullian (d. 240) who called "the blood of the martyrs . . . the seed of Christians." In mentioning the bishops' suggestion of "inter-congregational communities," Christian is at least noting the unusual possibility that individual religious from more than one institute who wished to stay in Algeria might do so by coming to live and work together.

"Offering up one's life as Jesus did . . ." What was and is in a way individual in the person of Jesus (in reality, the work of the Trinity) became communitarian through Jesus' command to repeat what he himself did. This command reaches the TWELVE, and through them the whole of the Church in every age, all the communities created in his Name. Of course, this GIFT remains personal to the one who consents to it, and the Church, like every Christian community, only exists in each of those by whom it is constituted: *you are Peter* . . . this is the name of a person, but the call that is addressed to Peter is the same for everyone: build the Church, be the living stone of a people whose unity is all the stronger because the life of each person is committed to a GIFT of love like that given by Jesus, for EVERYONE. Recall here again the fecundity of martyrs, of all life given, as the "seed of Christians,"[7] that is, as the capacity to inspire a living community of the same Gospel.

In this respect, it seems to me that we should be much less interested in the conversion of an individual than in the slower, more hidden, but very real transformation of a whole place. The first Pentecost was this current of fire passing through the TWELVE to the large and disparate assembly of listeners and witnesses present. There is thus something profoundly true and poignant in the call of each of our bishops asking modestly, and in poverty, for the constitution of a core of the

7. Tertullian: The blood of the martyrs is the seed of Christians (197): *sanguis martyrum est semen Christianorum.*

faithful around him so that the sign of CHRIST that is the making of the Church may still be present. The bishop alone, even with the fullness of the Holy Spirit (as it is said), knows that he will not be a legible sign if he remains isolated. And he knows this, even if the Church was able to affirm (at the Synod of 1971) that she was never as sure of being present, somewhere, as when she is there through the intermediary of a priest, *a fortiori* of a bishop repeating each day, in the Eucharist, the gift of Christ, the source of all communion.

Our bishops also know that the gift of life can be experienced by each person in a thousand different ways and that it must remain free, especially when there is a looming threat that, while endowing this gift with real fullness, at the same time abolishes the visible presence, the sacramental presence. And by respecting the choice of each individual, the bishops are still faithful both to their vocation to be a Church and to the vocation of the religious to be a community, when they recommend the creation of inter-congregational communities allowing individuals to give this country the gift of community presence, which ensures both the permanence of a personal call and the visibility of the church-communion.

Thursday, February 9, 1995
Our community "in its surroundings"

Christian rejoices that many rely on the community and suggests here that what they offer to their particular neighbors in Tibhirine is part of what constitutes their identity, with reference to the Prologue to John's gospel. Any departure from their neighborhood would contribute to a loss of meaning and purpose for their lives and common vocation. To be transplanted from a landscape of which they were an integral part into a relatively constricted but safer environment would break the "connective tissue" and risk "rejection" of the "transplant."

So we have privileged as far as possible the permanence of our community, as such, at the heart of this Church core, which feels itself called to continue to show forth the GIFT of Jesus' own life given by him, once and for all, on behalf of all people, and so also on behalf of Algerians today. And it is our joy—a little troubled and not at all certain—to feel that many of those who remain, like us, despite everything, rely on us, even if they do not come to tell us as much. This is what our bishop thought that he could tell the Presbyterium. You will no doubt have noticed that he spoke of the significance of our presence if it could get through this painful crisis "in its SURROUNDINGS."

This mention of our neighborhood is fair:[8] we cannot be the sign of a GIFT if there is no one there to receive and desire it. Or better . . . we cannot claim to give Jesus to our neighbors, in any way, without receiving JESUS from them, in any way. This is also part of the very conditioning of the Incarnation. There is mutual interdependence. Many have not received Jesus . . . but to those who have received him, he has granted them to become what he was himself: not only Christian, but a child of God. I also note that in speaking of our present surroundings as constitutive of the sign that we are, our bishop agrees more or less consciously with what is for us almost self-evident: it would not be easy, not to say impossible, at the present time to believe that we can be this sign anywhere else than here. Gathering together in a different place than this one in order to remain in Algeria—on the pretext of even greater safety or for any other reason—seems to me aleatory.[9]

8. Fr.: *est justice.*

9. Or, in a contemporary idiom, "random." Fr.: *aleatoire.*

Not only because I don't see how we can be "out of danger" in this country at the moment, but also because the consolation that our remaining would bring to our little church, which has been so badly managed, would be paid for at the cost of a loss of meaning insofar as our surroundings would no longer be involved in this presence as they can be here. It would be a bit like fish from a river being trapped in a goldfish bowl. Obviously, we can always imagine that the connective tissue with a new neighborhood would then be formed, day by day . . . but if the minimal conditions of mutual trust and shared life were not guaranteed, there is a risk that the transplant would be rejected. It is true that if we find it hard to see how this could happen, it is also because, right now, we still together think that we haven't reached this stage and that it is precisely our surroundings that convince us of this.

Saturday, February 11, 1995
Other communities . . .

Christian continues to speak of the links that the monastery has made with those who are around them, both in the common work of the monks and their associates and in the availability of medical care to the community in the monastery dispensary, but also in the shared enterprise of prayer. This mutual participation can be seen in other communities. The "attack at Bab el Oued" refers to the assassination, on October 23, 1994, of two Augustinian missionary sisters, Sr. Esther Paniagua Alonso and Sr. Caridad Alvarez Martín. Both were passionately committed to their work as nurses for their local community. Christian also refers to the massacre at Tizi Ouzou of the Pères Blancs, Christian Chessel, Alain Dieulagard, and Charles Decker.

Our bishops are thus aware, as far as I can see, of the importance of the sign of a community.[10] And it is just as important not to separate this sign from its natural environment, which is itself likewise community-based. Even a community such as ours, whose calling includes genuine separation from the world, has not been able to be imagined here as cut off or as independent from its neighborhood. No autonomy is possible without the risk of serious and futile confrontation. Links[11] have been forged through work and even prayer without forgetting the exchange that has been established around the dispensary. And all this has led us to a degree of interdependence rooted in respect for what makes each of us different: doubtless a fragile equilibrium, but one that proves its worth in the ordeal that we are living through together.

And we understand Sister Anne-Geneviève, who discovered that in leaving Ain Naadja she cut herself off from being present to (in) the area, as was the original aim of her community when she arrived in 1958 at Oued Ouchaya. We also know how much osmosis with the immediate vicinity is part of the vocation of the Little Brothers or of the Little Sisters, dictating their choice of settlement. We understand that after the attack at Bab el Oued the Little Sisters turned down the house of the Glycines that the White Sisters had just left and preferred to return to Oran, to the working-class district where they still had many friends. It is fair to note that, thank God, we are not the only community remaining in its place in order to be one with the country, each one according to its own vocation.

In this respect, the community of the Maternité at Blida seems to me a very important example and symbol. There too the community can only manage by relying upon a specific team in a natural group that is all the more characteristic

10. Fr.: *signe communautaire.*

11. Fr.: *Des courroies de transmission*, literally "transmission belts."

because it is in motion: there is the staff of the house, and especially the patients, who naturally replace one another, all the while participating in the mutual trust that is indispensable for offsetting the lack of safety and evading potential threats. In order better to protect them, each person manages it so that the Sisters do not need to go out. Their work is elsewhere, and people also keep watch over their prayer or community relaxation. At the Little Sisters of the Poor, the mixed community is stable. There is no shortage of external dedication to ensure the security of this group, whose constitutive parts seem inseparable.

Nonetheless, we must accept that this sign of a community can appear to be in itself provocative. It is a community as such that was destroyed at Tizi Ouzou, the only example up until now of a group that has been wiped out completely (with the seven Italians of Djijel).

[Tuesday and Thursday, February 14 and 16, 1995, on Algiers]

Saturday, February 18, 1995
From age to age . . .

Here Christian mentions the fragile health of Br. Luc, the irascible but much loved infirmarian who denied himself a brilliant medical career in order to pursue a religious vocation. His ministry in the monastery was, above all, to offer medical care to any who needed it, friend or foe. He was trusted and valued by the many locals who came to see him. Luc's vocation, together with the varied interests and vocations of the younger members of the community mentioned, are part of the ultimate vocation of the community—to anticipate the communion of saints in its variety.

I think that I have sufficiently highlighted the importance of the sign of a community and the value that our church assigns to this sign in knowing how to read it "in its surroundings," since the Church itself can only be deciphered in its rootedness. The Church is like the dove of Noah's ark, which does not return to the ark when it has found somewhere on dry land to rest its feet and to make its nest. With the community of Tizi Ouzou, we have gone from sign to reality . . . it is difficult to imagine what this passing[12] as a group must have felt like to those who went through it, and how reunion in the afterlife was experienced without there having been strictly speaking any separation. Those whom God united in one same lifelong consecration were not separated by death. The sign that they left us continues to express the ultimate meaning of all religious communities, which is that of anticipating the communion of the saints.

This is all the truer because we are mindful of the diversity of backgrounds, of temperaments, and also of the ages of our four brothers. Because he was so much younger, Christian, through his presence, brought to the community of Tizi Ouzou the element that would otherwise have been lacking, so bearing witness to the youth, vitality, and longevity of the Church. In order also to bear witness to the fact that here was a unique FAMILY bringing all the generations together, from age to age. We must rejoice that Providence has allowed our community likewise to express something of this, thanks to its successive rejuvenation: between Br. Luc, Fr. Jean-Baptiste (Fr. Étienne if desired[13]), and Br. François, there is a whole range, spanning more than half a century (fifty-three years). It is a richness that belongs to our church, as to those for whom the sign that we embody is destined. We are all grateful to Br. Luc for being with us despite his fatigue.

12. Fr.: *départ*.

13. Fr.: *si on veut*.

And we would very much like François to join us, just as we would wish Philippe to settle down with us.[14] At the meeting of the ACRCA, in January, Father Fisset intervened to beg those superiors present not to expose the younger members to the current dangers, highlighting specifically the irreplaceable loss represented by Christian's death for the White Fathers, who had placed so much hope in him. Our bishop immediately replied that age does not matter at all in this case, and that the life of each individual, facing murder, has the same value, however old he is.

I then thought to be able to intervene by explaining that the distinction was legitimate for brothers and sisters who have only committed themselves temporarily (which was not the case for Christian), because the situation risks leading them beyond their vows. At a minimum they need to agree to this on a personal level. But we cannot choose to leave in Africa only those brothers and sisters who are elderly, on the pretext that their loss would be less. At stake is the sign of herself that the Church has the right to give, and also respect for our younger brothers and their calling.

Tuesday, February 21, 1995
Individual, community, Church . . .

Saint Benedict says that it is for the abbot to "call the whole community together" for counsel "as often as anything important is to be done in the monastery" and to include even the younger brothers, for even they may receive insight from the Spirit: "the Lord often reveals what is better to the

14. Philippe Hemon of Tamié, who was a regular Visitor. Regular Visitations are carried out in Cistercian monasteries by nominated Visitors (monastic superiors), to evaluate the community's life and discipline.

younger" (RB 3). Christian continues here with the matter of the individual but interwoven vocations of members of a community, the so-called "communion of vocations, of individual callings that find a way to be conjugated," that is, con *(together)* + iugare *(to join/yoke/marry). Some of the individual callings of members of the Tibhirine community may be found in the last sentence . . .*

Thanks to different ages and personal commitments (which should normally be tested amongst the youngest), we return to the idea of individual faithfulness within a community vocation recognized and lived out in the Church. Every community is a communion of vocations, of individual callings that find a way to be conjugated—in the true meaning of the word—within the charism proper to each order or congregation. The community gets bigger and broader each time that it opens up to a brother or a sister who has come to join the community with a personal calling, whose specific features will enrich the whole group. This broadening happens without, of course, questioning the fundamental choice, since it is in this choice that each person recognizes himself or herself, including, it is assumed, the newcomer. It is necessary both to widen the space of the tent and to take the time to try out mutual adjustments. Saint Benedict had the wisdom to call for the novice to be consulted and listened to. If the novice has been obedient to the Spirit by committing to the path he finds himself in, he can help the community to clarify its mission and to correspond better to this mission.

There was a time when in our Order it was agreed that a community such as ours, in the surroundings that became its own following Algerian independence, was not VIABLE since there was no possibility of local recruitment. It is clear that our successive arrivals have been the only possible response to this preconceived idea, which did not sufficiently take into consideration the ingenuity of the Spirit. In the time in which we live, it is good to remember that we have thus been gathered together, one by one, from very different backgrounds, and that we have had to overcome quite a few obstacles, including within the Order, in order to reach our place. Each of us has a history, accordingly, and this history lends weight to each of our voices when it is a matter of clarifying community choices. The community has only been able to survive thanks to each of the paths that has brought us here.

But the community has at the same time had to allow itself to reconsider and review from top to bottom the why and the how of monastic presence in this country that wants to be MUSLIM. The old people have been jostled. Those who have stayed have known how to find anew something that was close to their heart when they arrived in an entirely different Algerian context. One person would always be there for poor sick people; another found it more important and easier to pray for Muslims; another remained tied to this country where he had always lived; another accepted African stability rich in meaning for everyone . . .

Thursday, February 2, [1995]
"Praying among other people at prayer . . ."

Thirty-three years seems to be a reference to the thirty-three years since Algerian independence in 1962, another occasion when the monks of Atlas decided to remain embedded in their community when other Europeans had fled. Christian describes Tibhirine as perhaps even a good place for monastic life: it offers "poverty, simplicity, and dependence," a remembrance of the starkness of Cîteaux. He sees inspiration in the words of Bernard Lefebvre: the autonomy of the monastery is defined by the specific situation that its members have defined.

So, we have all contributed to demonstrating, over the years (33 years . . .), that our "little thing" remains VIABLE through the grace of God. The presence of older members of the community, whom I have just recalled, enables us to talk about continuity . . . while those who have arrived at Atlas since independence are familiar with their connection with the new political status of Algeria as with the singular religious face that independence has, in a way, given back to this country. They could not have come here without accepting both aspects in advance. We became, almost without our knowledge, the only community of the Order buried in a completely non-Christian landscape.

Some people continued to tell us that this special feature of ours was not really important since the monastic vocation is the same everywhere. All that was necessary for community life was checking that our surroundings allowed us to live in them, and most Visitors one after the other agreed that this was true for us as long as we did not let ourselves be invaded. We even found ourselves in the conditions of poverty, simplicity, and dependence that lack elsewhere and that keep us closer to the origins of Cîteaux. Algerian law was a good "safeguard" for us. The sirens of consumption did not get too close to us. In 1982, a Visitor (from Timadeuc[15]) could tell us, "I feel very at ease with you; people often say that Atlas is very special, and that bothered me because I think that the monastic (Cistercian) vocation should be the same everywhere and that it can be the same because it is universal; you are 99% exactly the same as at Timadeuc."

Then I replied that the 1% was precisely what interested me . . . wherein the difference seemed to lie, because it is through this that we preserve a distinctive personality and actually respect and take into consideration the calls from God

15. The Abbaye Notre-Dame de Timadeuc, in Brittany.

that mean that, in the end, we are here and not at Timadeuc (nor at Bellefontaine, Tamié, or Aiguebelle). We must be grateful to Dom Bernard Lefebvre for having reminded us of this, starting from his first regular visitation in 1983, when he asked us to find ways to be autonomous: "Atlas is not Aiguebelle, and it is not healthy for your abbey to have been for so long the Abbey of Aiguebelle. Your autonomy is not connected to how many you are, a number that is what it is, but rather to your specific situation, which you yourselves have defined."

In 1975, as a matter of fact, we had wanted to define ourselves as "PRAYING among other people at PRAYER." A precise measurement of our "place" was necessary for us to get to this definition, which is at once simple and accurate: "praying among these people who pray differently . . ."[16] The new threat that weighs over us does not change anything about this reality. The best way for us to stay safe is to keep this in mind. This is the SIGN that God dared to make by gathering us here.

Saturday, February 25, 1995
Opus Dei . . . and continued presence

Christian refers to the vocation of the community using the first of the two formulae proposed in the previous chapter. He reflects that a regime of daily prayer is required not just of some

16. Translator's note: Christian is drawing a contrast between "*priants parmi d'autres priants*" (which I have translated as "praying among other people at prayer") and "*priants parmi ces priants autres*." The distinction is rather clunky to get across in English but plays on *autre* as both "other" and "different," and on the placement of *autre* before the noun (its usual position) versus after the noun (where it is emphasized). It is interesting that Christian chooses to keep the earlier version rather than the final definition as the title for this chapter.

Muslims but of all, as part of their calling. The Alawiyya are a Sufi confraternity that invited the monastery into dialogue.

This vocation of "praying in the middle of other people at prayer" is complemented, of course, by the vocation that leads us to earn our living through hard work: this is our Rule, and it is the common law of humanity. Happy are those who are spared unemployment, and those who are not overwhelmed by the harsh pressures of competition. For us too, it is a matter of balancing a family budget. All the while remaining modest in our standing,[17] because it is a personal Gospel choice and also because the presence of real material poverty around us would make it intolerable for us to be unfaithful to this important aspect of our monastic consecration. We know well that it is not easy morally, psychologically, to be clearly a "large landowner," even if we are one of the most reduced establishments in our Order. Nonetheless, it remains true that our vocation is practiced more directly as an *Opus Dei*: prefer nothing to the Work of God . . . And our neighbors notice this.

The SALÂT also gives a pattern to the day for *all* Muslims (and not only an elite). In Islam, it is not a matter of a personal calling . . . it is something that is shared by all Muslims, who, five times a day, know themselves to be called by the call to prayer, even if many of them do not respond visibly to this call. Fasting and almsgiving are also part of each person's life. It is understandable then that Cardinal Duval was able to tell us, one day, that the "Trappist life" (*sic*) was the best way to make the religious instinct of the Church understood in a Muslim context. In fact, our prayer times have always been respected. There has also been, in our more recent history, the request of the Alawis, then our own proposal of a prayer room, and the proximity that this involves . . .

17. Fr.: *standing*, a loan word for economic or social position, used as in English.

So many milestones that have sustained our own specific loyalty. Beyond the cardinal, many Christians in our church have reiterated to us—even in the present—how valuable they find our presence, our loyalty.

As a result, we can assert that if this sign were ever to be lacking, our Church would be mutilated, as would the Islamic-Christian dialogue in its current laborious, difficult investigations. As a result, our bishops' request about the much-discussed permanent "core" should also call out to us. As a result, we are led to the idea that if our community were to become unable to remain in its entirety—which is, I think, its preferred choice, as has been clearly expressed—there should be room for a solution for maintaining our presence, even if reduced to its simplest expression, which would demonstrate the stability of the vow connecting us to this people and to this church. The community is there where two or three are gathered in his name. This much is certain. And if there were only one left?

Tuesday, February 28, 1995
And if there were only one left?

Throughout the community's deliberations, amid the general preference that all members should remain, there had been the possibility that a few or even one might stay while the others departed for safety. In his reference to the "captain of a vessel" being last to abandon ship, perhaps Christian is imagining a possible or even likely scenario. In it, there would be a kind of separation, like that between two married people who are temporarily apart but who retain an unbreakable connection. In a similar way, when individuals pray, they do so as part of the whole Church and in collaboration with the whole communion of saints.

". . . and if there were only one left?" This question follows on from all the reflections that privilege the sign of the COMMUNITY, but that receive this sign from the CHURCH because it is the Church as the Body of Christ and the sacrament of universal communion that gives meaning to the community. Remember *ecclesiola*, little church. As we discover, our vocation is greater than the community that maintains it, as great as the Church that recognizes it by confirming Christ's call and the promise of the hundredfold increase[18] . . . It is necessary to be able to affirm that it would be possible for only a single member of the community to be left here without its being a personal choice, for that one to be treated like that of the hermits, whom our Constitutions accept as borderline cases.

The one who would be left in this way—of his own free will, of course—would not renounce anything of his community vocation. This vocation would be guaranteed by the mandate that he would receive from everyone, which would give his brief solitude the force of testimony of a clearly expressed common will. He would be there to express our FAITH in what has been experienced and, what is perhaps no longer possible . . . , our HOPE also that this shared life might/could/should be resumed, whatever the place and material conditions of the location, provided that these would guarantee us genuine monastic authenticity. This hope would be legitimate because we know from experience that humanity is magnified by welcoming each other in this way, mutually, in the most demanding spiritual emulation, that of prayer and common life.

We love the Algerians enough to continue to hope for this for them, with all those among them who have like us believed, and who have helped us to grow in this hope. In this way, the relationship with Algeria would clearly be kept going, following the vote that we have taken to return. (With-

18. Matt 13:23, the seed falling on good soil.

out this vote, remaining would lose its community meaning. This vote is a beautiful expression of our stability but also of our autonomy: it is different for other religious communities.) It is a bit like one spouse when the other spouse needs to be away from the conjugal home. The former remains there indefinitely, as proof of a dual fidelity that distance and the veil of absence can contribute to reinforcing.

It must then be admitted that I voted for this for myself, and I was not the only one to do so: in a personal capacity, first of all, because I believe that I could manage to live this out in a demanding but very real faithfulness that is different from that to which I have committed as regards the community within the Order. In my capacity as prior, too, as long as I have something of the instinct that holds that the captain of a vessel should logically be the last to abandon ship. Still, so doing would have to be possible and realistic in concrete terms depending on the other needs of the community. This is not the question at the moment.

The bishops asked us a question in principle, in the name of our Church. It is this question that needed to be heard today. When the time comes, we will all have what it takes to consent to the sacrifices of the time. In the every-man-for-himself attitude that might prevail (as for the Little Clares, for instance), we will know better what needs to be protected. Let us put this chapter and its investigation under the sign of the LOOKOUT. Grace to be thus stimulated to be vigilant in all directions.

Thursday, March 2, 1995
Ramadan and Lent in succession . . .

On the day after Ash Wednesday, Christian reminds the brethren that in the three previous years, Ramadan and Lent coincided. Given that the disciplines of each are easily compared, encompassing fasting, charitable action, and prayer, Christian finds that they differ in approaches to time. The reference to jewelry and the lamb is to Exodus 12:35-36 (the account of the first Passover), in which the Egyptians give the Israelites silver and gold.

Over the three years that they coincided (entirely, in the case of *Ramadan*), it is possible to argue that the two periods of time prompted one another, urging us on together . . . But now one comes after the other, and it is doubtless better this way, since this makes it easier to connect them both while respecting their distinct natures. Of course, both are community experiences, lived in faith, that is, for GOD above all—and both privilege fasting and charitable works, prayer and *lectio* . . these four "religious" pillars, which must offer sufficient guarantee of a particular effort of justice and charity without which one might wonder what these pillars are actually supporting. The main difference lies in their relationship to TIME, duration . . . Both involve what we call a PASCHAL rhythm, that is, the conjoining of death with life, but the passage from death to life takes place over a slow journey across the desert, lasting forty days and more, in the Christian tradition passed down from early Judaism . . . whereas the conjoining of death and life, in Islam, partakes of the daily rhythm of the alternate rising and setting of the sun and of the moon, of Providence in the present day.

The way to approach a long period of time is, as Saint Benedict says, to "take a little bit away." You must hold on. However, you can agree not to eat between dawn and dusk. Jesus, in the Gospel, managed to live through fasting completely for forty days. Some people have tried to do the same, following Jesus' example. The Benedictine Rule, in accordance with other monastic traditions, in this season of the year used to recommend only one meal a day, taken in the evening. During Lent, this meal is after Vespers, in the final hours of the day (RB 41). No doubt it is easier to give everything all at once than to let it be taken piecemeal, to give everything up rather than run the "house of God" in a humble manner . . . thus taking everything away rather than taking only a little away voluntarily . . . even though our reflexes may still be "parsimonious." What is certain is that we need to keep ourselves ready on all sides: today, tonight, God may call our souls back . . . just as it may please him for us to grow older and older under the yoke of conversion.

What is also certain is that the start of Lent recalls the flight from Egypt—when everything had to be left behind (except for jewelry and the lamb!)—and at the end of Lent we expect the cross of Jesus, the place where ALL renunciations converge. An extended period of time and a moment in time are joined together in these two necessary experiences. And perhaps we know better from now on that it is not all that easy to accept both of these at the same time: continuing to seek ways to stay here until the Last Judgment, if this pleases God and the cardinal, regardless of political developments over which we have no power, and being ready to leave within the hour to find a new home elsewhere, without ruling out the possibility that what is at stake is the eternal Passover.

Saturday, March 4, 1995
Propria voluntate . . .

According to the Rule of Saint Benedict, "the life of a monk ought to be a continuous Lent" (RB 49). On this Saturday before the first Sunday of Lent, Christian points out the value of "rediscovering a taste for basic food and of giving thanks for this food by celebrating it." Man does not live on bread alone, to be sure (a reference to the following day's Gospel, Luke 4:1-13); it is the sign of bread that Jesus chose as the taste of the resurrection.

Saint Benedict mainly refers to "*voluntas propria*" or "self-will" as a negative force, but in RB 49, he sees it as a force for good: during Lent, the brethren "will add to the usual measure of our service [some form of prayer or abstinence] so that each of us will have something above the assigned measure to offer God *of his own will* with the joy of the Holy Spirit."

In total fasting a constraint is imposed upon nature, and nature well knows that this violence could not be tolerated for long, even while acknowledging the benefits of imposing a healthy emptying out on the organism from time to time (N.B. abstaining entirely for one day is not sufficient!). But nature needs to learn that there are other forms of nourishment, *that man does not live on bread alone*. With this in mind, it is crucial to reiterate what the practice of a daytime fast such as that recommended during *Ramadan* can provide as an opening to a Word of God that wants to be nourishing, as a perception of the reality of the Eucharist, which is offered as "daily supra-substantial bread."[19] It is more difficult to view this fast as a way to join in the hunger of the poorest, particularly when this hunger decreed for a few hours ends in a celebratory meal, which often makes this month harder to bear for all those on a tight budget.

The Lenten way perhaps encourages a greater sense of sharing, at least if it is observed properly. Reducing one's usual fare is a way to get closer to those who are wholly focused on their daily bread, in all its simplicity and lack of fussiness. Our tradition of beginning and ending this time of increased austerity with a meal of bread and water is very rich in meaning. It is very much a question of rediscovering a taste for basic food and of giving thanks for this food by CELEBRATING it. It is this very BREAD that Jesus chose in order for us to taste the great joy of the resurrection. We sign ourselves up to the school of the poor person who knows how

19. *ἐπιούσιον*.

much celebration a simple piece of bread can embody. The eucharistic wine completes the sign by highlighting its utter gratuitousness and by inspiring us to give THANKS for the generosity of God who makes our cup overflow.

"The joy of spiritual desire"[20] is not limited to EASTER Day. According to Benedict, this joy can and must accompany the whole of Lent because, through this bread, the poor, and sharing, God's real PRESENCE is made known to us. Seeking this Presence, this companionship with Jesus who made himself Bread, Poor, and endlessly Shared, suffices to give us a foretaste of our own RESURRECTION. In my view, Benedict gives us a very eloquent sign of this Resurrection at work when he has the audacity to entrust our individual Lenten resolutions to *voluntas propria*. This famous "self-will" is mentioned eight times in the Rule of Saint Benedict . . . and presented as the most formidable enemy, to be wholly trampled under foot. Here, and only here, self-will is restored in its grandeur . . . since it is called to be united in love with the Beloved and so to have free rein when it uses the ways of God to get to God. The JOY emanating from the Holy Spirit will be the test to make sure that we have not ventured into the desert without being accompanied by the Only Companion who has caught our self-will in his.

Tuesday, March 7, 1995
The local church . . .

It may be that at this time we are discovering the spirit of the earliest monastic lives, says Christian, where a stubborn calling to particular circumstances results in a challenging but mutually supportive atmosphere. The abbot of Aiguebelle notes

20. RB 49 = Fr.: *l'allegresse de desir spirituel.*

how closely the monastery is linked to the life of its diocese and bishop, perhaps more so than in other circumstances, where they would be more closely connected to the Order.

It is the commemoration of Saints Perpetua and Felicity. In his journal for today, Br. Christophe writes, "during Vigils we read the account of their martyrdom, a true liturgy. Will our own liturgy be led all the way to this Christ-like truth . . . ?"[21]

Under the patronage of Saints Perpetua and Felicity, we can come back to our position within the local church. In his visiting card (which we reread yesterday), the father immediate[22] wrote to us that he was "pleased to observe how well you are integrated into the local church. Your bishop appreciates your influence in the diocese and the Algerian surroundings very much." This observation also applies to Fez,[23] since the letter likewise notes that "The Church in Morocco appreciates your presence . . ." It seems to me that this reference to the diocesan church is quite indicative. Such a reference is not very likely in the visiting cards of early Christian communities. For example, Aiguebelle has a genuine and cordial connection with the Church in Valence, but this connection is not of primary importance. There is even a particular tradition that basically guarantees practical autonomy in relation to the local bishop. This old reflex is the result of exemption.[24] In the event of any issues, help is sought first of all from within the Order, perhaps even from Rome.

21. Christophe Lebreton, *Born from the Gaze of God: The Tibhirine Journal of a Martyr Monk (1993–1996)*, trans. Mette Louise Nygård and Edith Scholl, Monastic Wisdom 37 (Collegeville, MN: Cistercian Publications, 2014).

22. The abbot of Aiguebelle Abbey.

23. The satellite priory in Fez.

24. Christian's listeners would have understood that beginning in the mid-twelfth century monasteries of the Cistercian Order were exempt from bishops' jurisdiction. See, e.g., Stuart A. Morgan, "Eugenius III's Privileges to Cistercian Houses," in *Pope Eugenius III (1145–1153): The First Cistercian Pope*, ed. Iben Fonnesberg-Schmidt and Andrew Jotischky (Amsterdam: Amsterdam University Press, 2018), 305–20.

The same is not true for us. This is very clear at the present time, as in other circumstances in our history, including our very foundation, to which the archbishop of Algeria at the time, Msgr. Leynaud, contributed so much. It might even be remarked that this situation of mutual dependence prevails in the case of most of the more or less recent foundations in countries where Christianity is relatively young. At heart, the title given to the two Commissions of the General Chapter that gather together most of these communities makes the same point. These communities are automatically described as "young churches." In our case, what is "young" or "rejuvenated" is not our church, whose venerableness is sufficiently proven by François and Philippe, but rather the type of belonging to this church, which is characterized by a very specific mission, which unequivocally colors all the forms of vocations that contribute to the constitution of this church.

The institution has lost its "works"; its structure is barely consistent anymore. Oddly, this constitutional weakness has fostered a whole range of connective tissue among the different modes of Christian presence. We have all had to invent ourselves freely in the service of this country, in the name of the Gospel and of a stubborn call from the Holy Spirit, and this creates connections: we respect each other, and we rely on each other. At present we are the only parishioners. We don't put things this way to one another, but what we are living through among us contributes to bestowing substance and meaning on our shared desire to be the Church, each of us according to our own charism. It is possible that in this way we may be rediscovering what happened in the early days of Christian monasticism. The life of Saint Anthony and his connection to Athanasius, the lives of Basil or of Saint Martin of Tours, the Eastern tradition of seeking bishops from among the monks—all these provide just as many pieces of evidence as to the ecclesial nature of our calling.

Thursday, March 9, 1995
Church and bishop in the Rule?

Following on from the comment about the monastery's life as part of the local church, it is interesting to note that neither "the Church" nor "the bishop" is a substantial figure in the Rule of Saint Benedict. These references do not explain what the Church is or what it should be. Rather, "what is important here is listening to the Spirit"—and what the Spirit's voice imparts as to the calling of each individual. The Second Vatican Council established norms for the relationship between the universal Church and the "particular churches" of each diocese and jurisdiction.

Curious to find out the place of the Church in the Rule . . . The word ECCLESIA only appears twice in it. In the Prologue through a quotation from Revelation: *Let anyone who has an ear listen to what the Spirit is saying to the churches* (Rev 2:7).[25] Benedict thus invites his disciples: "Let us open [. . .] our ears to the voice from heaven that every day calls out this charge." It is almost as if each one, and *a fortiori* the monastic community as a whole, were assimilated into the Church, into a church. What the Spirit says to the churches is addressed to each one of us, because the Spirit speaks to each individual in the very same language that it uses to the churches. And the call—the vocation—that the Spirit addresses to each one is very much meant for the Church. Let us not read too much more into Benedict's meaning in this quotation in which mention of the Church is secondary (and which is written a little in the heat of the moment). What is important here is LISTENING to the Spirit.

The other mention is in chapter thirteen, which discusses the celebration of the Office of Lauds on ordinary days. It is

25. RB Prol. 9.

expected that (after the Psalms) "a Canticle from the Prophets is said, according to the practice of the ROMAN CHURCH."[26] This reference to the Roman Church clearly situates the Rule in its Western context, and perhaps more narrowly still, in a local context; here we have a Roman man expressing himself and inviting us to follow the way of doing things that is customary in his local area. If we opt for this narrower interpretation, it leaves room for all the ecclesiastical pluralisms that have been able to surface in the wake of the recent Council. And this invitation to adopt the local church's way of doing things can very easily go beyond the remit of the Office and be applied to other practices linked to particular situations, times, and cultures. That's it for CHURCH!

What remains is to notice the role of the BISHOP in relation to the monastery. Once again we find two references to the bishop, both of which appear in a disciplinary context. In chapter sixty-two, which discusses the priests of the monastery, it is explained that if a priest who had been admitted into the community thought to disobey the Rule or the deans and priors, "he must be regarded as a rebel, not as a priest." And if, having been firmly reprimanded, he was not to mend his ways "let the bishop too be brought in as a witness" (and if this recourse likewise proves fruitless, the priest should be dismissed).

In chapter 64, the reference has to do with the election of an abbot. A community may happen to elect an abbot who is complicit with its misdemeanors: "if the BISHOP of the DIOCESE or the abbots or Christians in the area come to know of these evil ways." In a note: at that time, monasteries were not exempt . . . and it was the diocesan bishop who nominated the abbot after the presentation of the candidate by the community. As happened until very recently in the case of nuns. This power has passed since then to the abbot

26. RB 1980, p. 209, bilingual.

general, who "confirms." The *Exordium Parvum*[27] agrees with the Rule in leaving complete freedom to the bishop in resolving a situation created by a "transgressive" abbot. In conclusion, a stronger connection to the bishop, restored here as Tradition, with the nice thing being that this connection is "for better" and not only "for worse."

Saturday, March 11, 1995
Connection with the Church according to our Constitutions . . .

How does the Order (in this case the Trappists) relate to the wider Church? These relationships received special attention in the modern Constitutions of the Order, which were approved at Pentecost 1990, in the light of the new perspectives on religious life laid down in the documents of the Council and the Code of Canon Law. Each monastery is particularly connected to the Church through the jurisdiction of the abbot and the way that it participates in—and indeed models—the contemplative life, to which the whole Church is in some sense called.

It is not surprising to find in our recent Constitutions a much more developed approach to the connection that the Order and each community has with the Church. Starting with the preface, it is stated that Cîteaux's mission was received from God and recognized by the Church, in the past as in the present day. And the Constitutions are intended to

27. Fr.: *Le Petit Exorde*, a Cistercian treatise of the twelfth century giving the early customs of the Order (*The Exordium Parvum*, in *Narrative and Legislative Texts from Early Cîteaux*, ed. Chrysogonus Waddell, Studia et Documenta, vol. 9 [Cîteaux: Commentarii Cistercienses, 1999], 197–259).

be in the spirit of Vatican II, so that the Order "shows itself to be ever more capable of bringing to fruition its specific function in the Church and the world." The final Constitution, entitled "in the joy of the Holy Spirit," assures us that brotherly charity and faithfulness towards the Church in putting the Constitutions into practice are the conditions of a joyful journey towards the plenitude of love.

In Constitution 3, monasteries are presented as a "figure of the mystery of the Church." Monks are exhorted to take care "to be in communion with the whole of God's people," to work towards the aim of the unity of all Christians. This service to the whole of humanity (which is that of the Church) is specifically inspired by the faithful practice of monastic observance, which is exercised directly in the Eucharist (experienced in concert with the whole church, as CST 18 notes) and in *Opus Dei,* through which "the community accomplishes, in us, with the Church, Christ's priestly ministry" (CST 19).[28] It is also inspired by faithfulness in the use of the monastery's temporal goods, through respecting the "social doctrine of the Church" (CST 41) and looking after "the needs of the Church as well as offering relief to the poor and needy" (CST 41).

But CST 31, addressing the vocation of monks, directly confirms once again that "their way of participating in the mission of Christ and of his Church as well as of integrating into a local Church is their contemplative life." CST 33, which deals at length with the abbot's ministry, begins by stating very clearly that "The Abbot, chosen from among the brothers, receives his power from God through the ministry of the Church . . . ." Finally, in the chapter on FOUNDATIONS, the relationship with missions is presented as depending directly on the relationship with the Church herself (and her survival):

28. CST = Constitutions of the Cistercian Order of the Strict Observance.

"participating, in the monastic way, in the contemplative presence of the Church with a view to perfecting the Church's mission of proclaiming the Gospel" (CST 68). Monasteries are exhorted "to be especially attentive to Vatican II's call to implant monastic life in young Churches. This is why each church of the Order is dedicated to the Most Blessed Virgin Mary, mother and figure of the Church . . ."

Tuesday, March 14, 1995
The change in the COMMUNITY . . .

Christophe's journal entry for March 12 makes reference to "the question that brings us together in chapter this morning . . . 'What has changed in you?' Father Lépine asked Christian." This is presumably the "sharing" mentioned below, which took place on the Second Sunday of Lent (for which the Gospel was Luke's account of the Transfiguration, Luke 9:28-36). What has changed for the community, according to Christian, is the substance of this chapter: a renewed appreciation from the local church for the charism of the monastery, a renewal of hospitality, the nature of the work of the associates, and the realization that each member of the community has something to contribute, in confidence and in trust, to mutual discernment.

[after the sharing on Sunday: what has CHANGED . . .][29]

Following up on the sharing on Sunday as well as on Saturday's chapter on the connection with the Church according to our Constitutions (perhaps not "situated" very clearly by the letter from the abbot general?), I begin by noting what, in

29. Brackets placed by Christian.

my view, is the sign and site of a change between us and for us connected to the circumstances of the last eighteen months:

1. Our relationship with the local church: we have received from her an increase in appeals; through her, we have understood the necessity of staying, of carrying on as we are. We have recognized ourselves in what the Church is called to live through at the present time. And we have felt that the Church would live through this less successfully were it to be deprived of our specific contribution: prayer, silence, faith in day-to-day life, hope, peace with ALL.
2. It is true that this connection to the Church has to a great extent lost one of its clearest forms of expression: welcoming guests in prayer. But, at the same time, we have fallen back on two other forms of hospitality: that of prayer, knowing that Christians involved in Algiers are relying on this (they have told us as much), and that of our surroundings, in point of fact, the feeling of being welcome . . .
3. This has led us to new choices for our community: the different importance of those who work with us, of our associates. They too sense the change, and they have agreed to it. More generally, we have had to choose what events have dictated. To welcome an event is to disarm it; it becomes less of a constraint, an abuse, something violent, and more like a gift from God that means something to us . . . a meaning that is not always clear, but that we can discover if we really are disarmed.
4. It is in this respect that we have had to respond to a more urgent need for community discernment and consultation: realizing through experience that each one of us is called directly, and therefore has something to say, and that sharing will be illuminating, providing that

there is enough trust among us to believe that the opinion of another is more important than mine (or at least as important) . . . faced with a situation over which we have no control, and for which it is impossible to claim to have found the solution.

5. And it is in this regard that I feel very strongly that we have been guided, step by step, without necessarily seeing anything very clearly at the moment we had to decide on one thing over another.
6. It is also in this respect that I feel immensely grateful to the brothers who have been able to live through this global "climate" change, without changing their fundamental willingness in carrying out their service to the community: the image of an engine that changes speed but whose parts still have the same function, whether we think of Br. Luc and also of Fr. Jean-Pierre (errands), of the porters, of the brothers working with the associates, or of the associates themselves. Each one has had to be able to experience what is called a state of grace. Personally, I can attest that this grace has not been missing from my specific duty. There are moments when I have received from another what needed to be said or done. This grace was not linked to me but rather to the task with which I had been entrusted. A source of great abandonment.
7. And it is true (cf. Br. Christophe) that it was also important to record the change through concrete actions. Because there is also the danger of cloistering oneself in a protective "cocoon." And then we would inevitably be "uninstalled."

Tuesday, March 21, 1995
An external perspective on our church . . .

The "Spanish priest" mentioned here is Fr. Manuel, whose reflections are also mentioned in Christian's chapter for April 4.

[Thursday and Saturday: Major Superiors on Algiers]

A Spanish priest passing through, charged with gathering information about Sisters Esther and Caridad: his perspective on our church . . . and his dream:

1. A church of GRATUITOUS GRACE, with no ulterior motives of efficiency.
2. A church that makes its presence one of FRIENDSHIP, that believes in friendship because its presence facilitates being open to one another as the only way to be open to God . . . a love not for doing things but for being open to one another.
3. A church of FAITHFULNESS . . . faithful to the Father, through Jesus. The feminine face of this faithfulness: restore the place of women . . . Then "Leave!" or, listening to what they say to you, "Come back!" . . . no. Because these are words that come from flesh and blood. What is cancerous for you is the telephone (calls from outside), because it undermines your resolve; once you have resolved to remain, don't cast doubt on this resolve.

2nd part: my DREAM . . .

1. A much more internationalized church: its face is too French.
2. A church of Incarnation that takes Arabic culture seriously. We must start with this, if we want to be a church of Algeria (take time).

3. A church of Incarnation that has its own liturgy. Why not start by "saying nothing"? There is nothing missionary about the "prayerful" expression of the church when it continues to be Roman.
4. There are one billion people who belong to the MUSLIM world. In the Church, few people dedicate themselves to the world of Islam. There is no entry into this world; entering into it is said to be impossible. Our God is king of the impossible. The importance of being present. The importance of being present in all Muslim environments: you must tell this to the Church.
5. Give even more community value to your church: strange that congregations, communities, people can make decisions in their own corner, without any consultation. You need to share what you are. Your presence here belongs to the Church; it is your way of being the Church.

Saturday March 25, 1995
The conditions of being with . . .

Christian rejects the ability of the brethren, as foreigners, to escape the dangers facing them while the people of Algeria do not have a choice to do so. He identifies characteristics that their continued mission must embody.

[based on what Bernard Lapize, S.J. said]

His conference on Algiers to the Major Superiors: the conditions of religious commitment, in the mission in Algeria at the present time. For this brother who came back to Algeria because of the situation, it seems "unthinkable that Christians, those in religious orders *a fortiori*, could believe that the mission here is finished." Rather, we are ready to start the job. It is our opportunity to confirm, through our quality of *being-with*,[30] what we have "done" since 1962: to show that for us there is no break with that old decision to stay in Algeria; to demonstrate our church's Algerian nationality. We wanted to draw ever closer, to be ever more united, connected . . . we cannot take advantage of our status as foreigners in order to leave this country in its misfortune. We need to live the hidden side of our lifelong mission, along with the millions of Algerians who do not have a choice, nor control over any choices. "Even if I give in one day, I will not regret having said this." Our manner of remaining?

1. The necessity of a true spiritual life. It is not enough to pray in this situation but rather to pray, instead, about this situation, finding meaning day after day, preserving ourselves from the temptation of adopting a defiant attitude (towards the FIS,[31] towards ourselves). Like the second temptation of Jesus;[32] neither tempt God nor provoke people. If we stay, it is because this seems to us to be the will of God. Experience calm availability, which is the opposite of defiance. We are not called to a trial of strength but rather to a trial of faithfulness.
2. The necessity of preserving our love for the Algerians, our trust in them, at a time when they are uncertain about themselves. Maintain our kindness, which is the very kindness of God. Watch them "over God's shoulder." Contemplate people. Do not allow our forces to be exhausted by the storminess of a debate that escapes us, over which we have no control. Let our gaze go beyond, deeper.

30. Fr.: *etre-avec.*
31. *Front Islamique du Salut* (the Islamic Salvation Front).
32. Matthew 4: *Do not put the Lord your God to the test.*

3. In our communities, be humane in our relationships; have positive encounters based on shared humanity; create between us first of all the condition of remaining here. It is a matter of living through what we are living through together: our inadequacy in relation to Algeria, our waiting for Peace. Living through our present ministry, which is probably, essentially, that of SURVIVING.

Tuesday, March 28, 1995
"Nothing has changed . . . it continues!"

In the increasingly dangerous environment of the monastery, and as other religious are murdered nearby, Christian notices unexpected changes in the life of the community. The brethren "stumble less over the rougher aspects of [their] personalities." The daily work (prayer and manual labor, ora et labora*) remain unabated by invasive security measures, and relationships with the community have in fact improved.*

In what we have shared concerning the "change" in us and between us (over the last eighteen months), we have also experienced the same feeling as that described by Fr. Jean-Pierre: "for me, it continues!" In a way nothing has changed? This, too, is true, on two different levels. First, from the most external perspective. We are in the same place, in the same buildings, there are the same number of us (with a few setbacks), in the same surroundings . . . and in this, we truly feel that this is a wholly exceptional blessing in the present circumstances. The way people, our neighbors, behave towards us has not "changed" (except for the better), and Fr. Jean-Pierre tells us that the same is true at Médéa. Each one of us, at heart, remains the same, with our limitations and faults . . . but it seems as if this causes less trouble. There has been a sort of shift in our relationships that means that we stumble less over the rougher aspects of our personalities. At times, we still feel that normality is not far off and that it will soon gain the upper hand. It is at those times that we must firmly place ourselves at that intermediate level of change that we have tried to delineate.

But it is also true that, deep down, and as regards the crux of what we are and what we have vowed to ourselves, "it continues," as Jean-Pierre says. Saying this to each other, noticing it together, is a way for us to enter once more into communion with the particular grace of our calling in what is most altered in our being, first of all, and also in the face that the Church can show here. The reasons that led us here are still valid insofar as they were connected to this kind of office and this place of Incarnation, that is, to the Love of God and of this section of humanity that is Algeria, where we know that we can join the whole Body of Christ. A particular way "of being," mysteriously maintained by a dual choice of faithfulness: to prayer and to very banal, quotidian activities.

Some other people are no longer able to exercise their professional contract. Ours has not been called into question, quite the opposite: prayer and our different forms of work (the land, most notably) are in the present situation invested with renewed urgency. If we have refused most security measures, it is precisely because they were a threat to all our balance in this regard where we know that we depend only on the faithfulness of God, and that we can put our trust only in the means that he offers us to continue to believe in what we are by the call which is freely given. It is always the same paschal story, which is not surprised that the cross is the meeting place, which speaks of birth where we would see only death throes, and which knows the Presence in spite of the darkest shadows. It must be said that Islam likewise conveys something immutable that continues to inspire us. Then what is eternal in every relation becomes visible . . .

Tuesday, April 4, 1995

Christian makes reference here to Fr. Pierre Talec's book La Serenité, *a literary meditation or treatise, itself "existential" in character, on the concept of serenity through the varied challenges of life and the Christian approaches to them: gratuitousness, wisdom, faithfulness (*gratuité, sagesse, fidélité*). These are compared to the "characteristics" identified by the priest seeking information about Sisters Esther and Caridad, mentioned in the chapter for March 21.*

Christian sees a similar set of approaches that characterize the community's own work. The constant witness of Br. Luc in the dispensary is a sharing in the common life and witness of the community, even though he is the only one able to provide medical assistance. Like his work, the work of the whole community must be seen as an offering or gift to humanity.

I had considered looking with you at our life according to the tripartite approach that Fr. Talec proposes in his book in order to found SERENITY in grace: he speaks of GRATUITOUSNESS, WISDOM, FAITHFULNESS.[33] Since January these mini-chapters have taken a different turn, one that is even more existential, if you like. I note, however, that more or less the same trilogy can be found in the "characteristics" discerned by Fr. Manuel in our Church in Algeria. In his letter to the major superiors, he spoke of GRATUITOUSNESS, FRIENDSHIP, FAITHFULNESS. Perhaps we will want to follow this vein on my return . . . it is good while waiting that he summons us, and he has not been very absent from everything that we have been able to say to each other in the last few months. As in

33. Pierre Talec, *La Sérénité* (Paris: Le Centurion, 1993).

the two or three small things that I am suggesting this morning for your consideration:

1. Our brother the doctor . . . So, we state and accept that he heals everyone. He has always done so. That is the morality of his profession. A sick person or someone who is hurt breaks down the borders of their own factions, whatever their personal convictions. The doctor can even feel closer to the most affected, the most deprived, the most threatened. This is the case for Br. Luc. This medical attention certainly involves us in the name of the tie of community and vocation that binds us to "this" doctor. This means that it is not only his own business. Even if, as far as the practical matter of treatment goes, he is the only one who can take action. And if we refuse to provide other forms of help that are not of the order of a moral, humanitarian emergency (although we ought to be able to give a glass of water to anyone who is thirsty), it seems to me that this makes each of us enter more deeply into a choice *which* is also ours, that of HEALING. Algeria in its entirety is like someone who is very ill, and we can all contribute to the healing, which must concern all involved. Then we find ourselves with the same outlook as Jesus, the shepherd who wanted to be the "healer" of souls.[34] Prayer is, for us, a privileged site for this ministry. But in our daily life, in our relationships, we can have this care for mercy and compassion that expresses this commitment to healing (cf. the confessor).
2. We have chosen to STAY . . . and to stay here. Today we cannot see anywhere else. We have been borne out in this decision by our Church authorities, but also and especially by the appeals from our surroundings. There

34. 1 Pet 2:25.

is, in this choice, something like a renewal of the GIFT that we have made of our lives to humankind, to the men and women here. This gift must remain freely given. That is the Gospel today through the threat to which we are laying ourselves open. This gift must be freely given for tomorrow. We have not wanted to take out insurance against the future. It may happen, tomorrow, that we are driven to leave, perhaps even that we realize that we are surplus to requirements in this place. We might be made to understand this. There would be nothing to regret about our decision today. Impossible to live out in any other way the absolute disinterestedness that we seek to proclaim.

Thursday, April 6, 1995
Which GOD today?

On this Thursday before Palm Sunday, Christian (who would be absent for Holy Week and Easter) observes that the confrontation between the Jews and Jesus in John 8 relates to different "approaches" to God, and who God is. He leaves the community with an important question: how does their experience of God call them to live out their vocation? Who is God? Who do we say that he is? In today's Gospel (John 8:51-59), Jesus' opponents pick up stones to throw at him, but he hides himself. This is a striking story with which to end this series of chapters, and an unknowing foreshadowing of what was to come.

In this difficult debate in chapter 8 of Saint John (the Gospel for these days), we see very clearly a confrontation between two different approaches to God, that of the Jews and that of Jesus. These are also two different experiences, although you slightly get the impression that it is only Jesus who is speaking here from experience. The Jews are tempted to enclose God in their Law . . . and so this law becomes an idol, a dead word.[35] This is why I am going back, before leaving and especially before Holy Week, to the question that we were asked at the meeting of the major superiors: "What is the experience of God that we are called to live out in the situation in which we find ourselves?" It's a question that can occupy each one of us over the course of these Holy Days.

We ought to try not to answer too quickly, like the Catechism. It's the eternal question that Jesus made so personal: *And you, who do you say that I AM?* At the meeting, we had to divulge our answer instantaneously, without warning. Perhaps this was a good thing. It was impossible to evade the question and its relevance. And we were obliged to receive, at the same time, other answers as "partial" as mine, and as "vital" . . . as one another, on the move. I wanted then to let you know simply what I said in response . . . perhaps in order to invite you to commit yourselves more deeply to the recognition of our God. Five points about God:

1. A God who is a COMPANION . . . who no doubt goes ahead, but of whom it can be said, "He is there, He was there."
2. A God who has a horror of DEATH but who has overcome and vanquished fear of death, and who has made death part of life.
3. A God who LOVES Algerians . . . and who has chosen to need us, to need me, in order to tell them and show them as much (this dimension of love is quite low in Europe, and especially in France, according to the latest surveys).

35. Fr.: *une parle de mort.*

4. A God who is SILENT . . . more than he speaks. And I understand this silence better faced with the tendency to make him speak too much, to twist his Words.
5. A God who does not despise any part of creation . . . who has forbidden me to judge or condemn anyone. Greater than my heart.

PART 3

The Charism of the Martyr.
November 4, 1995–March 16, 1996

Saturday, November 4, 1995
The charism of the "martyr"

Christian presents here the theme of this final series: "to reiterate to the Church who she is," inspired by reflection on the Rule of Saint Benedict and on the Constitutions of the Order of Cistercians of the Strict Observance. He offers these notes inspired by a meditation on the Constitutions of another institute, the Congregation of Our Lady of the Apostles, which had suffered the loss of Sisters Angèle-Marie Littlejohn and Bibiane Leclercq on September 3, 1995. The sisters, who had worked with many Algerian girls to train them in dressmaking and needlework, were killed on their way home from Mass. For them, as for those listening to this chapter who ultimately joined them among the martyrs of Algeria, there was a consistency between the spirit and the letter of their vocation.

"How in the present situation do we join together with the CHARISM of our Congregation?" This is the question posed by USMDA (Union des Supérieurs Majeurs d'Algérie [the Union of the Major Superiors of Algeria]) and that we are going to have to reflect on and discuss in order to pass on something of this to our church, our response being associated with others so as to reiterate to the Church who she is. In order to introduce our discussions, a few mini-chapters on the place of the Paschal mystery of death and life in the Rule of Saint Benedict and in our Constitutions. These are directly connected to the use that the papal legate Msgr. Francisco Javier Errázuriz made, only two months ago, of the Constitutions of the Congregation of Our Lady of the Apostles[1] in order to contextualize the brutal deaths of Sisters Bibiane and Angèle-Marie[2] with their common vocation.

The Church recognized and formalized the charism of the Congregation. And in so doing, she gave "thanks" for the faithfulness to the end of two sisters who in spirit, in a death to which they had agreed in advance as an evangelical risk, truly gave LIFE to the letter. Among other articles he quoted the following to us: "We are ready to risk everything for the Lord" (article 7). "By accepting the austerity and challenges of each day, we enter, following Christ, into the Paschal mystery of death and resurrection which is inseparable from all apostolic life" (article 11). "Become a seed of unity, hope, and salvation, especially among the poorest" (article 13: the ideal of the Institute?). The two sisters still wanted to be ready for everything that "calls for devotion and generosity" (article 9).

And it is indeed this consistency between their ideal life and their concrete existence, lived out in their daily lives (for more than thirty years), and not only at the last minute, that struck us, just as it struck the legate. This was also the message of Br. Henri, whose life was wholly given in advance, even to those who took it from him.[3] It is true that dying

1. *recte* Congregation of the Missionary Sisters of Our Lady of the Apostles.

2. Sr. Angèle-Marie Littlejohn and Sr. Bibiane Leclercq, among the Martyrs of Algeria, d. September 3, 1995.

3. Br. Henri Vergès, Marist brother and Martyr of Algeria, d. May 8, 1994.

for proclaiming the Gospel is part of the call that the missionary institutions answer most directly: the White Fathers, the Augustinian Missionary Sisters (Esther and Caridad were killed on Mission Sunday!). As the bishop said (of the witness of Saint Charles Borromeo), they get closer than others "to torture, to martyrdom . . ." In our menology there are not many who are monks and "martyrs."[4]

Tuesday, November 7, 1995
"The Order needs monks more than it needs martyrs . . ."

Fr. Bernardo Olivera, abbot general of the Cistercian Order from 1990 to 2008, reported in his book How Far to Follow? *that Christian listened in silence to his observation that "the Order does not need martyrs. It needs monks." Then he looked at Bernardo and said, "There is no contradiction."*

Bernardo continued, "Today I see that he was right: monks and martyrs. The order, the Church, the world, we all need faithful witnesses who speak words of blood from the inexhaustible fountain of their first love. We need followers of Jesus who are ready to follow him to the end, eager to embrace the cross of forgiveness that gives freedom and salvation."[5]

The Croatians mentioned here are the twelve Croatian construction workers who were building a reservoir near the village of Tamesguida, two miles from Tibhirine, and were killed on December 15, 1993, on the orders of Sayah Attia, the GIA leader who subsequently invaded the monastery just over a week later on December 24 in what Br. Paul darkly termed the visit of "Father Christmas."

4. Cf. chapter on December 12, 1995.

5. Bernardo Olivera, *How Far to Follow? The Martyrs of Atlas* (Petersham, MA: Saint Bede's Publications, 1997), 12.

You know what the abbot general, Fr. Bernardo, said to me at Timadeuc in February last year, when I asked him for advice in relation to our recent experiences: "The Order," he said, "needs monks more than it needs martyrs. So you need to do everything you can to avoid a dramatic end that would be of no use to anybody."[6] He was incidentally in agreement with the dread of our bishop after the visit at Christmas: "the hardest thing for everyone would be for you to meet with the same fate as the Croatians. We cannot run this risk." These two concordant responses express something that I believe to be profoundly true, and traditional in the Church (especially in the Church in Africa. Cf. Saint Cyprian[7]): we do not have the right to hasten our own deaths, including through "martyrdom." We could not, without committing a sin, place our neighbors in the position of being tempted to kill by confronting them directly on their own ground, where temporary blindness encloses them.

For all that, it is not clear that it is necessary to leave this place. Indeed, in most such cases, leaving is not possible. Not without running the risk of being unfaithful to what we believe, to what we are, to our vows, to the urgently needed works of charity. Think of those who continue to care for people with contagious diseases. What to say about people like Fr. Damien, who shut themselves away with lepers? In fact, we are still here. With the grace of our state that made us aver that "here was our place for the moment." We have not turned this decision into something absolute. We will not stay "at any cost." In this situation, it is vital for us to be able to remain faithful to our conscience, to our monastic ideal, to our surroundings, and to our Church.

6. The reported conversation occurred in March 1994.

7. Saint Cyprian (d. 238), bishop of Carthage, martyred at Carthage, which is now in Tunisia.

And it is in this respect that there is something shocking about Fr. Bernardo's observation. It calls attention away from the essential question, which is that of knowing whether the Order needs us in this country, at the present time . . . If our Church, our surroundings need us? Our surroundings have given their answer in different ways, and we rely on this. Our Church likewise, through the support that she gives us, and this discernment throughout which she has been a constant companion. You could say that Scripture is also helping us from day to day. Only today, Saint Paul to the Romans: *Be patient in suffering, persevere in prayer.*[8] And our Order? Surely it is present. Surely it is asking itself questions. It has for that matter always asked itself questions about the meaning of our presence. Perhaps it is easier now to make our reasons for being here understood, like our Bosnian brothers in Bosnia? . . .

[Thursday, November 9: reading of the Declaration on the Order; Saturday, November 11: after the death of Sister Odette; a few texts by her]

Sister Odette Prévost, of the Little Sisters of the Sacred Heart, was a friend of the monastery and part of the Ribat-el-Salam. She worked in Algiers as a librarian and teacher. She was shot dead on her way to Mass on November 10. On November 11, Christophe wrote in his diary, "For 'others' to become an oblation sanctified by the Spirit, pleasing to God, there is NO? other means except offering oneself in You, with You, through You."[9]

8. Rom 12:12.
9. Born from the Gaze of God, 195.

Tuesday, November 14, 1995
After the *Declaration on Cistercian Life*, rereading of the GUIDELINES of the *Statute on Unity and Pluralism* (*SUP*)

The Order's Statute on Unity and Pluralism, codified in 1969, provides that "the fundamental values of our life are guaranteed without imposing a detailed uniformity, where in fact a legitimate diversity should exist. Conditions are laid down so that each community, in union with the other monasteries of the Order . . . may deepen its own living experience of the Cistercian life."[10] *Point 12 of the Statute indicates that "the monasteries of our Order are free to arrange the details of their observance. An effective consultation of the community should accompany these experiments—though the manner of it may vary."*

What is a "charism"? For Christian here, it is bigger than any individual or community and indeed bigger than the Order itself. A personal calling can be explored in community and, as observed in point 12, there can be legitimate diversity within the Order's various houses, "giving life" to the Order and to its mission.

Rereading the guidelines, from the perspective of a better approach and of a reminder of the "charism" of the Order, and within this search undertaken for the traces of the paschal mystery of death and resurrection, of death agreed to as word, parable, of a life given. The eleven points of the SUP tend to explain charism in terms of an objective that pre-exists each of us, as it does the community that it has

10. https://ocso.org/wp-content/uploads/2021/06/Statute-Unity-and-Pluralism-EN.pdf (last accessed January 4, 2024).

contributed to creating and that it maintains among us, and that in a way evades the "vagaries" of an individual or of a single community. The specificity of a personal calling that describes itself as and wants to be "Cistercian" must be able to recognize itself in this. Rejecting one or another of these points does not mean that there is no authentic vocation stemming from God; it would show that support must be sought elsewhere to avoid what could appear to be a conflict of charisms.

For all that, these eleven points, which could be summarized in eleven "words," are themselves susceptible to interpretation: it is here that your own personal calling, and even more that of a community such as ours, can find room for maneuver, that is, its total availability to the Spirit who is master of the letter, who keeps the letter alive. There is something like a perpetual Passover to be lived within each observance so that it is the site of a death to oneself in view of a life for and with God, for and with the community in its mission here and now. For this there is a precious twelfth point that anticipates the conditions of application and refers to the inventive FREEDOM of all those who, recognizing themselves in the original charism of the Order, have as their mission giving life to it today.

Thursday, November 16, 1995
Statute on Unity and Pluralism (SUP)

Offered in this chapter and the next two are Christian's interpretations of the Guidelines and Conditions of the Statute.[11]

11. *Statute on Unity and Pluralism* (1969): https://ocso.org/wp-content/uploads/2021/06/Statute-Unity-and-Pluralism-EN.pdf (last accessed January 1, 2024).

In this rereading of the *SUP*, we can bear in mind our two settlements[12] in their own specific circumstances. Both are exceptional on account of their exclusively Muslim surroundings . . . , which has sometimes seemed "suspect" to the Order. And they are even more exceptional . . . at Fez, because of their urban, reduced roots, which are quite original and unique at the present time. Is it still possible to be Cistercian in these conditions? We have received the abbot general's response . . . in this very place, because of the upheaval that surrounds us and threatens us, not directly as monks, but as foreigners, as Christians. What impact does this constraining reality, over which we have no control, have on our observance of the essential "guidelines" of the charism of our community? And conversely, what do these guidelines offer us as something helpful and stimulating that supports our faithfulness to the present day of our situation here?

Guidelines

1. Stability (effective in number and place!) / (greater) separation . . . through means (and not weapons): nationality, religion.
2. The abbot: has been taken as a "witness" ("pope of the place" solicited on both sides) and community gather ings, an often-taken means of discernment.
3. Our horarium: balance and more space accorded to *lectio*; the importance of work. *Opus Dei* as a way to regulate fear!

12. At Tibhirine and Fez.

Saturday, November 18, 1995
Statute on Unity and Pluralism (SUP) (continued)

1. Nocturnal prayer: "night" vocation, greater union with Christ interceding at night, turned at night towards his Father, including in his agony. This frees us from fear of the night that is inhabited by "others" . . . even if it is at nightfall that we have been "visited" three times (December 24, September 30, December 30 in the evening). "Watch for the coming of the Lord": a positive meaning (not only that of fighting against the Prince of Darkness). This is one of the "rare" mentions of the paschal mystery: the time of resurrection (and not only a place of death).
2. Tending towards continual prayer . . . when the end seems to be nearing, it is easier to reach towards it in the more constant company of the one who waits for us. *Walk in my Presence*. Which does not exclude a fixed, free time of prayer. Each day: here too, the daily aspect emerges as increased by the ordeal.
3. An atmosphere of recollection and silence: we reflected on this not long ago; it is clear that this depends even more on us. A degree of agitation and anxiety linked to events can harm this atmosphere, which is always delicate. Each one of us must face up to these new difficulties. We confirm that the "great silence," which has passed into our habits, our reflexes, has had a beneficial role, renewing tranquillity . . . as long as it is experienced together, as an appropriate language of compassion, hope, and communion despite everything with EVERYONE if possible.
4. Separation from the world: going out infrequently . . . this remains. I have often insisted that Fr. Jean-Pierre

keep an eye on this.[13] The prudence recommended by our bishop goes in the same direction as this "guideline" (appreciated that Fr. Jean-Pierre on his own initiative canceled his going out on Wednesday: could this be repeated? Why not?) Radio: more room, certainly. TV? Other media: newspapers . . . letters (delivery time!).[14]

Tuesday November 21, 1995
Statute on Unity and Pluralism (SUP) (continued)

1. Hospitality: "generous" in the sense of given freely or "abundantly"? It has been said that our welcome has moved to the gatehouse: the hospitality of "generous" material sharing; we might wonder, if the situation were to continue, how we could use our building for hospitality without "interfer[ing] with the contemplative nature of our way of life"?
2. Diet: simple, I think. "Frugal": really? There is everything that we only find rarely . . . and if we compare our table with that of other monasteries in Europe . . . and with that of our neighbors? There are these luxury products which come from the garden . . . and which we could never allow ourselves if we had to buy them: should these be given up? It seems to me that there is an "art" also and especially of knowing when to use something and when to give it up. Cf. Saint Paul, the example of WINE.[15]

13. Jean-Pierre lived in the gatehouse.

14. Guideline 7 states, "The use of radio and television will be exceptional. Discretion is needed in the use of other media of communication."

15. See 1 Tim 3:8; 1 Cor 5:11.

3. Habits: nothing very new about this point. I feel a little as if with our unwelcome "visitors" our habits rather facilitated the welcome of another language, used internally.
4. The life of the community: simplicity and poverty (the reference to the world of the poor is thus rather accidental in points 8, 9, 11 . . .) and more through identification whatever the context in which we find ourselves. This is easier to realize in our context. Mention of "fraternal correction": we reach for the Gospel.
5. Question of details . . . It is in this respect that charism is something living for the living. There is always room for interpretation, discernment, no one owns charism, not even the founder, nor past generations however admirable they were. The fact remains that what is crucial is that charism must be the site of mutual understanding and of communion in faithfulness to a specific vocation in the Body of Christ whose members are diverse. Above all this (and not on the margins!) let there be LOVE.

Tuesday, December 12, 1995
Cistercian heritage

I said, rather hastily, that there were not many "martyrs" in our Order's menology.[16] Our contemporary age provides us, all the same, with some examples of martyrs whom the church has already more or less retained. There are the three brothers beatified on October 1 who died of exhaustion in the docks of Rochefort in 1794: two brothers from Sept-Fons

16. Compare chapter talk for November 4, 1995.

and the former prior of La Trappe.[17] Other monks belonging to the Order died in "concentration camps," but their case has not been successful. We know that the process for our brothers in China is progressing well.[18] We will be able to ask Dom Armand, as the postulator, to tell us how this is going. There are also brothers who were victims of persecution in Spain's dark years. And then the survivor of Akbès who was crucified on the door of his monastery, which was destroyed during a Druze revolt.

For all these, and no doubt others too whom it would be worth including, there is a special place in what our Constitutions, in their preface, call the Order's "substantial spiritual heritage," constituted by "the lives and labours of innumerable brothers and sisters," and which "found expression in writing, chant, architecture and crafts, and in the skillful management of their lands."[19] It is evident that this list refers more to daily life and its diverse demands of beauty and "regular" creativity than it does to the witness of bloodshed, which can only be exceptional. Faced with this witness, to me monks do not seem to differ from Christians in general (and *a fortiori* from members of any other religion).

Monks know that their life does not belong to them, that it is definitively united with the love of God that their faith inspires in them. Monks know that the GIFT of their life is given one day at a time, with humility and tenacity. Because monks want to be friends with the whole of humankind, they cannot imagine any death that would hurt another person, whoever they are, making them their brother's murderers. If such a situation should arise, God ALONE provides the lamb for the sacrifice! I was rereading Saint Jane Frances de Chantal

17. The Martyrs of Rochefort, who were killed in 1794 and beatified by John Paul II earlier on October 1, 1995.

18. Presumably the Trappist martyrs of China, killed in 1947–1948.

19. OCSO Constitutions, Preface 1.

speaking to her daughters: "Neither S. Basil nor the majority of our holy fathers and pillars of the Church were martyred. Why do you think it was so? [. . .] [F]or my part, I believe there is a kind of martyrdom that is called the *martyrdom of love*, in which, God preserving the life of his servants to work for his glory, makes them both martyrs and confessors at once."[20]

Thursday, December 14, 1995
["CONSTANCY" of love]

Saint Jane Frances de Chantal was then asked how long this "martyrdom" lasts. Her reply: "From the time that we give up ourselves unreservedly to God, till our death; but this is to be understood of generous hearts, who are faithful to love; for our Lord does not make martyrs of weak and inconstant hearts; he is content to let them go their own low road, lest they should escape him, for he will never do violence to free will."[21] She added, "Love is STRONG[22] as death, and the martyrs of love suffer infinitely more in preserving their life to do the will of God than if they laid it down as a testimony of their faith, their love, and their constancy." We very much feel that these are words of wisdom. And that God does not invite people to live mediocre lives. He judges us. It is very easy to take the "low road," to imagine oneself a slow

20. Citing here from *Life of S. Jane Frances de Chantal: Foundress of the Order of the Visitation by Françoise Madeleine de Chaugy* [translator unknown] (London: Richardson, 1852), 19.

21. Chaugy, *Life of S. Jane*, 20.

22. Christian writes here, "L'amour est FOU [mad] comme la mort," while the English translation translates it as it is familiarly found in Song of Solomon 8:6. The word in Hebrew is עַז.

train while lounging around. You could say, perhaps, that for the last two years we have especially been pressured to maintain the pace and, what's more, to have a better understanding of the common madness that connects love and death. In risking the one, we risk the other.

Yet even in this even greater urgency, we have quickly recovered! I still have the cardinal's reply after Christmas 1993 ringing in my ears: "What is your advice for us?" His reply: "CONSTANCY. . ."[23] The very same that, for Jane Frances de Chantal (also from the Savoy region!), is an indication of strong hearts. It is therefore a matter of HOLDING out and of doing so TOGETHER: *cum-stare*, as the city of God where *everything is one BODY*. There is in this something like an initial note of the STABILITY that dedicates us permanently to one another: constancy of place and constancy with our brothers, love of the place and love of our brothers, *amator loci et fratrum*, according to Benedict's definition of the monk as relayed by Saint Gregory. With this slight difference that the events have perhaps added to our charism: this place has other people who live here and who are also our brothers through shared steadfastness in this difficult day-to-day existence.

We are united, at least for the moment and by mutual consent, with the happiness of peace that the small group of people who surround us do not cease to hope for the country as a whole by continuing, most notably, to make space for us, and who in this way refuse to identify themselves with an Algeria that would drive out strangers or with an Islam that would execute non-Muslims. Two years ago today this solicitude around us was intensified in horror at the tragedy in Tamesguida.[24] Our stability and its constancy respond to the spontaneous behavior of the majority of our neighbors. And

23. Léon-Étienne Cardinal Duval, who was from Chênex, Haute-Savoie.

24. Tamesguida (Algeria): where the twelve Croatian workers were killed by the GIA (Armed Islamic Group) in December 1993.

the risk that we run is also a testimony (martyrdom) offered to their rejection of violence and bloodshed.

Saturday, December 16, 1995
At the historic intersection of martyrdom and monasticism

Even in March 1994 Christian had reminded Fr. Bernardo Olivera that there was "no contradiction" between being a monk and being a martyr—and indeed both monks and martyrs die to the world. The abbas in the desert battled the devil and not other human beings, but theirs too was an "offering of martyrdom."

From the very beginnings of Christian monasticism there has been both continuity and discontinuity between martyrdom and choosing the monastic life. The continuity is, as we know, of its time. The early centuries of persecution were certainly familiar with vocations to a solitary life, dedicated to prayer, to intercession for everyone. It is easy to imagine John the Evangelist retreating from the world and inspiring followers. But the threat is still there, for them as for everyone else, and it is a question of supporting the courage and faith of the faithful in that immediate form of *sequela Christi*[25] that is the offering of martyrdom, and to which we are exposed through the mere fact of being Christian. And there is discontinuity, since the intervention of the "peace of the church" under Constantine was necessary in order for monasticism to establish itself in its particular character at a time when ease and relaxation were quick to threaten the vitality of evangelical witness.

25. "following in the footsteps of Christ."

It was indeed the GOSPEL that inspired Anthony to "lose his life," differently from that of blood shed as a result of the hatred of "pagans." Paganism is not dead. It has been transplanted into the Church, where "secularization" is rife. So Anthony was "pursued" by the Word. He listened to the Word and solidified it by following it to the letter, in but an instant. It was almost as quick as the blow of an axe on the neck of Cecilia or Lucy. But for him that was only the first step of the Passover, of the passing over. It would then take decades for the letter truly to be written in terms of the spirit, in order to find in following Jesus the ways and means of a jubilatory Passover uniting time and eternity, earth and heaven.

Anthony and many others instinctively went and found the site of the first Passover, the desert, for their particular "martyrdom." In the past, persecutors preferred towns, and even cities, where the spectacle of faith would be presented as if it were a sport to the crowds in the amphitheaters. The persecutors have been replaced, but our adversary is still there and is having a good time. So it is he who must be tackled directly. Anthony's "battle" was not with any people, whether pagan or not, but rather with the traditional Enemy of the human race, whom he confronted single-handedly, certain of contributing in this way to vanquishing him at the very site of his attack. And this flight of the spirit from the world, this solitude that is at once fierce and humble, strangely becomes the "seed of Christians," to borrow Tertullian's description of the first martyrs.[26] It is this shedding of flesh and blood drop by drop in the desert to which we must constantly return in order to adhere to the specific fecundity of our lives *hic et nunc*.

26. Also noted in the chapter on February 7, 1995.

Saturday, December 23, 1995
Christ is FORMED . . .

*Two days before Christmas, Christian calls the monastic life "a perpetual Advent" and indeed "a constant nativity," perhaps a reference to Saint Benedict's injunction that "the life of a monk ought to be a continuous Lent" (RB 49). This chapter also plays on the language of paschal mystery and Passover (*mystère pascale, Pâque, passage*)*[27] *and the imagery of the hymn of Philippians 2. The mystery of the Incarnation could only be fully understood after the time of Pentecost, when the church was formed. In the monastery this formation continues in the "school of the Lord's service."*

In this investigation of the place of the "paschal mystery" in our Constitutions and in the Rule, it is doubtless necessary to have, from the outset, an all-encompassing vision of the "paschal mystery." Everything is Passover, passage, in the life of our Lord among mortals, God's passing down to earth, God's participation in human mortality, and the progressive introduction of humankind into the glory of God. The hymn of Philippians 2:1-11 rightly makes the Son's obedience the dynamic principle of this Passover. And this obedience is signified fully in the humbling of the Incarnation. Christmas is to be understood entirely in the light of Easter. The evangelists help us to make this reading in the faith of an event that is linked to our history only so as better to lead this history in a venture that transcends it. They could only receive and understand the Christmas mystery after everything had been accomplished up to the gift of Pentecost.

The liturgical time that we are celebrating incites us to compare our monastic life to that wholly new face of the paschal mystery to which we must constantly return in order

27. See similar wordplay in the chapter on March 22, 1994.

to be sure of properly interpreting the passion, cross, and resurrection. The face of a small child formed on his mother's breast, then growing up in a family, modestly, laboriously, joyously too in the simplicity of a daily existence like anyone else's, with everyone else. We have rightly said that the monastic instinct is experienced first of all as waiting, desire, a perpetual ADVENT. And this truly is one way to follow Christ, who came from the Father and who returns to the Father through everything, by being "about his Father's business"[28] everywhere and in everything.

There is also the meaning that the time of our consecration assumes when we allow it to take on the task of shaping us bit by bit like Christ, of giving birth in us to a "son of the Father" in the image of his Beloved Son. Is this not a constant nativity? This interpretation is confirmed for us in the very beautiful Constitution 3.2: "The monastery is a school of the Lord's service where Christ is FORMED in the hearts of the brothers through the liturgy, the abbot's teaching and the fraternal way of life." Find in this something of that which Mary lived out in waiting for the Child who already LIVES, and also, of course, something of that which will "come to pass" in JESUS of Nazareth so that, at length, in him too "Christ may be FORMED."

Saturday, December 30, 1995
And Nazareth?

Christian remarks that there is little in the Constitutions to remind members of the Order of the connection between their formation and the Incarnation. Reference is made here

28. Luke 2:49: the young Jesus in the Temple.

to Charles de Foucauld ("Brother Charles," also known as Brother Marie-Alberic when he was for seven years a member of the Order). Foucauld left the abbey of La Trappe (in Akbès) in order to move to devote himself to an even more austere existence in Nazareth.

Beginning an excursus on "work," a central pillar of Trappist life, Christian notes the connections between the revised Constitutions of the Order and John Paul II's encyclical Laborem Exercens *"on Human Work" (September 14, 1981), as well as the conciliar theology on religious life.*

One would expect to find an explicit trace in our Constitutions of the mystery of the INCARNATION as such; our fathers of Cîteaux, and most especially Saint Bernard, lovingly bent over the Infant's cradle, tirelessly contemplating the marvel of God's Presence, such a new and extraordinary Presence, all-encompassing too, to the point of leaving none of our human sins in the shadows. And yet in reading and rereading these Constitutions, we find barely a trace of the Cistercian life's relation to the slow maturing of the Word made flesh. This is even more surprising given that the spirituality of NAZARETH truly belongs to our age . . . and even that it owes a lot to everything that has been able to grow around the witness of Brother Charles.[29] I even wonder whether Brother Albéric's joining our Order had some influence on the expression of his later attachment to the hidden life of Nazareth. Did he take this from us, by entering into a "life of abjection" that was so different from his past life . . . or did he end up finding later, at Nazareth precisely, the "unique model" that La Trappe had not been enough to provide him with?

Constitution 26 on WORK seems important to me. It is a matter of participating "in the divine work of creation and

29. de Foucauld.

restoration." Here you would expect at least an indirect reference to the work done by the Son of Man at the carpenter's school in Nazareth. A note to this Constitution cites a passage from the encyclical of John Paul II on work that makes the imitation of Christ, through toil and sweat, much more explicit. The mention of CREATION surely refers to the influence of the Council, and of the theology that has prevailed since the 50s, in part thanks to Teilhard and Fr. Chenu.[30] It is tempting to think that this Constitution falls within an area of Christianity barely explored by Father de Foucauld and his disciples (the chief editor: Australian). Cf. Little Sister Magdeleine and the very minimal impact of the Fraternity in the anglophone world.[31]

Neither is there a reference to the "Holy Family," or to the time spent in Nazareth, not even in the Constitution on "simplicity": the term "SCHOOL" used several times refers more to the Rule than to an idea of growth, of maturing childhood. The expression closest to all that which is lived out in the "hidden life" can perhaps be found in Constitution 2: "in solitude and silence, in assiduous prayer and joyful penitence [. . .], thus rendering to the divine majesty a service that is at once humble and noble." But this is borrowed from the *Perfectae Caritatis*.[32] And the note seems to say that it relates

30. Pierre Teilhard de Chardin, palaeontologist and Jesuit, and Marie-Dominique Chenu, OP, both liberal Catholic theologians who had a significant influence on the Fathers of the Second Vatican Council.

31. Little Sister Magdeleine of Jesus (d. 1989), founder of the Little Sisters of Jesus, a religious institute inspired by the life and work of Charles de Foucauld. "The Fraternity" is a term applied to Charles and those who followed his example.

32. Decree on the Adaptation and Renewal of Religious Life *Perfectae Caritatis* 7 (October 28, 1965): "[Communities in which] in solitude and silence, with constant prayer and penance willingly undertaken, [contemplatives] occupy themselves with God alone, retain at all times, no matter how pressing the needs of the active apostolate may be, an honorable place in the Mystical Body of Christ."

instead to the imitation of MARY, as the *Declaration on Cistercian Life* explained.[33]

Thursday, January 4, 1996
Christmas . . . and us

The Ratio Institutionis. *(Guidelines on Formation) of the Order (1990) includes a significant passage on work as one of the central aspects of the Trappist vocation. The thirty years of Jesus' life before his public ministry, writes Christian, would have been a time in which the mysteries of the Incarnation and the death and resurrection would have been held in tension. It is in the continued presence of the community and its apostolates that aspects of the mystery of the Incarnation can be glimpsed. Gilles Nicolas wrote (according to Christian in a retreat address), "We must find in the mystery of the Incarnation the true reasons for our staying here despite the threats and torment of the people . . . What is true for Christmas is true for Easter. The mystery of the Incarnation. We, too, have to live the mystery of the Incarnation, for that is the deepest of all the reasons why we stay at Tibhirine . . . Our witness is here in Algeria. The only way for us to give witness is to live where we do, and be what we are in the midst of banal, everyday realities . . ."*[34]

33. Declaration of the General Chapter of 1969 on the Cistercian Life: "[The community] lives in an atmosphere of silence and separation from the world, and fosters and expresses its openness to God in contemplation . . . treasuring, as Mary did, 'all these things, pondering them in her heart' " (https://ocso.org/history/historical-texts/declaration-on-cistercian-life/) (last accessed January 1, 2024).

34. Cited in John W. Kiser, *The Monks of Tibhirine: Faith, Love, and Terror in Algeria* (New York: St Martin's Press, 2002), 217–18.

In addition to what has been said about our Constitutions, an equivalent observation should be made regarding the *Ratio* for formation. No explicit evocation of the very mystery of the Incarnation. In the paragraph on formation through WORK, it says, "Through work, especially manual work, monks and nuns participate in the CREATIVE activity of the Father and share in the experience of all workers, particularly the poor. At times this work may be marked by fatigue, tension or frustration: a sharing in the CROSS of Christ . . ."[35] No reference to the school of Nazareth, which enables an understanding of the constant interpenetration, over more than thirty years of Jesus' earthly life, of the mysteries of the Incarnation and the redemption. But mention is always more willingly made of the latter, even though it is in a way subordinate to the former according to the order of succession and of revelation over time.

As for us, I am strongly in agreement with what Gilles [Nicolas] told us in his Christmas homily about seeking in the mystery of the Incarnation for the true rootedness of our reasons for "remaining" despite the threat and turbulence. In a letter to his loved ones, he confirms, "Christmas is EMMANUEL, God silently present, but the presence of Love which alone is revolutionary, which alone transforms the hearts of one another." To which he adds the following, which cannot leave us indifferent: "For the Eucharist to be celebrated on the TIBHIRINE mountain, inhabited by down-to-earth, hardy people who are attached to Islam and to 'their' monks, seems to me to have a

35. *Ratio Institutionis* 10 (https://ocso.org/download-attachment/1372) (last accessed January 1, 2024). It continues: "As one of the principal ways of serving the community and exercising responsibility towards it, work is a powerful instrument in drawing the community closer together. It is also a means of self discipline that promotes health of mind and body and fosters maturity. When the necessary conditions of simplicity and peace are provided, work is an opportunity for the exercise of the continual prayer that flows from lectio and the liturgy."

very important meaning and one that is not only symbolic." In fact, I think that it is much healthier psychologically, mentally, for us who have to experience this, as well as more in conformity with the monastic tradition, that we join the imitation of CHRIST here through this offering of a continual Incarnation in "the humble consecration of a hidden life"[36] of prayer and work (the expression of *Perfectae Caritatis* no. 9), rather than assimilating it directly to the solitary reality of the CROSS and of a martyrdom isolated from their material context of a life lived together over many years.

Mary's presence at Calvary also indicates a continuation there of what had long been experienced in the familial intimacy (in a broad sense) of Nazareth. In response to our abbot general's quip that our Order needs monks more than it needs martyrs, our answer must therefore be that we are truly monks by continuing to live out, here, the very mystery of Christmas, of GOD LIVING among humankind . . . and exposing himself in this way, from the cradle to the massacre of the Innocents. As if to demonstrate more clearly that before the cross, multitudes of innocents had been massacred, just as multitudes have been massacred since then, including all around us. Nor can we ever forget that our direct encounter with the great tragedy that is affecting this country happened in this liturgical context, between the night of 14 December and that of 24 December.[37]

36. A paraphrase perhaps of the French of *Perfectae Caritatis* 9, which read, "l'humble et noble service de la divine Majesté dans le cadre du monastère, soit qu'ils se consacrent entièrement dans une vie cachée au culte divin" (https://www.vatican.va/archive/hist_councils/ii_vatican_council/documents/vat-ii_decree_19651028_perfectae-caritatis_fr.html) (last accessed 1 January 2024).

37. The date of the murder of the Croatian workers and that of the visit of their murderers to the monastery.

Saturday, January 6, 1996
"In praise of old age" . . .

Christian once more invites the brethren to reflect on the monastic vocation they are living in the light of the Incarnation, remarking that the two invasions "that have directly knocked on your door" fell the day before and several days after the feast of the Nativity. It was, too, the apostle and evangelist who by tradition lived to an old age (John the Evangelist) who "made himself the evangelist of the Incarnation," imitating Christ in situations such as old age that Christ did not experience in his human life.

Sayah Attia, as reported in Kiser's account, apologized to Christian for barging in on Christmas Eve, by saying, "Excuse me. I didn't know."[38]

The reading at Vigils this evening (Jean-Claude Sagne, *Traité de théologie spirituelle* [*Treatise of Spiritual Theology*], p. 85)[39] is a beautiful illustration of what I have been trying to say all along in seeking to situate the impetus and dynamism of the monastic life and of our presence here, at this moment, in the light of the Incarnation: "In the detail of daily life, the Virgin Mary gives us, as criteria for discernment, the life of NAZARETH, with the imitation of Jesus. This discreet development from day to day in patience and forgetfulness of oneself is the preparatory school for the whole gift of oneself in a more heroic form, when the Holy Spirit draws us into the baptism of fire that is the passion of Jesus." It is MARY again, at the foot of the cross, "who helps us bear peacefully what is beyond us" (to give our preference to that which we cannot avoid) "by reminding us that the secret of

38. Kiser, *Monks of Tibhirine*, 147.

39. Jean-Claude Sagne, *Traité de théologie spirituelle* (Paris: Éditions de l'Emmanuel, 1995).

the strength of the Spirit is received in the meekness of the heart of a CHILD."

Leaving to you the task of rereading the events that have directly knocked on your door (I am too involved to suggest mine to you!), I would just like to underline once more their connection with the Christmas mystery (12/24/93 and 12/30/94), a connection that has been expressed and recognized, and that has led both emir and lieutenant to apologize . . . . and, I would say, to depart "meekly" (and to return no more . . .). It seems to me that it is a long habit of day-to-day existence shared among us and with our surroundings that has ended up giving us, in these circumstances, the internal logic of the life of Nazareth as the ultimate criteria of discernment. We carry on, we remain at our work today at least, in patience and forgetfulness of our legitimate fears . . . waiting for a sign given by the Holy Spirit telling us to act differently.

We know that such an attitude, in its apparent passivity, has had to destroy in us any instinctual defenses. We have had to let ourselves be DISARMED by ourselves. Happily, we have had the CHRISTMAS Child to help us . . . and perhaps to remind us that we could not "drink the cup with him" without starting out for a long time like him, without going through this WORK hidden in the hollow of humanity that, for us, is also work on ourselves.[40] Have you noticed that it is the "son of thunder,"[41] the only apostle present at both the agony and the foot of the cross, who made himself the evangelist of the Incarnation, the only one incidentally who was not a "martyr." The long life of John, the beloved, who followed and desired his Master up to that period of old age that Jesus did not experience and during which he had to invent in the Spirit the imitation of Jesus, just as it is given

40. Cf. Matt 20:22.
41. Cf. Mark 3:17.

to us to do in each of our situations in life. A lot of wisdom in this respect in the book *In Praise of Old Age*.[42]

Tuesday, January 9, 1996
The Church's Ordinary Time: continual

This day marked the beginning of "week 1 in Ordinary Time" in the lectionary, the feast of the Baptism of the Lord having taken place the previous day. In so-called "Ordinary Time," a term for the parts of the church year not set apart by a season such as Advent or Lent, "the ordinary of the Christian takes over from the 'ordinary' of the Lord." In some sense (implicitly, says Christian), we leave Jesus to grow up in Nazareth after the Epiphany, and we begin to read (explicitly) the stories of the beginning of his public ministry.

In Gaudium et Spes *(1965), the Pastoral Constitution on the Church in the Modern World, Christian points to the section on "principles governing socio-economic life." Here we read that "we hold that through labor offered to God man is associated with the redemptive work of Jesus Christ, who conferred an eminent dignity on labor when at Nazareth he worked with his own hands. From this there follows for every man the duty of working faithfully and also the right to work."*

The Church season, or ORDINARY time, which starts as soon as the solemnities of Christmas and Epiphany are over, is clearly part of a continuity that can be read in two ways: implicitly, we leave Jesus to undertake in Nazareth his slow

42. Most likely Christian Combaz, *Éloge de l'âge dans un monde jeune et bronzé* (Paris: Laffont, 1987).

and long period of growing up as a man. Explicitly, we undertake the regular reading of his activity and teaching after his baptism, which marks his entry into public life. A dual continuity, then, each of which comes under the mystery "made manifest" at Christmas and which is the INCARNATION of the Word, his dwelling in human society. Church time is continual. And here indeed the ordinary of the Christian takes over from the "ordinary" of the Lord.

Taking on this continuity is not something easy, whether in actions or in texts. We have seen as much in relation to our Constitutions. It is even more astonishing across the texts of the Council. The mystery of the Incarnation is almost entirely absent as such from the great Constitution on the Church, *Lumen Gentium*, just as it is from the Constitutions on the liturgy or revelation. It is mentioned quite interestingly in the decree *Ad Gentes* (3, 8, 10) as a point of reference for the need for missions. But there is nothing in *Perfectae Caritatis*. However, it acts as the framework, the "background of the picture," in the very innovative fresco of *Gaudium et Spes: On the Church in the Modern World*. Here again we must discern the decisive influence of the theology developed by Fr. Chenu and strongly supported by Teilhard de Chardin's cosmic vision (and perhaps, as well, in a latent way, by the spiritual movement awakened by Brother Charles?).

It is not surprising that the whole section on WORK (nos. 67ff.) makes reference to the "eminent dignity" bestowed on labor by Jesus "when at NAZARETH He worked with His own hands" (the only mention of Nazareth?). There is also the very beautiful text of no. 22 . . . : "For by His Incarnation the Son of God has united Himself in some fashion with EVERY man. He worked with human hands, He thought with a human mind, acted by human choice and loved with a human heart." In the same no. 22, this frequently cited text: "we ought to believe that the Holy Spirit in a manner known only to God offers to every man the possibility of being associated with this paschal mystery" . . . We could just as well say "with the mystery of the INCARNATION." We are happy to speak of the incarnate Word (passive) and the redeeming Word (active). If the Word is not "redeemed," it must be said to be "INCARNATING."[43]

This again is very clear in the very beautiful no. 32, which describes the community character of all the deeds and acts of the incarnate Word: "He revealed the love of the Father and the sublime vocation of man in terms of the most common of social realities and by making use of the speech and the imagery of plain everyday life." It is clear that our VOCATION in its very specificity finds here its *raison d'être* and its most quotidian impetus.

Tuesday, January 30, 1996
Community character of the INCARNATION

[after the Regular Visitation from January 11 to 20][44]

Four days before this chapter, the abbot general (Dom Bernardo Olivera) had announced that the central theme for the next General Chapter would be "The Community, School of Charity." Charity, for Dom Bernardo (and following Saint Bernard), is "the unblemished law of the Lord, because it does not seek what is useful for itself but rather for others. For this reason charity is 'light' and 'purity.'" [45]

[The reading at Vigils this evening picks up the thread where we left it with *Gaudium et Spes*. One of the last issues of *La*

43. An intentional neologism?

44. A visitation of Dom Armand Veilleux from Rome. Of his visit, Christophe wrote, "I feel real happiness . . . a Cistercian who draws me toward a more complete self-surrender" (Christophe's diary, p. 203).

45. Letter from the abbot general, January 26, 1996 (ref 96/AG/01).

Croix received (but from 4 December!) expresses the importance of this document, which is thirty years old, the age of Nazareth! See in addition the present from Gilles Nicolas: three cassettes of Fr. Varillon on the Incarnation.] With *Gaudium et Spes* 32, we have joined with the theme of the next General Chapter, since this text underlines the COMMUNITY character of the whole history of salvation manifested in all the acts and deeds of the incarnate Word: "Willingly obeying the laws of his country He sanctified those human ties . . . He chose to lead the life proper to an artisan of His time and place. In His preaching He clearly taught the sons of God to treat one another as brothers. In His prayers He pleaded that all His disciples might be 'one.' . . . He offered Himself for ALL . . . He commanded His Apostles to preach to ALL peoples the Gospel's message," etc.

And no. 38 picks up on the same teaching by basing all this activity on the command of LOVE whose "way [. . .] lies open to ALL men."[46] It is this life shared together day by day that enables the experience of the certainty of a "universal brotherhood," to which an individual is warranted to dedicate all his effort as to a legitimate and ultimate aim. This charity is not principally the fruit of specific important matters, but is chiefly pursued "in the ordinary circumstances of life" (as the Council emphasizes!).[47] *Giving your life for those you love* is not an isolated gesture that would necessitate seeking martyrdom or that ought to be identified, in Jesus' life, with the supreme gift consummated on Calvary. Jesus took care to warn that the CROSS itself is "every day" and that it is the sign that gives value and weight to "all works in favor of justice and peace."

46. Translator's note: The published English text of *Gaudium et Spes* reads here "the way of love lies open to men," but the above amended translation takes account of Christian's highlighting of "TOUS les hommes."

47. Paraphrased from *Gaudium et Spes* 38.

What took place during the hours of the passion was continual Incarnation: the Word became human flesh and bone then as in the days of his birth and upbringing. He came to inhabit suffering and death like all the other realities shared by all people in this world. But he did so in order to bring the great dynamism of Incarnation to its conclusion by enabling it to establish a foothold in the glory that he has from his Father from the very beginning. For the outcome of our Redemption is indeed this of a humanity similar to ours in the glory even of God . . . and in this way, God's entering into human community through the communion of the saints.

Thursday, February 1, 1996
CST 86 "and so JOYFULLY make their way . . ."

On the eve of the feast of the Presentation of the Lord, Christian reminded his listeners that the objective of this series of chapters was to look at the paschal mystery and the Cistercian charism. Advent, Christmas, Lent, and Eastertide are all read in light of the paschal mystery and their resonance with one another, just as the mysteries of the Rosary are interconnected.

I proposed to look with you for the traces of the "paschal mystery" in the Cistercian charism . . . , and this is how we allowed ourselves to be led into a meditation on the mystery of the Incarnation, discovering perhaps even more to what degree it represents the specificity of the Christian message to the extent that this does not match the specificity of the Incarnate Word. The season of Advent and Christmas made this approach even more topical. Traditionally, tomorrow's feast day marked the end of this season, forty days after the Nativity. We thought that we had thus finished telling the "joyful mysteries" and that we were going to move, with Lent already so close, on to the "sorrowful mysteries," which seemed to give true weight to the mission of Christ come to heal and save all people by the blood of the cross.

This other forty-day period has always weighed very heavily on our approach to the "paschal mystery," much more heavily at certain times, seemingly, than the final forty days destined to familiarize us, between Easter and the Ascension, with the "glorious mysteries." Yet in telling these traditional mysteries of the ROSARY with Mary, how can one not be struck by their mutual interpenetration, by their constant resonance with one another? The Cross and Glory are fully present in the Joy expressed by Simeon and Anna. And this is what in truth points to the Incarnate Word. It is also what accomplishes the mission of the Word, which is to SAVE, to REDEEM all people by teaching them to appreciate this new combination of joy and suffering, of death and life, through which the individual can quench his most radical thirst, that for God for ever.

This is why the paschal mystery must be held to be as extensive as the Incarnation, that is, as extensive as human LIFE and vice versa. And Jesus teaches us that human life is destined for eternity, including and perhaps especially in its passing through (bodily) death. In Christ's Passover, Incarnation is the method and redemption the motive. The cross is part of the method but does not exhaust the motive. Our Fathers said, by analogy, that the cradle was already the cross where the Son will be laid; they also said that the cross is like the cradle of the first-born among the dead. It seems to me that the final Constitution, 86, says much the same by inviting us to "joyfully make [our] way to the fullness of love" (what David called: *to go the way of all the earth*, in 1 Kgs 2:2 today!).

Tuesday, February 6, 1996
"That in all things . . ."

Christian argues that it is not for the monastic community or individual to be focused on either pleasure or the cross. Christ knew all sorts and conditions of human experience, apart from sin, and including both sorrow and joy. There is no contradiction between asceticism and joy in monastic life. Absolutely everything is to be received as a gift from God: God can even be glorified in failing to over-price monastic produce!

Our way (*tariqa*)[48] of following Christ more closely is thus "a joyful way to the fullness of love." And it is for this very reason a way of INCARNATION, assuming all the conditions of humanity that Christ himself knew: nothing belonging to humanity was unknown to him, apart from sin, which he told us is not "of man," that it does not belong to the image and likeness. Sorrow and joy, happiness and suffering can thus be closely connected, perhaps even imbricated, conjoined in the way that Saint Paul found joy in his tribulations. It is not for us fixedly to adopt either a purely hedonist attitude ("everything is great") or, on the contrary, a sort of pain-obsessed perspective that seeks nothing but the cross for oneself and others.

At the very moment when it appears a choice of asceticism and deprivation, the monastic way seeks to be a way of peace and authentic freedom leading to what Jesus himself experienced by calling it "perfect joy." What matters is that EVERYTHING be received "with an even temper" as a GIFT from the Father and experienced for the glory of God. It is all the same astonishing that this greater glory of God should be tucked away in the Rule of Saint Benedict in a place where you

48. Arabic: "road" or "way," the spiritual path toward God.

wouldn't immediately go looking for it: in the chapter on the artisans of the monastery (chap. 57), and more precisely in a discussion about commerce: "The evil of avarice must have no part in establishing prices, which should, therefore, always be set a little lower than people outside the monastery are able to set, *so that in all things God may be glorified*."[49]

Historically, we have managed to invent all sorts of macerations, flagellations, etc., . . . by seeking in them the glory of God. Without realizing that we were running the risk of reducing this glory to those means that come from us. And to no longer see the "other" things, all these other things that happen to us like everyone else. It is our way of welcoming these other things "in the presence of the Father"[50] that means that we remain in the world without being of the world. It is doubtless because of this that the very mention of the mysteries of Christ is ultimately rare in our Constitutions as well as in the Rule. Almost as if this were to be self-evident. I have already noted that nowhere is any mention made of "MARTYRDOM" (in the sense in which we understand this word when today we speak, for example, of the martyrs of Japan[51]). Only once in the Constitutions is there mention of "SUFFERINGS." In the very beautiful Constitution 3, which talks about the spirit of the Order: "The Cistercian way of life is CENOBITIC. [. . .] By bearing one another's burdens they fulfill Christ's Law, participating in his SUFFERINGS in the hope of entering the Kingdom of heaven" (CST 3.1).

49. 1 Pet 4:11.

50. Cf 1 John 2:1?

51. The Martyrs of Japan, persecuted for their faith, of whom forty-two have been canonized.

Thursday, February 8, 1996
Through the patience of the Gospel

The Prologue to the Rule of Saint Benedict suggests that nothing in the school of the Lord's service should be "harsh" or "burdensome" but at the same time invites the community patiently to share in Christ's suffering. This can be experienced in the quotidian nature of community life in whatever the context, and it is accomplished by (as Christian puts it) "a sharing in community in the joys and sorrows of human existence."

The mention of the SUFFERINGS of Christ in Constitution 3.1 harks back of course to the Prologue to the Rule, in its closing words: "Never swerving from his [God's] instructions, then, but faithfully observing his teaching in the monastery until death, we shall *through* PATIENCE *share in the sufferings of Christ* that we may deserve also to share in his kingdom. Amen!"[52] In both places, then, unique use of the word "sufferings" (passion). And it has to do with the sufferings of Christ in which we are invited to participate . . . In the Rule, this is expected to come about through the patience of lifelong personal faithfulness without requiring anything especially "extra-ordinary." Benedict himself specifies that he wanted to institute in his school "nothing harsh [*asperum*], nothing burdensome," except in so far as it always takes "a little strictness in order to amend faults and to safeguard love."[53]

In the Constitutions, the point of application of this participation in the passion becomes almost exclusively communal life, mutual support (Gal 6:2).[54] And we know that

52. RB Prol. 50. Translator's note: The closing exclamation mark follows Christian's punctuation rather than that of the critical edition and English translation.

53. RB Prol. 47.

54. "Bear one another's burdens, and in this way you will fulfill the law of Christ."

this is what inaugurates the kingdom of heaven, which, for us, is participation in LIFE in God through the communion of the saints. And it is truly the passion's victory that it transfigured the multitude of sinners into a people of the ELECT destined for the same beatitude as Christ. This is how Redemption (the word is absent) is accomplished, certainly, but the means of this accomplishment remains, for each of us as for Jesus himself, a sharing in community in the joys and sorrows of human existence. Certainly, the PATIENCE that this requires has, at its very root, more to do with "sorrow": it is necessary to suffer, for prolonged periods of time.

But at the same time, Benedict tells us that patience is the key to the "overflowing" of the heart that starts to run joyfully in "the inexpressible delight of LOVE."[55] This is indeed the "joyful way towards the fullness of love" that sums up all the Constitutions; this indeed is our *sharia* . . .[56] This is again what Saint Bernard wrote to the monks of Aulps in a famous letter: "Our *ordo* is debasement, humility, and voluntary poverty. It is obedience, JOY and PEACE in the Holy Spirit. Our *ordo* is to be under a master, under an abbot, under a rule, under discipline. Our *ordo* is to be zealous for silence, to practice fasting, vigils, prayer, and manual work, and above all to keep to the more excellent way of CHARITY."[57] Thus it is that, according to the same Constitution 3.4, "the common life in its entirety conforms to the GOSPEL, which is the supreme law. In this way the community will not be

55. RB Prol. 49.

56. Arabic, "a correct path," e.g., a religion as a whole.

57. Translator's note: Here we follow the text of Saint Bernard's letter in the following English translation: Bernard of Clairvaux, Ep 151, in *The Letters of St Bernard of Clairvaux*, trans. Bruno Scott James, rev. Beverly Kienzle [Stroud: Sutton Publishing, 1998], 219–21). The middle part of the quotation in Christian's citation is more abbreviated: "elle [la vie] est soumission, application, pratique, exercice" [the *life* is submission, application, practice, exercise].

lacking in any spiritual gift" (see 1 Cor 1:7), united as it is by waiting for the revelation of Christ in its heart.

Saturday, February 10, 1996
"On earth, their minds are occupied with heavenly things"

On this day of the memorial of Saint Scholastica, sister of Saint Benedict, Christian reflects on the familial love of the monastery as akin to that of siblings. Indeed, by the end of Scholastica's life her love for her brother was enlarged by their common vocation, and by the "sweet complicity of a shared desire." Three days before her death (a story recorded in the books of Dialogues *of Gregory the Great), Scholastica and Gregory were deep in spiritual conversation in the hut where they were meeting midway between their two dwellings, and a heavy storm prevented him from going back to his cell. Their falling asleep in the Lord, for Christian, seemed a "logical and happy consequence of that last exchange against the backdrop of a stormy night." Such was Christian's own life with his brethren.*

The memorial of Saint Scholastica illustrates well "the inexpressible delight of LOVE." The relationship between brother and sister is just like that which must be established between the members of a community as the days go by over the whole course of a lifetime. This is what, already here on earth, fulfills the promise of the Gospel, which assures that those who have left everything to follow Jesus will find brothers, sisters, mothers, children A HUNDRED TIMES OVER . . .[58] The Father alone remaining the unique cornerstone of this

58. See Matt 19:29: anyone who has left family or property for Christ's sake "will receive a hundredfold, and will inherit eternal life."

necessarily disparate gathering that is transfigured by the Spirit. A way of saying concretely that the communion of saints also relates to the Incarnation, on earth as in heaven.

If we ask ourselves where the paschal mystery is applicable in our lives, it is doubtless very much within community relations that we should look . . . more so than in each one of us taken individually. Christians, through their ecclesial vocation, must know that they cannot save themselves alone. They have received shared responsibility for the salvation of all people, of all time. "What have you done with your brother?"[59] . . . This is the question that is asked of everyone at the moment when we are "judged on our love."[60] Even the hermit is "separated from all only in order to be more closely UNITED with all" (Evagrius Ponticus); otherwise he is nothing but an old boy (or an old girl). Saint Maron and the "hypaethrals"[61] that we were speaking about yesterday remained open to the community, "open to the winds."

We are also told that this is what Saint Scholastica was seeking with Saint Benedict in their last conversation, where the joy of being together was no longer linked to their close family ties (as twins) but rather to the sweet complicity of a shared desire enabling them to be in communion, through one another, as if in anticipation, with the heavenly bliss. Scholastica's passing over "three days later," then that of her brother, seem then like the logical and happy consequence of that last exchange against the backdrop of a stormy night. One thinks of the ecstasy at Ostia between Augustine and his mother.[62] If it is thus the community itself that is the site of a permanent Passover, all the elements of life in the community must be able to contribute to this passing over while shaping

59. See Gen 4: Cain and Abel.

60. Reference to a saying of Saint John of the Cross: "At the end of our life we will be judged on our love."

61. Roofless buildings.

62. A reference to Augustine, *Confessions* 9.10.

us in the image of the Word made flesh, who chose to "abide" among people in order to share the Passover, his Passover, with them. It is in this spirit that Constitution 22 on the heart's vigilance must be received . . . "While dwelling on earth, their minds are occupied with heavenly things, desiring eternal life with all spiritual longing."

Tuesday, February 13, 1996
Is there anything about DEATH?

Christian uses imagery of verticality, contrasting the ordinary work of the "things below" while aspiring to the "things above," noting that the incarnate God "passed through" the earthly in order to raise God's people to the heavenly. We must not "cling . . . onto the rungs of the ladder."

Is there anything else in the Constitutions about death? Its appearance there is almost incidental to the principles: fidelity to vows made, for instance, "until death." Martyrdom, Christian says, "is of the same nature as the violence that is sometimes necessitated by simple fidelity to ordinary things."

It is thus a matter of "dwelling on earth," of having one's feet on the ground, all the while keeping the "heavenly skies" in view and never losing sight of the aim, the endpoint: tree-tops do not point towards their roots. There is no reason for us to be exempt from this law of creation that aspires "to the things above."[63] It is up to us to turn this into an orientation towards the choice of freedom and of perpetually renewed longing, whose sap irrigates all our desires without ceasing to be drawn from the fertile ground of everyday life. The tree

63. Col 3:2.

of the cross enables this comparison. It reveals all human dimensions, both vertical and horizontal in its outstretched arms. And if we contemplate it tirelessly, it is indeed because the true CROSS is not the wood of torture that causes death, but the tree of life, which is similar to us in all aspects, whose head touches the sky and where everyone can make his nest in the breach of an open heart.

Because the Incarnation of the Son of God passed through this in order to declare, in the fullness of human communion, his own death, the meaning of our death has been irrevocably changed. It is not a site of decay. It is no longer an uprooting, but rather a definitive taking root there where the head has taken root. The great movement of the Incarnation is that of Jacob's ladder, where there is no end of descending and ascending in order to embrace everything relating to the human condition, which is thus accomplished as "spiritual ardor": death, no doubt, means not clinging onto the rungs of the ladder, no more on the first than on the last of them!

So, is there anything about DEATH in our Constitutions? About death by violence especially? We have said as much: that martyrdom, "dying for the faith," is not envisaged. Is this because the monk should avoid this, or should never be exposed to it? It is perhaps because it does not add anything substantial to the dynamism of Incarnation that feeds and confirms his consecration. It is of the same nature as the violence that is sometimes necessitated by simple fidelity to ordinary things. (What we alluded to [Michel][64] by talking about our successive moments of "departure": from family, country, etc.) And then, as we have said, nobody should seek or even desire such a death. It can befall us only within the logic of a continuous desire for LIFE. So our Constitutions

64. What Christian intended to say here is not clear, but mentioning Michel is probably a reminder to him to make it clearer when the chapter talk was delivered orally.

express this well when they speak about death almost incidentally. Thus in Constitution 8 (on monastic consecration): "[t]he brother binds himself in faithful stability to a sincere conversion of LIFE through ready obedience until DEATH."[65]

Thursday, February 15, 1996
"Renouncing his own will"

Continuing the theme of the previous chapter, Christian observes that life is more important for monastic profession than its end. Death, while an obvious endpoint in many senses, is indeed "included in our gift." Following Constitution 46 and RB 58, the postulant must indeed be reminded about all the difficult challenges of life in search of God; indeed (in Benedict's Rule) he "should behold all the hardships and difficulties that will lead him *to God" (emphasis added).*

*There is a contrasting note (*perinde ac cadaver*) mentioned in the Constitutions of the Society of Jesus, in which one must obey "as if he were a lifeless body, which allows itself to be carried to any place and treated in any way."*

We are not surprised to find the very terms of this Constitution on monastic consecration in the phrasing for the solemn confession as set out in Constitution 56.3 (it involves a Constitution, that is, a fixed text that cannot easily be modified): "I, Brother N . . . , promise my stability, my fidelity to the monastic way of life, and obedience until death in accordance with the Rule of Saint Benedict (RB 58), Abbot. I do this

65. Translator's note: It seems noteworthy that the phrase in French "en obéissant joyeusement jusqu'à la MORT" reiterates more explicitly the theme of joy and joyfulness explored in the recent chapters, something that the translation of "ready obedience" does not capture.

before God and all his saints, in this monastery of N[. . .] of the Cistercian Order, etc." It is noticeable that the three monastic vows are expressed here as concerning LIFE, with death present as a natural endpoint over which the monastic consecration has no hold. It will take place at its appointed time that only God knows, as is true for everyone. The form of this death doubtless depends on the three notes of our consecrated life, since it relates to this, but as such, it does not have the power to free us from our commitment. Does not another neighboring religious tradition state that it is necessary to obey *perinde ac cadaver*, or "like a corpse in the hands of the person responsible for washing the dead"?

It is not death but what comes "after" that renders stability, conversion of life, and a certain form of obedience obsolete. This is to say that our DEATH is included in our gift, that it does not belong to us, and so can only be risked in the same Gospel atmosphere as all our other moments offered to God in the heart of this monastic community to which we are united through love "in life as in death" or "for better and for worse." It is thus normal that the third mention of DEATH in our Constitutions should be in Constitution 11, which is about obedience . . . "In thus renouncing his own will he [the brother] follows the example of Christ who was obedient until death, and commits himself to the school of the Lord's service." The death that is intended here is that of Christ, directly linked to his obedience. It is the supreme mark of the Servant who knows to obey "to the end . . . to the very end,"[66] in the same manner as he LOVES.

And we are told that this service is to be learned, and that the community, if it is faithful to itself, puts us in a good school for the duration of our lives. Upon admission to the monastery, it is reiterated in Constitution 46 (as in the RB)

66. See John 13:1, "Jesus knew that his hour had come . . . having loved his own who were in the world, he loved them to the end."

that the postulant must be warned about "all the hard and difficult things that are to be found on the way to God." It is not a question of "digging one's grave every day," as a rather morbid tradition would have it, nor even of ensuring a "peaceful death" for those who have had a "hard life" (cf. Staouéli).[67] But our death, which is a slow and difficult death, is that of our own will. The paschal mystery, which is continually implicit in our Constitutions as in the Rule, is this slow passage of obedience that renounces one's own will in order to appreciate LIFE only in the life of God. Gethsemane is our place (cf. G. Thibon).[68]

Saturday, February 17, 1996
And the other congregations represented here?

Christian names here a number of the other religious congregations present in Algeria and points to the ways in which their constitutions too offer a vision of endurance and patience in difficulty, on the search for God.

It is thus not a question of "martyrdom" or of a violent death, nor even of the "gift of one's life" in the classic and "realist" sense of the word in our Constitutions. The only mention of violence is the violence that we choose to impose on our own wills. Those who have experienced this know that this is indeed a true "martyrdom" in the popular under-

67. Christian perhaps refers to the inscription on the wall of the monastery at Staoüeli: *S'il est triste de vivre à la Trappe, qu'il est doux d'y mourir* (While it is sad to live here, it is sweet to die here).

68. Undoubtedly a reference to Gustave Thibon, though the work referred to here is not known.

standing of the term. This is indeed the great JIHAD, the true fight, spoken of in the spiritual tradition of Islam.

Today let us make a little foray into the answers given by other religious families represented in Algeria in order to discover a more directly concrete evocation of what we are living through here at present down to the expression of charism in these congregations. This is what Msgr. Errázuriz already raised with the Sisters of Our Lady of Apostles. Thus the White Sisters cite their Constitution 9: "Christ's love compels us . . . it leads us to do everything for everyone, not withdrawing from any suffering, not even from death, in order to continue to extend the Kingdom of God." With quotations from Cardinal Lavigerie (1867), "It is probably nicer to live in Lyon, but it will certainly be less hard to live in Algiers, even and especially if there is, as people have assured me, much to be suffered there" (cf. Staouéli?). In addition, several texts in their constitutions or regional capitular proceedings speak about sharing a distressing situation, about proximity to a people who are suffering, about patient endurance in impossible situations . . .

The Little Sisters (Oran) cite in their Constitutions, "Immersed in suffering with our people, and hurt in our innermost being, it is here that we encounter God who preceded us and who comes to free us from weakness, poverty, the cross. The Resurrection of Jesus, the source from which life springs . . . will nourish the Little Sisters with hope in situations where death seems to prevail." And they also cite from the green booklet of Little Sister Magdeleine: "You will not retreat from any danger so as to accept the risk of a violent death."

The Little Brothers: their answer is entirely made up of extracts from their Constitutions put side by side:

> The Holy Spirit teaches them to love to the point of giving their life for Jesus and for their brothers . . . They will perhaps have to endure persecution [37]. Like Jesus,

> they choose the path of non-violence . . . [92]. If they find themselves misunderstood, rejected, persecuted, they remember the Lord's words: "Love your enemies and pray for them." They refrain from all violence towards anyone, praying God to be able to follow their Master to the end in the gift of their blood, if this supreme proof of love is demanded of them [93].

Hence their conclusion: "natural that no brother has left, especially in the country where Fr. de Foucauld gave his life." But Br. Bruno adds that this is not what matters most: "If I give my body up to the flames and I do not have love, I am NOTHING."[69]

Tuesday, February 20, 1996
Through patience . . . our PASSION

Psalm 43 is "permanently attached," for Christian, to the eleven Croatians, presumably because it was sung at None on December 14, 1993, after they had heard of the Croatians' murder.[70] *The passage about being "kept in the darkness of a dungeon" is an eerie foreshadowing of the monks' own captivity before their execution. The mention of the "eleven dead" reminds us that in a short time both the seven martyrs of Atlas and Bishop Pierre Claverie will join them to form the nineteen martyrs of Algeria.*

On this Tuesday before Ash Wednesday, Christian turns toward the Prologue of the Rule of Saint Benedict. From verse 39, the Prologue turns specifically to the "battle of holy obedience": "Let us call the 'PASSION' that is ours, he says, more

69. See 1 Cor 13.

70. Noted by Kiser, *Monks of Tibhirine*, 142.

prosaically PATIENCE, *and our inevitable 'C*ROSS,*'* OBEDIENCE *. . . ." Again, Christian insists that death to self and desire for life in God are far more important to the monastic vocation than physical death: they are "permanently at stake."*

We are finishing this series of mini chapters on the expression of the paschal mystery in our founding texts (RB and CST), before getting more actively into their application during Lent, by returning to the text of the Prologue of the Rule of Saint Benedict that connects participation in the sufferings of Christ first and foremost with PATIENCE in stability as experienced joyfully in everyday life. Here, every word is important . . . and what is not said is also important! Br. Christophe brought to my attention a reading note (A. Borias[71]) that refers to the Rule of the Master, where these five notes (the sufferings of Christ, patience, joy, stability, the everyday) are associated with MARTYRDOM, precisely. It is in the chapter on OBEDIENCE (we cannot escape this inevitable passage), chapter 7.59–60: "In the monastery their will is daily thwarted for the sake of the Lord, and *velut in martyrio*[72] they patiently endure whatever commands they receive to test them . . .[73] they will assuredly say to the Lord, with the prophet, "*In the monastery, for your sake we are being slain all the day; we are looked upon as sheep to be slaughtered*"[74] (Ps 43:22 . . . for me this psalm is permanently attached to the message of the Croatians).

71. André Borias, OSB, *En relisant Saint Benoît*, Vie Monastique no. 23 (Abbaye de Bellefontaine, 1990).

72. Christian here keeps the phrase in Latin, which the English translation renders as "in the spirit of martyrdom."

73. Christian omits here the phrase "In the monastery," which he instead transposes to the start of the cited psalm verse.

74. English translation from *The Rule of the Master*, trans. Luke Eberle, Cistercian Studies 6 (Kalamazoo, MI: Cistercian Publications, 1977), 123.

This same psalm is cited again in another chapter of the Rule of the Master (90.26–33), in relation to the reception of novices:

> It is right and proper therefore that fasting and abstinence should make us suffer . . . for the sake of the Lord . . . For the sake of God we are kept in the darkness of a dungeon . . . For the sake of God we embrace DEATH for the moment, so that we may be forever freed from the eternal death of hell. Finally, even when there is no persecution, even when Christianity is in peace, we serve in the school of the monastery under the ABBOT's command through testing and thwarting of the will, so that when, after the pilgrimage of life in this world, our Lord summons us to his Judgment, we may present to him . . . the patience with which we submitted to all the diverse and difficult things that the abbot commanded us . . . saying to the Lord, "*For your sake we are being slain all the day; we are looked upon as sheep to be slaughtered.*"[75]

(He adds, "*you set men over our heads!*").[76]

The Master's verbosity at least has the advantage of clearly situating, historically, the passage between the time of martyrdom and that of monasticism . . . and also of more clearly situating our dependence on a Benedictine school that is more SOBER in its evocations. Nobody can declare himself a "martyr," nor even make a claim to martyrdom. Let us call the "PASSION" that is ours more prosaically PATIENCE, and our inevitable "CROSS," OBEDIENCE . . . without its being necessary to turn the abbot into a PERSECUTOR, if however, as we are invited by the Rule of Saint Benedict and our Constitu-

75. English translation from *The Rule of the Master*, 262.

76. The parenthetical addition is from 90.39 (*The Rule of the Master*, 263), citing Ps 66:12. The same passage is also quoted in 7.63 (123).

tions, differently from the Rule of the Master, we know how to find JOY in the things that are at times "harsh and bitter," which "are pleasing to God" (cf. the very peaceful and calming "PASCHAL" atmosphere that emerges from CST 3.5, the charter of a LIFE in CHRIST).

N.B. The grace of the eleven dead who have left such a strong mark on us because they signify a common vocation, more even (and better!) than the threat confronted together. We have recognized in this something that connected us to one another in the name of the same logic of consecration, to the communion of saints in the church, in the heart of a community. It is perhaps good that the reality of even physical death should be hardly mentioned in our Constitutions, if not as if in passing . . . while both death to oneself and the desire for life consummated in God are permanently at stake in everything which we commit to together.

Tuesday, March 12, 1996
In connection with the theme of the next General Chapter

[after our retreat] contemplative community as a "school of charity"

Christian had been invited to lead a diocesan retreat on the theme of "The Church: the Incarnation Continued." In his conference, he reiterated many of the themes on which these chapters had focused, including embracing the Incarnation as the principal reason for staying in Tibhirine, and the value of Gaudium et Spes 22 *("By his Incarnation the Son of God in some way united himself with all men"). Christian observed, "Our witness is here in Algeria. The only way for us to give witness is to live where we do, and be what we are in the midst of banal, everyday realities . . . If redemption is the motive for the coming of Christ, then Incarnation is the method. Intent belongs to the Son. He wanted to save something in us that only he could save. But the method is up to us." He then gave again the charming example of not over-pricing monastic goods (as in the chapter on February 6, 1996) as a reminder that one should act "in order that in everything, God may be glorified."*[77]

To introduce the shared discussions announced yesterday evening around the question "What have I LEARNED in the last three years?" let us go back to the homily given at Tamié on this topic [FSO, Tamié, April 27, 1995, 2nd Sunday of Easter].[78]

The Father LOVES *the Son and has placed all things in his hands* . . . John 3:31-36[79]

This brings us back, as if taking us by the hand, to the theme of our next General Chapter, which greatly occupied us yesterday morning: "The community as the foundation, confirmation, and manifestation of our contemplation," in the words of Father Bernardo.

We wanted to simplify matters by saying "the community, a school of charity," and here we were stammering: we do not really know how to approach this subject. Very probably because we do not really know how to go about getting into that particular school.

A primary school, a nursery school even, for the youngest children . . . and we are too old, especially when we consider ourselves to be "superior."[80] A school of higher education . . .

77. Cited in Kiser, *The Monks of Tibhirine*, 217–18.

78. FSO = "France-Sud-et-Ouest." April 27 was in fact the Thursday of the second week of Easter.

79. The Gospel of the day.

80. Translator's note: There is a pun here on *supérieur* as "superior" and referring to *l'enseignement supérieur* (higher education).

and we are not up to it: nobody among us has already received the title of "doctor" in this school!

And then, what is charity? We have confirmed that it is easier to say what it is not . . . neither "jam" nor "gelatin," we clarified; not even cream . . . nor exactly any of the things that I do well or any of the things that I would like to do; it cannot be identified with any law, commandment, or observance, even if it contains and fulfills all of these.

Let us not be surprised by all this ignorance and stammering. The first school of charity—the only one really—is the trinitarian context, the divine context. In God mutual love and contemplation are perfectly simultaneous. Impossible to make them the successive themes of two different General Chapters!

The trinitarian context is a "school" of contemplation, in imitation of the Son who is eternally turned towards the Father; this is even his way of offering obedience (first reading[81]): God obeying God. And the Father himself is sight alone: "He sees—he saw—that everything is good." The pure heart of the Father who sees God in everything and everyone . . .

The trinitarian context is also a "school" of charity, of course, a school of communion, communication, relationships. "The Father loves the Son, and gives him the Spirit, without counting . . . ."[82] This kind of Charity is not the wholly merged unity that some people dream of: each person retains his individuality, in the wonder of a community of Persons who are freely and wholly in harmony. The wonderful richness of each of our communities . . . Nor is this kind of Charity simple unity on the surface. Perhaps there is "jam" in God—it's the work of the Spirit!—but there is never just jam. Saint John tells us above all that there is bread in God; it's more filling! What is being sought between us, in our

81. Acts 5:27-33: "Peter and the apostles said, 'Obedience to God comes before obedience to men.' "

82. Cf. John 3:34?

communities, is not skin-deep, nor even heart-deep.[83] We end up knowing that it is truly deep within us![84]

Thus contemplation is only possible where there is openness to community life, to communion, and to the whole human family . . .

And community is only possible where there is an openness to the contemplation of the wonders of God hidden in each person, signs of the Unique that are written on our faces as so many differences destined for the communion of saints.

Even if it is still necessary, for a little while, for us to find this difficult to perceive.

Thursday, March 14, 1996

(Homily: continued) The Trinitarian context as a "school" of CHARITY. We can speak of a SCHOOL in God to the extent that each Person has to receive something from the others, to learn from the Other who they are. Where there is CHARITY, there is necessarily a "school."

Saturday, March 16, 1996
Of good ZEAL . . . RB 72

Christian intended to stand down as superior of the monastery on March 31 (Palm Sunday), two weeks after he gave this

83. Translator's note: The wording here plays on a parallel between the actual phrase *à fleur de peau* (skin-deep, thin-skinned, sensitive . . .) and the invented equivalent *à fleur de cœur*.

84. *Ça nous tient profonde.*

chapter.[85] *While the text here ends abruptly, and there would have been much more to say, one imagines that Christian was beginning to think carefully about his final addresses to the brethren as superior. It is a terrible irony that he was prevented from standing down by his own capture and assassination.*

Christian invites the brethren to re-read chapter 72 of the Rule ("The Good Zeal of Monks") in view of the abbot general's invitation to see the community as a "school of charity." We are reminded of the "school for the Lord's service" referred to in the Prologue to the Rule of Saint Benedict, which Christian has referenced in the previous brief chapter.

Fr. Bernardo himself offers some reflections on chapter 72 in his letter to the Order:

> *"No one is to pursue what he judges better for himself, but instead, what he judges better for someone else" (RB 72.7). This maxim on disinterested and selfless love . . . incarnates concretely the good zeal or most fervent love proper to a heart overflowing with the inexpressible delight of love . . . This love is quite different from new or first fervor. And what is more, it is compatible with the fact of feeling and judging oneself "a poor monk or nun," "just one of the community" . . .*
>
> *Given that Christ alone takes us to heaven, we can say that the exercise of most fervent love, which only looks to the good of others, conforms us to Christ, who strove for our good and not for his own, and brings us all together to the kingdom of heaven.*[86]

For Christian, the principles of RB 72 are "self-evident," as are the beatitudes.

85. Suggested in Kiser, *Monks of Tibhirine*, 220.
86. Letter from the abbot general, January 26, 1996 (ref 96/AG/01).

After this preamble on CHARITY–CONTEMPLATION as one same SCHOOL . . . . it seems almost natural to return to the school of Saint Benedict, that "master to whom we have attended with something of our inner ear,"[87] so that he may educate us in both the contemplative life and in the life of charity. Already in its Prologue, as we know, the Rule presents its project as follows: "we intend to establish a SCHOOL for the Lord's service (*Dominici* SCHOLA *servitii*)."[88] This is the only place where the word "SCHOOL" is used. Soon after, the word *CARITAS* appears . . .[89] and it seems truly to mark the Prologue's culminating moment and thus the ultimate aim of the whole Rule, and of the Benedictine school that it describes: CHARITY, the DELIGHT OF LOVE, the OVERFLOWING of the heart . . .[90] all this in the PATIENCE of stability and perseverance, our way of "shar[ing] in the sufferings of Christ," our "MARTYRDOM," which should thus be a "martyrdom of love," and just as well a "martyrdom of HOPE" since this passage is all about movement, about walking and running towards the kingdom of which the community is the image, but not yet the full reality.

Most of the commentators on the Rule have drawn a parallel between the Prologue (especially its conclusion) and, at the opposite end, the chapter on GOOD ZEAL, *zelum bonum*. It is this chapter that we are going to try to REREAD together, still from the perspective of the theme of the General Chapter, not directly as preparation for the General Chapter, but in order to let us be encouraged in our daily lives in the direction in which it points us and that says EVERYTHING, in fact, about what we want to be. Of course, it is the abbot general's letter

87. See RB Prol. 1

88. RB Prol. 45.

89. Cf. RB Prol. 47.

90. Christian returns here to a passage he glossed in a recent chapter on February 8.

that aroused my curiosity and drew my thoughts to this quite short chapter in our Rule, where everything seems to be stated so simply and naturally that it would be easy almost to see in it merely a list of self-evident truths. The same thing happens to us when we encounter the BEATITUDES, as if we lived with them on a day-to-day basis, as if our lives had only their language through which to be deciphered. Strangely, I have noticed that there are as many "NOTES" of "good zeal" as there are BEATITUDES: EIGHT. The same number as there are harmonics in a scale going from DO to DO, the precise span of an octave. Let us just read the whole passage together . . .

This is where the chapter ends, but we wanted to follow Christian's invitation by including the chapter from the Rule of Saint Benedict to which he directs us.

Chapter 72. The good zeal of monks

> Just as there is a wicked zeal of bitterness which separates from God and leads to hell, so there is a good zeal which separates from evil and leads to God and everlasting life. This, then, is the good zeal which monks must foster with fervent love: They should each try to be the first to show respect to the other (Rom 12:10), supporting with the greatest patience one another's weaknesses of body or behavior, and earnestly competing in obedience to one another. No one is to pursue what he judges better for himself, but instead, what he judges better for someone else. To their fellow monks they show the pure love of brothers; to God, loving fear; to their abbot, unfeigned and humble love. Let them prefer nothing whatever to Christ, and may he bring us all together to everlasting life.

Selected Bibliography

Edition of the Chapter Talks

De Chergé, Christian. *Dieu pour tout jour: chapitres de père Christian de Chergé à la communauté de Tibhirine (1985–1996).* 2nd ed. Les Cahiers de Tibhirine 1bis. Montjoyer: Éditions de Bellefontaine, for the Abbaye Notre-Dame d'Aiguebelle, 2006.

Other Primary Sources

[Benedict.] *RB 1980: The Rule of St. Benedict in Latin and English with Notes.* Edited by Timothy Fry et al. Collegeville, MN: Liturgical Press, 1981.

The Exordium Parvum. In *Narrative and Legislative Texts from Early Cîteaux,* edited by Chrysogonus Waddell. Studia et Documenta, vol. 9. Cîteaux: Commentarii Cistercienses, 1999. 197–259.

Lebreton, Christophe. *Born from the Gaze of God: The Tibhirine Journal of a Martyr Monk (1993–1996).* Translated by Mette Louise Nygård and Edith Scholl. Monastic Wisdom 37. Collegeville, MN: Cistercian Publications, 2014.

Olivera, Bernardo. *How Far to Follow? The Martyrs of Atlas.* Petersham, MA: Saint Bede's Publications, 1997.

The Rule of the Master. Translated by Luke Eberle. Cistercian Studies 6. Kalamazoo, MI: Cistercian Publications, 1977.

Ecclesiastical Documents

Catholic Church. *Catechism of the Catholic Church.* Rome: Libreria Editrice Vaticana, 1993.

Order of Cistercians of the Strict Observance. *Declaration of the General Chapter of 1969 on the Cistercian Life.* https://ocso.org/history/historical-texts/declaration-on-cistercian-life/.

Paul VI. Constitution on the Sacred Liturgy. *Sacrosanctum Concilium.* https://www.vatican.va/archive/hist_councils/ii_vatican_council/documents/vat-ii_const_19631204_sacrosanctum-concilium_en.html.

Paul VI. Declaration of the Relation of the Church to Non-Christian Religions. *Nostra Aetate.* October 28, 1965. https://www.vatican.va/archive/hist_councils/ii_vatican_council/documents/vat-ii_decl_19651028_nostra-aetate_en.html.

Paul VI. Decree on the Adaptation and Renewal of Religious Life. *Perfectae Caritatis.* October 28, 1965. https://www.vatican.va/archive/hist_councils/ii_vatican_council/documents/vat-ii_decree_19651028_perfectae-caritatis_en.html.

Paul VI. Dogmatic Constitution on the Church. *Lumen Gentium.* November 21, 1964. https://www.vatican.va/archive/hist_councils/ii_vatican_council/documents/vat-ii_const_19641121_lumen-gentium_en.html.

Paul VI. Pastoral Constitution on the Church in the Modern World. *Gaudium et Spes.* December 7, 1965. https://www.vatican.va/archive/hist_councils/ii_vatican_council/documents/vat-ii_const_19651207_gaudium-et-spes_en.html.

Secondary Sources

Foulcher, Jane. "Nuit de feu: Christian de Chergé and Prayer with the Other." *Spiritus: A Journal of Christian Spirituality* 18 (2018): 218–30.

Kiser, John W. *The Monks of Tibhirine: Faith, Love, and Terror in Algeria.* New York: St Martin's Press, 2002.

Salenson, Christian. *Christian de Chergé: A Theology of Hope.* Translated by Nada Conic. Cistercian Studies 247. Collegeville, MN: Cistercian Publications, 2012.